NEW YORK STATE'S SPECIAL PLACES

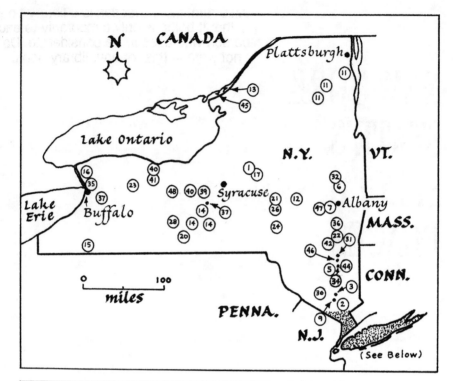

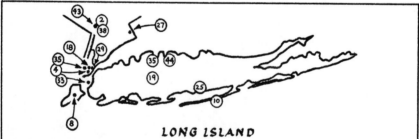

LONG ISLAND

1. Fort Stanwix National Monument
2. Philipsburg and Van Cortlandt Manors
3. West Point
4. Federal Hall National Memorial
5. Huguenot Street Houses
6. Saratoga National Historic Park
7. New York State Museum
8. Richmondtown Restoration

9. Bear Mountain and Harriman State Parks
10. Fire Island National Seashore
11. Adirondack Sampler (Ausable Chasm, High Falls Gorge, White Face Mountain)
12. Howe Caverns
13. The Thousand Islands

14. Waterfalls and Gorges of the Finger Lakes
15. Allegany State Park
16. Niagara Falls

17. Erie Canal Village
18. New York Stock Exchange
19. Old Bethpage Village Restoration
20. Corning Glass Center
21. Farmers' Museum
22. American Museum of Fire Fighting
23. Genesee Country Museum
24. Hanford Mills Museum
25. Suffolk Marine Museum

26. National Baseball Hall of Fame
27. Museum of Cartoon Art
28. Bully Hill Vineyards
29. South Street Seaport
30. Hall of Fame of the Trotter

31. Old Rhinebeck Aerodrome
32. The Canfield Casino

33. The Statue of Liberty
34. Franklin and Eleanor Roosevelt
35. Theodore Roosevelt
36. Martin Van Buren
37. Millard Fillmore
38. Washington Irving
39. William Seward
40. Elizabeth Cady Stanton and Susan B. Anthony
41. George Eastman

42. Olana
43. Lyndhurst
44. Vanderbilt Mansions
45. Boldt Castle
46. Mills Mansion
47. Schuyler Mansion
48. Sonnenberg Gardens

NEW YORK STATE'S SPECIAL PLACES

Day Trips, Weekends, and Outings in the Empire State

Michael A. Schuman

The Countryman Press, Woodstock, Vermont

For David and Fay Schuman and Patti Jensen Schuman with love and admiration, without whom this book would never have come to be.

The Countryman Press
P.O. Box 175
Woodstock, Vermont 05091

Library of Congress Cataloging-in-Publication Data
Schuman, Michael.
  New York State special places.
  1. New York (State)—Description and travel—
1981–   —Guide-books. 2. Historic sites—New York
(State)—Guide-books. I. Title.
F117.3.S38   1988   917.47'0443   87-37991
ISBN 0-88150-107-7 (pbk.)

Designed by Leslie Fry
Printed in the United States of America

CONTENTS

INTRODUCTION

NEW YORK STATE IS LIKELY THE MOST MISUNDERSTOOD STATE IN THE nation. You don't have to be from California to think that the state's borders start in Staten Island and end in Westchester County. There are people who live much closer who associate the Empire State with New York City and little else.

Certainly the Big Apple is one of the greatest cities in the world, maybe the greatest, and worth many visits. But New York is a state filled with diversity, and you would be hard-pressed to find more between any other state's borders.

The Hudson is one of the country's most storied rivers; it rolls past handsome estates, past bluffs that hug it like an apron, past farms and cities. Its valley is rich with heritage. The Adirondacks offer miles and miles of wilderness, with a vastness you will find in few other northeastern states.

The Finger Lakes and their surrounding hills and valleys serve up enticing recreation and views that change and impress at every turn. Leatherstocking country—Cooperstown and the rest—looks more like New England than parts of New England.

Simply put, there is a lot of state between the Niagara Frontier and eastern Long Island.

So how could we narrow down the list to present the best in a single book?

It was hard work, but fun. We traversed the entire state, investigating the cornucopia of places where one can spend his or her free time. And we found they fit into six major categories.

Heritage. Colonists from all over Europe came to New York: the Dutch, the English, the Huguenots from France. More Revolutionary War battles were fought on New York State soil than in all of New England. When the war was over, George Washington was inaugurated as president at Federal Hall in Manhattan.

Beauty. New York has the best in mountains, rivers, lakes, caverns, *and* the seashore. What more could an outdoors person want?

Work and play. New Yorkers have earned their livings on whaling ships and on farms, in resounding mills and on the floor of the stock exchange, by manufacturing glass and selling herbs.

And they spend their valuable leisure time in so many ways: tasting the wine, sailing the waters, shopping at reborn markets, and relaxing at the old ball game.

Famous personalities. New Yorkers have made their marks on the world in all fields; there have been presidents, authors, inventors, reformers, and, of course, the lady in the harbor.

And, finally, there are magnificent mansions. The wealthy and the eccentric had a passion for building Corinthian castles in the most beautiful of settings; here we present the lifestyles of New York State's rich and famous.

As with my book, *New England's Special Places: A Daytripper's Guide,* I used three basic criteria in selecting attractions to be included. First, each place must offer insights into an aspect of New York State's character. Second, I wanted to touch as many of New York State's corners as possible. Third, I included only quality attractions, only those I would recommend to a friend.

I visited and personally researched every place featured in this book. I didn't just breeze through them in 10 minutes. I took every tour, screened every film and slide show, and spoke with curators, rangers, and other staff personnel to find special information visitors should know.

Please keep in mind two factors as you read on. While every detail has been verified at press time, changes in operating procedures, hours and days open, or admission charges can always occur. For specific information about hours, costs, or special events, we recommend calling or writing in advance.

Also, just about all attractions included—even those that keep year-round hours—shut down on Thanksgiving, Christmas, and New Year's Day. If you plan a special trip on any of those days, we again ask you to call ahead so your trip will not be wasted.

Finally, a note about the overnight accommodations mentioned in this book. For the most part, the listings are not places we have personally visited, and their listing does not represent a recommendation. However, the information was compiled from reliable sources, and we hope it will be a convenience for travelers in this far-flung state.

We are certain that whether you are making your first or 51st visit to any of these special places, you will find them to be wholly enjoyable and reflective of a special part of New York State's character.

Happy traveling!

EARLY
NEW YORK

FORT STANWIX NATIONAL MONUMENT

Cross the moat at Fort Stanwix and you are suddenly frozen in the year 1777.

National Park Service photo by Richard Frear

Benedict Arnold is a great guy, you hear when you visit the American troops stationed at Fort Stanwix National Monument in Rome.

Arnold is a hero, a highly praised general who helped defeat the British at Saratoga the year before.

It is 1778 at Fort Stanwix. The enlisted men and officers and their wives whom you meet cannot answer a question relating to a later time. If you ask where is the nearest McDonald's, you will be sent to the quarters of Corporal Donald McDonald, a man who actually served here in 1778.

You see, the staff members at Fort Stanwix National Monument, an accurate reconstruction of the real Fort Stanwix that existed here more than 200 years ago, don't simply interpret life during the Revolutionary War. They play the roles of actual men and women who lived here. There is Corporal McDonald, Sergeant Stephen Adams, Captain and Mrs.

Joseph Savage, and drummer Cornelius Buttson. And they are stuck in a time warp.

It is summer, 1778. If you ask any question about a later time or an unheard-of country called the United States of America, you will get a blank stare as a response. If you ask a question beyond the scope of soldiers at Fort Stanwix in 1778, you will be directed towards the visitor center, the only place inside the fort where staff members are living in the present; they will be pleased to answer questions.

As with most National Park Service sites, the visitor center is the first place you should stop; it is located in the west barracks inside a door marked "GREGG." A sentry will show you the way if you need help. An audiovisual presentation will describe the true-to-life setting and acquaint you with this site's unique method of living history interpretation; you will absorb the background you need to converse with the 1778 fort residents.

Ask Sergeant Adams, for example, how the war is going and he might say that there is no end in sight—the war should be raging for some time—but it doesn't look hopeless. After all, just last fall General Burgoyne surrendered his army at the Battle of Saratoga, a major victory for the Americans.

And two months before that, the very men to whom you are talking successfully staved off a 20-day siege by the British army, composed mainly of Canadian Loyalists and Indians. Much of the credit went to Colonel Peter Gansevoort, commanding officer of the fort, but reliable and trustworthy Major General Benedict Arnold also played an important role. Arnold was sent from Albany to assist the men at besieged Fort Stanwix and, soon, rumors reached the British camp that Arnold was coming with a tremendous force of Americans. The British commander, General Barry St. Leger, seeing low morale and desertion by Indians who had joined his cause, ultimately lifted the siege and retreated to Canada.

The residents are incredibly cordial to visitors from the 20th century. They will let you enter their living quarters and put your hands on just about anything inside. Feel a straw mattress on which they slept, lumpy as a sack of soiled laundry, and keep in mind that none had the luxury of a pillow.

We wanted a closer look at the portable writing table in the staff dining room, the place where Colonel Gansevoort and his high-ranking officers would have eaten. The table comes with a quill pen and some cloth covering its surface; an officer explained that the cloth was necessary because quills break when used directly on wood. Inside the table are maps and currency; the maps, too, had cloth attached to them to make them last longer. It's easy to forget that things weren't disposable and replaceable as they are today; 1778 on the edge of the wilderness was hardly a throw-away society.

Survival here means making do. Ask an officer's wife what's cooking in the hearth of her coarse quarters and she will likely respond chicken pie or stew. Bread was mostly corn bread; there wasn't much wheat grown around here.

Ask an officer what his garb is made from and you will probably be told it's linen; you could count on the fingers of one hand the number of bales of cotton that arrived in Boston annually.

Ask to pick up some draughts (in our time, they are called checkers) on the checkerboard in the enlisted men's bunkhouse and you will see they are made of melted down bullets. You may find up to 10 soldiers here on the busiest days, but in 1778 there would have been 28, four in each of the seven bunk beds. The 28 cooked over one fireplace and ate at one table, all sharing a space the size of your living room. Sanitary conditions were primitive; no visitor from the 20th century would have been able to stand the stench of a real bunkhouse.

That is one of the few cases where lines are drawn short of complete realism. You see the past as it was but up to a point. Says Fort Stanwix staff member Bill Curtis, "We're not going to get typhoid or eat bad meat or go without showering for months."

But they do accurately depict everyday events that would have occurred in such an outpost. Some weapon is commonly fired each day as part of a drill or ceremony. At times, a misbehaving soldier is led to the whipping post in the middle of the parade ground where everyone can see. It was up to the company drummer to apply the lashes to the miscreant, but before the whip is cracked today, an officer will rush out to stop the punishment, calling out something like, "There are enough injured people here already."

Drummer Cornelius Buttson, played adeptly by staff member Bill Sawyer, is seen throughout the day on the parade grounds, where he dispells the false images of young drummer boys.

Drummers ranged in age from their teens into their thirties and forties and were found all over the battlefield. They acted as orderlies for officers and gofers for doctors, helping collect the wounded or doing light hospital work, tasks which could not have been handled competently by a boy.

Most important, they gave signals with their drums. Everyday at noon, drummer Buttson marches to the parade grounds and calls the militia men to rations; then at 4:30 he plays retreat, signalling to the soldiers that it is time to come back inside the fort. The drummer's responsibilities were never cancelled on account of the weather; he's out there in any condition, summer sun to upstate New York drizzle.

In one sector of the fort, time warp is suspended. Inside the west casemate is a museum, serving as a repository for relics from the original fort found during excavation. Articles like cloth and woodwork have long disintegrated, but buttons on French or British uniforms have survived the centuries. So have digging tools, pottery and pieces thereof, scissors, and toothbrushes. A short slide show on the process of reconstructing the fort is also shown there.

Location: Fort Stanwix National Monument is in the center of downtown Rome. Westbound: from the New York State Thruway, exit 31, take Route 49, which becomes East Dominick Street in Rome; when you reach the fort, circle around it to reach the parking garage on North James Street on the west side of the fort; there is free parking for three hours in the garage. Eastbound: from the New York State Thruway, exit 33, take Route 365, which becomes Erie Boulevard East in Rome; just before you pass the fort, take a right onto North James Street to the parking garage. **Admission** is charged. **Hours:** April through December, daily. The full living history program is in effect from Memorial Day through Labor Day. A modified program is in effect at other times. **Allow** 90 minutes to two hours in peak season, up to 90 minutes in the off-season. **Information:** Fort Stanwix National Monument, 112 East Park Street, Rome, NY 13440; (315) 336-2090.

Events: Late May, Soldiers on the De-o-wain-sta, a living history comparison of 18th- and 20th-century soldiers; May, June, October, November, Sunday sampler, a series of programs on regional 18th-century history; two separate summer weekends, reenacted encampments; August, 18th-century entertainment by balladeer Linda Russell from Federal Hall National Monument; August, September, December, Candlelight tours.

Note: Separate tours of the outside and the inside of the fort, black powder demonstrations, and a topical talk called, "Ranger's Choice" are usually offered once daily in peak season.

If you are staying overnight: Quality Inn, 200 S. James Street (in the center of Rome on Routes 46, 49, and 69), (315) 336-4300; Paul Revere Motor Lodge, 7900 Turin Road (three miles north of Rome on Route 26), (315) 336-1776; Family Inns of America, 145 E. Whitesboro (in the center of Rome off Route 49), (315) 357-9400; Esquire Motor Lodge, 1801 Black River Road, Rome, (315) 336-5320.

PHILIPSBURG AND VAN CORTLANDT MANORS

Courtesy: Historic Hudson Valley

Springtime at Philipsburg Manor means dancing, games and, of course, flowers.

OUR GUIDE WELCOMED US INTO THE MAIN HOUSE AT PHILIPSBURG Manor, Upper Mills, a colonial home and mill complex in North Tarrytown, by saying, "You've heard of the family room, the living room, the dining room, and the play room? Well, you're in it."

The time portrayed at Philipsburg Manor is the period when this modern commuter-land was sparsely settled, and even the busy borough of Brooklyn to the south was little more than cows, sheep, and an occasional farm.

This was a time when conditions were Spartan, even for a wealthy family like that of Frederick Philipse, who came here in the 1650s as Governor Peter Stuyvesant's carpenter but later built up a great fortune that included this 20-acre parcel of land on which he operated a gristmill and granary; reconstructions of both are here today.

People at Philipsburg Manor also had an aquatic setting in its still mill pond; today's visitors cross over the pond's reconstructed dam on their way from the reception center to the main attractions here: the manor house, grist mill, granary, and the new world Dutch barn.

In the white stone manor house the floors are bare, the windows have no curtains, and as you can tell from the guide's opening remarks, a single room usually had many purposes.

The multi-purpose room our guide referred to as the family room, etc., is the first stop in the manor house. Its walls are whitewashed since it was thought that light colors promoted good health; the centerpiece is a Dutch draw-top table, appropriately covered with a colorful carpet.

A Dutch kas, or cabinet, dominates the parlor, and the upper kitchen has shelves lined with delftware and pewter serving dishes. Anybody heading upstairs had to pass through the upper kitchen so it was natural that the family's best possessions were put on display here. The furniture is simple but handsome, crafted by country joiners and turners.

Upstairs are bedchambers with rope beds; this is one of the sites where you learn that the phrase "sleep tight" derived from the action of tightening the ropes with a rope key before bedtime.

In addition, each bed was filled with two inches of straw, creating an appetizing breeding ground for insects and giving birth to another time-worn expression, "Don't let the bedbugs bite." Again, here's proof positive that in those times even a lot of money couldn't buy comfort.

The upper kitchen, despite its name, was mainly a show place, used often for dining and occasionally for cooking. Most meal preparation took place down in the lower kitchen with its stone floor, insurance against fires caused by flying sparks.

The spicy scent of apples filled the air when we visited, as staff members garbed in mop hats, shawls, blue aprons, and wooden shoes baked apple puffs. One woman rolled dough on a wooden table while another tended apples simmering in wine and a six-pack of spices in a Dutch oven, a squatty little pot with legs. After one whiff of the hot, spicy scene, there were many requests for the recipe from our group.

The Philipsburg Manor tour ends with a look inside the dairy, an underground chamber with gold milk containers from Holland, and the mill house; visit at the right time and you can watch corn or another grain being ground while a staffperson explains all the processes involved.

The explanation of milling, mechanics and all, is less complex than the roots of the Van Cortlandt family, whose manor house and ferry house in Croton-on-Hudson, just a few miles north of Philipsburg Manor, guard the confluence of the Hudson and Croton Rivers. Here you can have another look at early New York life, and you'll hear the background on the family's generations and marriages—and more generations and marriages—as you stand outside the sturdy home on a path paved with oyster shells. In brief, the first Van Cortlandt arrived in New Amsterdam in 1638, and over the decades, they married into prestigious New York families like the Schuylers, Livingstons and Philipses.

The manor house, which has occupied this site for over 200 years, has been restored to reflect its appearance from 1790 to 1814. The upper half is built in the Palladian style, the bottom half like a hunting lodge.

Guide Herb Lerner entered through the rear of the house while we climbed up the outdoor staircase in the front. Lerner was there to greet us, peering over the bottom half of a split Dutch door; he told us that the closed bottom door was a device to keep children in and animals out, while the open upper door allowed a breeze to sweep inside.

Lerner gave us a mini-course in furniture design; we saw Chippendale chairs with their ball and claw feet and Queen Anne chairs with typical rounded backs. And there were neo-classical pieces designed in Greek and Roman styles along with Duncan Phyfe and William and Mary furnishings.

But for all the showpieces, we saw reminders of the lack of comforts, even for the wealthy, as in the Philipsburg Manor. We stepped over a doormat made of corn husks upon entering the kitchen. Upstairs in a bedroom is a Chippendale toilet chair, elegantly styled but with a practical chamber pot under the seat. Behind the manor, of course, is the outdoor necessary house, certainly necessary but definitely unpleasant on freezing January mornings.

As at Philipsburg Manor, foods are prepared in the downstairs kitchen. On our visit, a fire raged in the huge hearth, while cooks in colonial dress baked chocolate almond cookies.

The tour leaves the manor and following the brick path known as "the long walk" (though it's really a short walk), takes you to the ferry house. In this tavern, travelers could have a few drinks, conversation, and a

Courtesy: Historic Hudson Valley

Philipsburg Manor bridges the centuries, offering visitors a look at life in a Dutch manor in colonial New York.

view of the rushing river before taking a ferry across the Croton or a stagecoach on the Albany Post Road.

Stagecoach operators delivering the mail often stopped here, evidenced by the bull whip resting by a bar room table; that room's raison d'être is symbolized by gin and Madeira bottles, while five rows of the Van Cortlandt family's pewter ware—tankards and plates and mugs—line the shelves of the sprawling hutch.

Take a look at the posted signs outside the ferry house before you leave. They were the travelers' best friends, whether relating reports of runaway slaves (slavery was common in New York then and the Van Cortlandts had about a dozen slaves) or giving the latest Albany stage-coach schedule. According to the posted timetable, the trip from Croton-on-Hudson to Albany lasted two and a half days.

Location: Philipsburg Manor, Upper Mills, is on Route 9, two miles north of the Tappan Zee Bridge, also two miles north of Interstate 87, exit 9. Van Cortlandt Manor is one-quarter mile south of the Croton Point Avenue exit off Route 9. It is nine miles north of the Tappan Zee Bridge, also nine miles north of Interstate 87, exit 9. **Admission** is charged to both. **Hours:** For both, April through November, daily; December through

March, Wednesday through Sunday. **Allow** an hour to an hour and fifteen minutes for the Philipsburg Manor tour and an extra hour if you want to walk the grounds. Allow an hour and a half for the tour of Van Cortlandt Manor and at least another hour to walk the old Albany Post Road past the ferry house or to see the gardens. **Information:** For both, Historic Hudson Valley, 150 White Plains Road, Tarrytown, NY 10591; (914) 631-8200.

Events: Philipsburg Manor, Upper Mills: mid-May, Pinkster Celebration, Dutch colonial spring festival with music, country dancing, children's games; early November, King George II's birthday, songs, dancing, fireworks, militia on parade; early December, Candlelight tours. Van Cortlandt Manor: early January, Candlelight Tours; early and mid-October, Marketplace, handcrafts, apples, ciders, pumpkins for sale; mid-October, Autumn Crafts and Tasks, demonstrations of farm and horse labor in preparation for 18th-century winter, handcrafts. Garden lovers should keep in mind that parts of the Sleepy Hollow Restorations gardens are in bloom from early April to mid-June; write to Historic Hudson Valley at the above address for their calendar of bloom.

Note: Discounted combination tickets for Philipsburg Manor, Upper Mills, Van Cortlandt Manor and Washington Irving's home, Sunnyside, (see page 176) are available. Although all of these Historic Hudson Valley properties have quality gift stores, the one at Philipsburg Manor is the most complete, and you can buy corn meal or grains made right at the mill. Both sites maintain picnic areas.

If you are staying overnight: Westchester Marriott Hotel, 670 White Plains Road (Route 119, just west of Interstate 287, exit 1), Tarrytown, (914) 631-2200; Howard Johnson's Motor Lodge, 290 Tarrytown Road (Route 119, off Interstate 287, exit 4), Elmsford, (914) 592-8000; Holiday Inn, Tarrytown Road (Route 119, take Interstate 287, exit 1 or Interstate 87, exit 8), Elmsford, (914) 592-5680; County Center Motel, 20 County Center Road (Routes 100 and 119), White Plains, (914) 948-2400.

WEST POINT

Photo by Michael Schuman

The nation's oldest and one of the largest military museums is at West Point.

"AT WEST POINT, MUCH OF THE HISTORY WE TEACH WAS MADE BY people we taught."

These words are displayed in a poster above an artist's rendition of the faces of arguably the four most famous American generals.

There's Ulysses S. Grant, hard-faced and bearded in his Union uniform; Robert E. Lee, with his light flowing beard blending into his Confederate greys; Dwight D. Eisenhower, looking determined and intent; and the jaunty profile of Douglas MacArthur, his ever-present corn cob pipe protruding like a natural extension of his mouth.

The poster sums up the attraction of West Point to visitors; this is an institution of higher learning with a past as full of color and adventure as any storied college or university in the world.

But the poster omits an additional lure to visitors: the stunning view looking down to the Hudson River.

It is the setting that many casual visitors recall long after they have forgotten how many pipes the great Cadet Chapel organ has or the year that Ike graduated. Yet even the academy's beautiful cliff-side locale, a granite promontory jutting out into the Hudson, carries a macho, no-nonsense militaristic name: the American Gibraltar, coined by George Washington.

It was Washington who gave West Point its first role of service to the nation in January 1778. The British had hoped to control navigation of the Hudson in order to split the colonies and isolate New England. Anticipating this, Washington stationed the first permanent garrison of troops here. The men threw a chain, more than 600 yards long and weighing 150 tons, across the river to Constitution Island, making enemy use of the Hudson impossible.

The states were bound together, linked literally and figuratively. The academy has taken this metaphor and run with it, boasting of its "long gray line" of living human links still providing service to the country. Several links of the famous chain can be seen at the west side of Trophy Point.

Most of what visitors wish to see can be toured on one's own. Parts of the campus that are off limits to visitors are clearly marked; unfortunately, the famous Flirtation Walk is one place visitors can't go, since this riverside trail is saved for cadets and their guests.

Trophy Point is where civilians will want to go. The view is stellar and the setting is as romantic as Flirtation Walk. The crowds may be oppressive, but that's the penalty for being a civilian. From Trophy Point step up to the Battle Monument and cast your eyes downward and you will see why this is called "The Million Dollar View."

The West Point Museum, which is worth a million dollars to military historians, means a stop even if you don't know the difference between a bayonet and the Bay of Pigs. Here is the nation's oldest and among the largest public collection of military arms and equipment, arranged so that any visitor can appreciate and understand it, even those whose major interests lie elsewhere.

Yes, there are weapons of all types, and some people may feel uncomfortable admiring cases filled with mankind's tools for killing one another. However, the museum doesn't glorify the displayed weapons; instead, it chronicles their development.

You start your visit with a look at 14th-century English long bows and arrows and finish your tour with an inspection of the ballistic case for the "fat man" atomic bomb, the type dropped over Nagasaki, Japan, at the end of World War II. You can decide for yourself whether this is progress or regression.

The museum also contains more light-hearted material, such as a somewhat whimsical life-sized diorama of a French cafe scene during World War I and John Chapman's youthful-looking portrayal of *George Wash-*

ington as a Colonel in 1772 (in the Craighead Gallery of Military Paintings inside the museum).

The unforgettable agony of *Reveille on a Winter Morning* is immortalized on canvas by Henry Bacon, a field artist for *Leslie's Weekly* during the Civil War. Each soldier is frozen in a moment of early morning routine, and the detail in each waking soldier's face is as amusing as it is fascinating. Don't neglect to notice the drummer boy blowing on his hands to warm frozen fingers.

The Civil War uniforms these soldiers would have worn are displayed among other military garb, including Dwight Eisenhower's winter service uniform, General Joseph (Vinegar Joe) Stillwell's hat and boots, and Douglas MacArthur's cadet bathrobe.

In many cultures, a soldier's uniform was extended to include his hair. You will read that Napoleon's light horsemen wore braids and long, curling mustaches, and those who were physically unable to grow a mustache had to paint them on their faces.

One of the most popular exhibits at West Point would never fit inside the museum's walls. Fort Putnam, built in 1778 to protect the Hudson River, was refurbished for the bicentennial in 1976 using the drawings of a Revolutionary War topographic engineer. It was threatened twice during the war—once by Benedict Arnold—but the men stationed there never saw combat.

What you see today when taking the self-guided fort tour are the weapons, casemates, embrasures, and redoubts similar to those the Revolutionary soldier would have found more than 200 years ago.

The colonial era uniformed man probably uttered informal prayers for safety when in the old fort's vulnerable location, but today West Point is blessed with several handsome chapels, all open to visitors.

What is recognized as the largest church organ in the world sits inside the Gothic-style cadet chapel. With 18,000 pipes, it is the building's most notable attraction, although the stained glass, vaulted ceiling, and buttresses are also impressive. Windows are dedicated to each class from 1802 to 1976, and you should try to be here on a sunny day when the sun filters in through the stained glass.

The Chapel of the Most Holy Trinity, which serves Catholic cadets, was dedicated in 1900 and widely expanded in the late 1950s. Though there have been Jewish cadets since the first class in 1802—Simon Levy was one of the ten-man Corps of Cadets in the Academy's first graduating class and one of two men commissioned a second lieutenant—and separate Jewish services since 1939, there was never a separate house of worship until the Jewish chapel was completed in 1984. The gallery and museum inside highlight contributions Jews have made to the nation and the military.

Finally, there is the Old Cadet Chapel built in 1837, the only existing chapel until the present Cadet Chapel was built in 1910. Robert Wier's mural, *Peace and War*, hangs above the altar; black marble tablets pay tribute to general officers of the Continental Line and officers killed in the Mexican-American War. Each lists the officer's name, rank, and dates of birth and death, with one exception: Benedict Arnold. While he is honored for his service in the invasion of Canada and the Battle of Saratoga, he is noted by just his date of birth and rank; his name is omitted.

Location: From the north, take Interstate 84 onto Route 9W south through Newburgh to the exit for Thayer Gate and follow the signs. From the south, take Interstate 87 onto 9W north onto Route 218 through Highland Falls, which will take you to Thayer Gate. A visitors information center is located just outside Thayer Gate. A public parking lot is off Thayer Road between Clinton Field and "The Plain" parade ground. **Admission** to all sites is free. **Hours:** West Point Museum, year round, daily; Fort Putnam, mid-May through mid-November, daily; Chapels, year round, daily (on weekends the Jewish chapel is open only in the afternoon). **Allow** three to four hours to see all the major sites. **Information:** West Point Visitors Information Center, USMA, West Point, NY 10996; (914) 938-2638.

Events: Parades are held on "The Plain" parade ground from late August through early November and in April and May usually on Saturday or late weekday afternoons. Athletic events take place throughout the school year. Contact the visitors information center (number listed above) or the West Point Public Affairs Office, (914) 938-3507, for specific information.

Note: The visitors information center located outside Thayer Gate is open daily throughout the year and is helpful, although it is not essential to stop there. The academy offers no guided tours; there is a self-guided walking tour, and you can pick up a brochure at the visitors information center. A private company, West Point Tours, gives hour-long guided tours of the campus in the warm weather months; contact them at (914) 446-4724 or call the visitors information center. There are no public eating facilities on the academy grounds.

If you are staying overnight: Hotel Thayer (on USMA campus, inside Thayer Gate), West Point, (914) 446-4731; Palisade Motel, Route 218 at the junction with Route 9W, Highland Falls, (914) 446-9400; West Point Motel, Route 218 east of junction with Route 9W, Highland Falls, (914) 446-4180.

FEDERAL HALL NATIONAL MEMORIAL

National Park Service photo by Richard Frear

It was not in Philadelphia or Virginia that George Washington took the oath of office. It was in New York City and Federal Hall marks the spot.

Ask someone to name an American city with a colonial heritage and most will answer Boston or Philadelphia. Press further and they may bring up Williamsburg or Charleston.

Perhaps because New York City is so often associated with its more modern diversions—Broadway, Rockefeller Center, the Metropolitan Museum of Art—Americans neglect to think of its long history. In addition to being the center of publishing and theatrical and business activity in the country, Manhattan is home to Federal Hall National Memorial, one of the country's most important colonial historic sites.

It was on the site of Federal Hall that George Washington was inaugurated as the first president of the United States. This occurrence alone makes it noteworthy. A bronze statue of Washington on the steps of this building depicts him lifting his hand from the Bible immediately after taking the oath of office on April 30, 1789.

However, it was also here that one of the landmark trials in colonial America was held. In a case which inspired our forefathers to adopt the cherished liberty of freedom of the press, John Peter Zenger was found not guilty of "seditious libel" against Royal Governor William Cosby. Zenger's attorney claimed that the bitingly critical songs attacking Cosby that Zenger printed were truthful criticism of the government and, therefore, could not rightly be considered libelous. The jury agreed with Zenger and his attorney.

This spot was the scene of other momentous acts, specifically the Stamp Act and various acts of Congress. The Stamp Act Congress met here in 1765 to formally protest the hated taxing scheme and, as a result, adopted the Declaration of Rights and Grievances, stating that the English in the colonies had the same rights as those in England and could not be taxed without their consent.

Some 24 years later, the first United States Congress under the Constitution met here and ratified the first ten amendments to the Constitution, the Bill of Rights.

All those illustrious events happened on this spot, but not in the Greek Revival building that sits here today. This structure is the third one to occupy the site, and an audio tape inside describes scale models of all three, telling their intriguing histories.

First built as a customs house, the current building later served as a subtreasury from 1862 to 1920. After becoming a home for various government agencies, the structure was pronounced a national memorial in 1955, administered by the National Park Service.

A mammoth statue of George Washington greets visitors at the Wall Street entrance, while the Messmore Kendall Collection of Washingtoniana awaits anyone who heads to the building's upper level. The collection starred at the 1939 New York World's Fair with its own pavilion, and today the snuffboxes, jasper ware, ceramics, mourning pieces, and many other objects bearing the first president's image, or once owned by him or his family, are permanently on view here.

Dioramas inside Federal Hall present scale versions of the first presidential inauguration. One depicts the inaugural parade from Washington's home on Cherry Street near the Brooklyn Bridge to Federal Hall. Another presents a view of the inauguration from the Federal Hall balcony with flags hanging from windows and bunting on the pillars.

Then there is a diorama of the Federal Hall interior depicting the first House of Representatives debating the Bill of Rights; notice details like quill pens at each seat, candles distributed at every four or five seats, and knives and scissors at just a few.

The sweet sounds of Linda Russell's dulcimer bring 18th-century popular music to 20th-century visitors at Federal Hall.

The most memorable feature of the building is the massive rotunda, 60 feet in diameter with 27-foot-high Corinthian columns. When this was a customs house, a big round desk occupied the rotunda center. Today, you will likely find a classical pianist, an operatic tenor, or a Gospel choir here as a part of regularly scheduled lunchtime concerts.

An additional bonus here is balladeer Linda Russell, who dresses in period costume and imparts colonial musical renditions on period instruments such as a dulcimer, guitar, pennywhistle, or limberjack, the latter of which looks like a little wooden marionette and is tapped against a board to appear as if he is dancing up a storm. Russell offers daily performances of popular music— 18th-century style. She also offers another reminder of George Washington, his impact on the American people and their admiration for him.

Russell says, "George Washington's birthday was celebrated as early as 1781. He was such a hero and one song dedicated to him, called a broadside in its day, was ironically set to the tune of 'God Save the King.' "

She then offers a sample verse:
"Fill the glass to the brink.
To Washington's health we'll drink.
Tis his birthday."
Broadsides were songs, patriotic or political in tone, that discussed

topical news events, be they about an increase in taxes or a senseless murder. They were sung to oft-heard tunes like "Yankee Doodle" or "Derry, Derry Down" and were usually full of passion.

Most important, Russell further explains, broadsides were one 18th-century news medium, and citizens could buy a broadside for about two pennies during the years just prior to the American Revolution.

As you listen to Russell sing, it is apparent that basic human passions and feelings never change, although politics and boundary lines do. This is evident whether the broadside eulogized a hero like George Washington or lamented the cruelty of war; anyone hearing Russell's melodic rendition of "Johnny's Gone for a Soldier," could imagine it springing from Joan Baez's lungs almost 200 years later.

Look at Russell's hands while you listen to her voice and see her capably handling early America's folk instruments. There are few other places where you can see musical accompaniment on a dancing limberjack or a dulcimer plucked with a quill pen.

Location: Federal Hall National Memorial is at 26 Wall Street on the corner of Wall and Nassau Streets. **Admission** is free. **Hours:** Year round, Monday through Friday, including Washington's Birthday and July 4, but closed other major holidays. **Allow** 30 minutes to an hour, more to hear Linda Russell or other musical performers. **Information:** Federal Hall National Memorial, 26 Wall Street, New York, NY 10005; (212) 264-8711.

Events: Weekly midday concerts are scheduled regularly. Special programs take place on Washington's Birthday and July 4, usually including colonial music, films, and other entertainment. A costumed reenactment of George Washington's inauguration takes place April 30.

Note: Federal Hall National Memorial has a significant film library relating to George Washington and colonial America, and films can be shown upon request. The staff prefers to receive such requests at least three days in advance.

If you are staying overnight: Get information on conventional lodging and tour packages from the New York Convention and Visitors Bureau, Inc., 2 Columbus Circle, New York, NY 10019; (212) 397-8222. For information on alternative lodging, contact City Lights Bed & Breakfast, Ltd., P.O. Box 20355, Cherokee Station, New York, NY 10028; (212) 737-7049. Also try Urban Ventures, another bed and breakfast service, P.O. Box 426, New York, NY 10024; (212) 594-5650.

HUGUENOT STREET HOUSES

Stone houses in New York are a rarity and those on Huguenot Street date as far back as 1692.

HOUSES MADE OF STONE ARE NOT COMMONLY SEEN IN THE UNITED States, so when you first set eyes on the group of stone houses near the banks of the Wallkill River in New Paltz, your first feeling will likely be one of curiosity.

The houses were built as early as 1692 by Huguenots, French Protestants, who, despite the abundance of natural hardwoods in the Hudson Valley, chose to build their new homes in stone as they had back in France.

Who were the Huguenots? They emerged during the Protestant Reformation in 16th-century Europe and were ultimately forced to flee their homes because of relentless persecution.

In 1685, King Louis XIV revoked an official edict that granted Huguenots religious and political freedom. Over the next several years, more than a quarter million Huguenots fled France, settling in England, Holland, Prussia, and the colonies of America.

These were hardly the stereotyped dirt-poor refugees. Most were successful upper middle-class merchants, artisans, and craftsmen. While these immigrants had the financial capabilities to build large homes, they were lacking in manpower. So they started with two basic rooms, one with a loft for sleeping and a kitchen in the cellar. Most of the houses were expanded within a decade and, in time, were further altered by later generations. Some you will see still look European in style, others have been remodeled to reflect styles of later periods.

An example is the Hugo Freer House, which is believed to date from 1694. Within 20 years it had doubled in size, and late in the 18th century a wooden extension was added.

While the Huguenots emigrated to escape religious persecution, they were not resistant to assimilation. Their children were not discouraged from marrying offspring of Dutch settlers and adopting their ways of living.

And they were willing to borrow and learn from their new neighbors. In the Abraham Hasbrouck House, you will see examples of Dutch influence. Wooden shoes rest silently in the cellar kitchen, and a wall bed, ascended by ladder and with a door to shut out drafts, is seen in an upstairs bedroom. A big wooden kas (cabinet) is also in that bedroom; a smaller one is in a bedroom next to it.

The Huguenots adopted the Dutch kas not simply for practicality or aesthetics. There was a closet tax then so the kas and other storing alternatives like a three-section wardrobe in a bedroom were common. A similar tax was levied on glass; little wonder that several houses, like the Hasbrouck House, have tiny windows with no more than six panes, making rooms depressingly dark. There is also the Dutch door, a handy development seen in the Bevier-Elting House, circa 1698.

In addition to serving as showcases for antiques and oddities, each of the six houses (and one church) open to the public on Huguenot Street is warmed by its own distinct personality. The Hugo Freer House is basic stone adapted to afford comfortable latter-day living; the Abraham Hasbrouck House is known for its big hearth in the expansive cellar kitchen with its bumpy stone floor; the Bevier-Elting House also served as a general store (note the 30-paned window, pure decadence in a time of heavy glass taxes).

Another store was across the street in the Jean Hasbrouck House. This store also served as a tavern, and in spite of the hardened Calvinistic attitudes towards religion, the residents of Huguenot Street were known to bend an elbow there now and then; old bottles resting on the tavern counter attest to that.

The Jean Hasbrouck House has a rare central hallway, dividing the residential portion of the house from the store; it also has an unusually handsome kitchen. But even though the pots, roaster, toaster, wafer irons, and pewter ware all surround the expansive hearth, the Hasbroucks leaned towards frugality; the room still has its original six-paned window, which makes the interior as dark as twilight in the nearby Hudson River woods.

Getting tired of Dutch colonial New York? Then step inside the LeFevre House and the Deyo House. The Federal-style LeFevre House first took shape in 1799 and was built by a member of the Elting family. (Many Elting women married into the LeFevre family, giving the home its name.)

The LeFevre House also served as a store, but it appears that business was not good enough. Since brick construction was a status symbol, Ezekiel Elting cleverly put brick on the front and side so people arriving by ferry on the Wallkill River would think it was a wealthy family's home.

Should you need a reason to be thankful you live in the 20th century, climb upstairs and enter the re-created early 19th-century doctor's office. The friendly country doctor served as a dentist, too, and this one was thoughtful enough to place rings on his patients' chair so they could hold onto something while having their teeth yanked out in the days before anesthetics.

Victoriana rules the Deyo House, which, though hard to believe, was once a little stone structure. Remodeled in 1890, this rambling home features a wedding cake ceiling with plaster of paris frills and Tiffany glass globes on the lights.

Only one building in the grouping is not an original. A French Reformed Church was built in this neighborhood in 1717 and destroyed in 1795. After seven years of tedious research, a reproduction was raised in 1972 near the spot where the first one stood.

The most cumbersome part of reconstructing the church was the placement of the cupola, which had to be lowered into place via helicopter. In the 1700s, a man or boy would climb to the cupola and blow a conch shell to let area residents know services were about to begin.

Services were austere, lasting from morning to sunset with a break only for lunch. Cold hard-backed wooden pews and a man hired to watch over the congregators made sure nobody slept when they should be praying.

Before leaving the area, make one last stop in Deyo Hall (not to be confused with the Deyo House). The museum on the second floor, called the Howard H. Grimm Memorial Gallery, contains a variety of Huguenot possessions and a smattering of paintings. You can see anything from silver teapots to swords and pistols to a circa 1714 chocolate pot, evidence that chocoholics were around long before modern times.

Location: From New York State Thruway (Interstate 87), take exit 18 to Route 299 into New Paltz where the road becomes Main Street. After the junction with Route 32, take a right onto Huguenot Street, then a right onto Brodhead Street to Deyo Hall where the tours start. **Admission** is charged to all buildings with the exception of the Howard H. Grimm Gallery in Deyo Hall. **Hours:** Memorial Day through September, Wednesday through Sunday; weekends only in October. **Allow** two and a half to three hours for the full seven-building tour; one and a quarter to one and a half hours for the smaller three-building tour (two houses and the church); a half hour to 45 minutes for the tour of the Jean Hasbrouck House, the only house you can see without taking a longer tour; and 15 minutes to see the Grimm Gallery in Deyo Hall. **Information:** Huguenot Historical Society, P.O. Box 339, New Paltz, NY 12561; (914) 255-1660.

Note: We recommend that casual visitors take the three-building tour. The complete tour is best for persons with specific interests in this period of history or architecture. Those with little time and passing interest will be satisfied with a visit to just the Jean Hasbrouck House. Tickets are purchased at Deyo Hall on Brodhead Street (not to be confused with the Deyo House that is seen only on guided tours).

If you are staying overnight: Mohonk Mountain House (a national historic landmark and noted resort), off Route 299, New Paltz, (914) 255-1000; Anzor Motel, Route 299 (Main Street), New Paltz, (914) 883-7373; Thunderbird Motel, Route 299 (Main Street), New Paltz, (914) 255-6200.

SARATOGA NATIONAL HISTORICAL PARK

The victory at Saratoga lifted the spirits of the colonists, who no longer saw their struggle as David against a powerful Goliath.

WHEN GENERAL JOHN "GENTLEMAN JOHNNY" BURGOYNE SURRENdered to the colonists at Saratoga in October 1777, it was enough to make one American supporter break out in song. He wrote an anthem, 46 verses long, to commemorate the event. A sample verse, number 29, went like this:

"Our brave soldiers all with powderhorn and ball
Each man with a gun on his shoulder.
With courage so stout directly turn'd out
No men in New England were bolder."

The victory was as vital as it was sweet. Most historians believe that if the colonists had lost at Saratoga, they never would have gotten needed help from France; without that aid, they would have ultimately lost the revolution. In addition, the battle lifted the sagging spirits of the colonists who had seen themselves as David up against a towering Goliath.

One colonist said, following Burgoyne's surrender, "Rebellion, which a twelve-month ago was a contemptible pygmy, is now in appearance a giant."

The British had been hoping to control the Hudson River, cutting off New England from the rest of the colonies. They planned for Burgoyne's forces to meet with those of two other generals in Albany.

Burgoyne was moving his army south from Montreal. As a diversion, Colonel Barry St. Leger was to start out at (present day) Oswego on Lake Ontario and penetrate the upper Mohawk Valley, while Sir William Howe planned to march north from New York City in order to join his forces with Burgoyne's.

The plan was approved by the British Crown and orders were sent from London to Burgoyne. However, orders never reached Howe, and he decided to move his forces to the colonial capital in Philadelphia. St. Leger, meanwhile, held Fort Stanwix in (present day) Rome under siege, only to retreat back towards Canada after hearing that General Benedict Arnold (still with the colonies at the time) was bringing a substantial force to the fort.

Burgoyne and his men were left on their own, a weak and lonely fragment of loyalists in strange and unfriendly terrain. They met the colonists under General Horatio Gates at Freeman's Farm on September 19. The British were staved off, but three weeks later on October 7, the British attacked again only to be beaten back once more. The British suffered 1,000 casualties, more than twice as many as the Americans, and the next day they retreated north. The American army swelled in size as more militiamen joined Gates; they surrounded Burgoyne's troops, causing him to surrender on October 17.

To keep yourself from surrendering in confusion, plan to make the park visitor center your first stop. Here you can pick up a park brochure with a map of the nine-mile-long battlefield auto-tour route.

The visitor center is also the place to take a close look at the battle and get a feel for life as a colonial soldier. *Checkmate on the Hudson* is the 21-minute-long film that re-creates the battle through the use of visual and aural effects including regiments of toy soldiers, a chess board, and a tense drum roll. There are two theaters so even in the busiest seasons long waits are rare.

While *Checkmate on the Hudson* interprets the strategy and political implications of the battle, the visitor center museum shows you the human side of 18th-century warfare. On view are soldiers' crude eating implements such as a wooden bowl, two-pronged forks, a rusty old butter knife, a squat little camp stove, and colonial toothbrushes. In addition, there are trivia facts, some of which are extraordinary; the Continental Army was not segregated by race—that would not happen again until the Korean Conflict in the 1950s.

To offer news for those in the military and at home, broadsides were posted on faded clapboard barns and city building walls throughout the colonies. An example is the song mentioned at the start of this section celebrating Burgoyne's surrender.

To see where that surrender took place, head for the auto-tour route, which has ten stops where important incidents in the battle took place; you will find audio tapes at most stops, each lasting one to three minutes.

Perhaps the most popular point to pause is site #7, the Breymann Redoubt. General Benedict Arnold was injured in the leg here in an incident immortalized by the "boot monument," a favorite photo spot. Arnold, of course, survived. Had he died from the wound he would have gone down in history as one of America's finest generals and patriots.

Expect to confront militia men in the flesh if you visit in summer. Living history encampments are regularly scheduled at the Nielson Farm (site #2), which American generals used as headquarters. Catch these "18th-century" soldiers in their acts and you can learn everything from how meals were fixed in an army encampment to what was involved in a colonial military drill. You can even show your patriotism by putting your John Hancock on the muster roll at the Officer's Marquee on Company Street.

Then raise your Saratoga visit to new heights by walking the 190 steps to the top of Saratoga Monument. You will have to drive to get there, though; it's in Schuylerville, eight miles from the battlefield. The 155-foot-high monument was built from 1877 to 1883 and stands on a portion of Burgoyne's October 1777 camp.

From the top you have a panoramic view of rolling hills in a vast landscape; in good weather you can see the Hudson River in the distance. Park staff member Bill Ward says that some people have reported seeing church steeples in the distance, but he hasn't found them yet.

Near the monument and also part of the park is the Schuyler House, built in three weeks as the home of General Philip Schuyler, who preceded Horatio Gates as the commander of American forces. Schuyler once described his wilderness retreat in this manner:

"My hobby horse has long been a country life; I dismounted once with reluctance and now saddle him again with a very considerable share of satisfaction, and hope to canter him on to the end of the journey of life."

The two-story frame building was actually Schuyler's third home here, the others being destroyed during the French and Indian Wars and by Burgoyne. But this one survived marauders, and three pieces inside belonged to Schuyler: a Chippendale drop-leaf dining room table, a linen press in an upstairs vestibule, and a dresser in the master bedroom.

Location: From Interstate 87, take exit 12 onto Route 67 towards Malta; at Malta, take Route 108 east to Route 9P and follow it around the southeastern shore of Saratoga Lake; then take Route 423 east for three and a half miles to Route 32 north and follow signs to the visitor center.

To reach Schuylerville, site of the Schuyler House and the Saratoga Monument, follow the signs for Route 4 from the visitor center parking lot and take Route 4 north for eight miles. The Schuyler House is on Route 4 on the right side, just before you cross Fish Creek and head into town. To reach the monument, follow Route 4 into town where it becomes Broad Street; take a left onto Burgoyne Street; the monument is on your left side between Gates Street and Cemetery Avenue.

Admission is charged May through October. **Hours:** Visitor center: year round, daily. Auto-tour route: Mid-April through November, daily, weather permitting; the road is not plowed so it's not unusual for a late spring or fall snowstorm to close it. Schuyler House and Saratoga Monument: Mid-June to Labor Day, daily. **Allow** three to four hours to explore the entire park if you are a casual visitor. Park service staff member Bill Ward recommends 45 minutes to see the film and museum in the visitor center; an hour and a half to drive the auto-tour route; 20 to 30 minutes to tour the Schuyler House and 15 to 20 minutes to climb the Saratoga Monument. Anyone with more than a casual interest in the topic could spend three to four hours just on the auto loop road and should plan a full day to see all. **Information:** Saratoga National Historical Park, RD #2, Box 33, Stillwater, NY 12170; (518) 664-9821.

Events: Lectures, slide programs, and living history demonstrations are presented throughout the summer. A sampling of topics includes: "Eighteenth-Century Herbs and their Many Uses," "The British and German Soldiers at Saratoga," "Songs and Ballads of the Burgoyne Campaign," "Wildflowers," and "A Revolutionary Fourth of July."

Note: There are two picnic areas in the park: one with grills is by the visitor center parking lot, one with no grills is by site #10 on the auto-tour route. Some small hiking trails and horseback riding trails, which become cross-country ski trails in winter, are also in the park.

If you are staying overnight: Burgoyne Motor Inn, 220 N. Broad Street (on Routes 4 and 32), Schuylerville; (518) 695-3282. Empress Motel, 173 Broad Street (Route 4), Schuylerville; (518) 695-3231. Also see the Saratoga Springs lodging listing.

NEW YORK STATE MUSEUM

Courtesy: New York State Museum

So you want to see early New York? The life-size diorama of this massive mastodon takes you back 10,000 years.

" . . . WITH ALL THE OPULENCE AND SPLENDOR OF THIS CITY, THERE IS very little good breeding to be found . . . they talk loud, very fast, and all together."

John Adams, 1774, on New York City

Reading Adams's quote in the New York State Museum in Albany may lead one to think that some things never change. Yet a little further along you see a diorama of a wilderness setting that includes a timber rattler in repose. The locale is not the Adirondacks but upper Manhattan, three centuries ago.

Things have changed, immensely so, and the New York State Museum chronicles the changes brought by both man and nature. The museum, one of the best we have seen in any state, shows visitors through life-sized dioramas, films, video exhibits, transplanted antique vehicles, and reconstructed building interiors the "intricate relationship between man and a wilderness environment."

You see this in many massive displays, not just those one would expect like pre-historic hunters sleuthing a wolverine, but also urban scenes, including a 1930-ish barbershop from Manhattan's upper west side and a 1920s Texaco gas station with a hand-cranked gasoline pump, the kind everyone's grandfather remembers.

The museum is divided into three huge halls, each focusing on major regions of the state: the New York metropolis, the Adirondack Wilderness, and upstate New York. The upstate exhibition is not yet complete; it will be opening gradually throughout the next several years.

Wander through each hall and you will be accompanied by music peculiar to each region. In the metropolis, Liza Minelli's "New York, New York" sets the tone; in the Adirondack region, it's the songs of the birds and the rushing water of mountain streams.

The songs of the city, however, also can be heard in Chinese, Spanish, Yiddish, or Italian. New York is a city of neighborhoods, as one exhibit explicitly points out. It is here that you see the Hispanic depression-era barbershop. Prices in the 1930s were 80 cents for a haircut and 40 cents for a shave; the prices fell to 30 and 20 cents respectively after 1937.

24 Mott Street in Chinatown, home of the Tuck High Company, which sold foods, dry goods, spices, and utensils is reproduced here, too.

Then there is the turn-of-the-century sweatshop with five garment workers and an infant crowded into a rat trap of a room. As untold refugees fled Europe, the companion commentary reads, Americans were making a habit of wearing machine-sewn clothing; the sweatshop was the logical result.

Another neighborhood depicted belongs to Big Bird and Oscar the Grouch. The brownstone set from Sesame Street is fully replicated, complete with Oscar poking his head up out of a steel garbage can. Hard to believe that this so recognizable television set is made of nothing but papier mache, canvas, wood, and paint.

Continue wandering through the maze of the re-created metropolis. The stock market trading post from the thirties, the Broadway area tableau from the day when *Showboat* was the biggest thing to hit the stage, and the subway car made in 1940 will educate as well as ring nostalgic. And you didn't have to be alive in 1940 to appreciate it today.

The metropolis exhibit isn't limited to man-made effects. Keeping in tune with the museum's theme, you see that nature won't let go of the city. Check out the model of a vacant lot where house finches, English sparrows, a brown snake, common plantains, and dandelions make their home.

Some upstate residents may be surprised to find that New York City is a wonderful spot for bird watchers. The city is located along the Atlantic Flyway, a major north-south bird migration route, and thousands of species are found in Central and Van Cordtlandt parks every year; photos of birds that fall victim to urban air conditions show that many don't make it out of the city.

Maybe they should stop instead in the Adirondacks, New York State's purest wilderness. The Adirondack rocks were formed deep below the earth's surface over 1,000 million years ago. But even here, the presence of man has taken its toll on native animal life, most significantly in the last 200 years.

As in the metropolis hall, life-sized dioramas show all angles of this. One presents two men trying to cooperate with nature in the crudest form of early wilderness camping. They camp in a basic shelter of wood and bark; no Coleman canvas tents here. Another shows a tangled log jam on the upper Hudson River, a common occurrence when lumbering companies commenced their log drives during the gushing snow melt of early spring.

The diorama dominated by the ponderous moose is a paean to animals that man has driven from the Adirondacks. The moose, whose meat became meals and whose hide went for snowshoe webbing and moccasins, was gone by the 1860s. The elk vanished by the 1830s, the wolverine by the 1840s, and the lynx by the 1890s.

About that time, many parts of the Adirondacks were rapidly becoming a haven for New Yorkers with leisure time on their minds. The ca. 1900 wagon, locally called a "mountain taxi," was typical of those which carried passengers and their luggage from the railroad station to hotels.

But other New Yorkers came because of doctor's orders. Patients afflicted with tuberculosis were often given this prescription for rest and recuperation: the clean air, pristine water, and tranquility of the Adirondacks.

The model of the 'Rondack combination couch and chair, displayed on a typical resort deck surrounded by a birch wood fence, was a common sight around the turn of the century. An accompanying advertisement proclaims the 'Rondack "highly endorsed by leading physicians for tuberculosis patients and convalescents."

Museum visitors journey even further into the state's past. A diorama of ice age hunters, the state's first residents, highlights a representation of the Hudson Valley tens of thousands of years ago. A mastodon and her calf stand in a frigid setting of glaciated terrain; Syracuse in February never looked colder.

There also are many smaller exhibits on other topics like state gems, state birds, old fire fighting equipment, and Holocaust refugees who were interned in Oswego during one of the state's coldest winters prior to being relocated. All are worth seeking out.

Location: The New York State Museum is in the Cultural Education

Center in Empire State Plaza in downtown Albany. From Interstate 87 southbound, take Interstate 90 east to Interstate 787 south to US 20 west (Madison Avenue) to the museum. From Interstate 87 northbound, take Interstate 787 north (exit 23) to US 20 west (Madison Avenue) to the museum. From Interstate 90 westbound, take the Albany/Troy exit and bear left onto Interstate 787 south; exit at US 20 west (Madison Avenue) to the museum. From Interstate 90 eastbound, take Interstate 787 south to US 20 west (Madison Avenue) to the museum. Parking is available at the museum visitor lot off Madison Avenue, at lots on the corners of Madison and Pearl Street and Madison and Philip Streets, and in the Empire State Plaza underground garage. **Admission** is free. Parking is free on weekends. **Hours:** Year round, daily. **Allow** two to three hours. **Information:** New York State Museum, Cultural Education Center, State Education Department, Empire State Plaza, Albany, NY 12230; (518) 474-5877 or (518) 474-5842.

Events: Films, temporary exhibitions, and programs are scheduled regularly.

If you are staying overnight: Albany Hilton, Ten Eyck Plaza, State and Lodge Streets, (518) 462-6611; Albany Marriott, 189 Wolf Road (off Interstate 87, exit 4), (518) 458-8444; Jeremy's Inn, 500 Northern Boulevard (off Interstate 90, exit 6), (518) 462-5562; La Siesta, 1579 Central Avenue (off Interstate 90, exit 24, and Interstate 87, exit 2W), (518) 869-8471.

RICHMONDTOWN RESTORATION

Two apprentices learn the art of candle dipping during Richmondtown's summer season.

"THERE WAS AN EXPRESSION HEARD OFTEN ON STATEN ISLAND," WE were told by Stephen Nutt, the resident potter at Richmondtown Restoration. "The rich man has a canopy over his bed. The poor man has a canopy under his bed."

The canopy under the bed, an expression used regionally, referred to a chamber pot. In Staten Island, it was likely made from redware, a type of pottery commonly used here, which Nutt works with while you watch.

You will hear other similar tales of long ago days in Staten Island when you visit Richmondtown, a burgeoning living history museum on 96 acres in the island's Greenbelt area.

The Richmondtown staff refers to the complex as "New York City's only historic village," and that point is well taken. Walk in lower Manhattan or Queens or Brooklyn and there is virtually no vestige of the colonial heritage of the city other than a few isolated historic buildings, rubbing elbows with steel and glass skyscrapers, row houses, or commercial blocks.

But Staten Islanders had foresight. As far back as the 1920s, members of the Staten Island Historical Society began acquiring historic buildings with an eye towards preservation.

The original village of Richmond first took root in the 1690s as a minor crossroads on an island dotted with farms and country estates. Its name then was Cocclestown and the Richmondtown staff is fortunate to have the Voorlezer's House as a link to those earliest days on the island.

"Voorlezer" was not a family name. It was the title of the Reformed Dutch Church's lay minister and teacher, who lived here from the time the structure was built (about 1695) until 1700; the house stands as the oldest surviving elementary school in the country and the oldest building on its original site in Richmondtown.

Cocclestown eventually became Richmondtown and the village grew to finally become the seat of county government. Representing this period of growth on the restoration are the Guyon-Lake-Tysen House, a sizable Dutch colonial farmhouse, and the Treasure House. The Treasure House is the second oldest original building in the village; it dates to the turn of the 18th century, with several later additions, and got its name from the story that a bundle of gold coins, concealed by the British during the American Revolution, was uncovered during a renovation in 1860. The Treasure House is under renovation and closed to the public for the time being.

On the other hand, if you enter the Guyon-Lake-Tysen House in peak season, you will probably see the early American lady of the house engaged in weaving at the loom upstairs or concocting the midday meal downstairs in the kitchen brick oven.

Our guide said there was a simple way for a cook to tell whether or not the bricks were hot enough for baking. She would put her arm inside the oven and count to ten; if the hairs on her arm were still not singed, the oven was not yet ready. It often took an hour and a half of pre-heating for the oven to reach the proper cooking temperature.

The Guyon-Lake-Tysen house had several face lifts in the 19th century. The kitchen was added about 1820 and dormers about 20 years later. So it's not inappropriate that the upstairs bedrooms depict different periods. The 1815 room, for example, is heavy on Shaker-style boxes. Across the hall is the 1815-1830 Classical Revival room with a sleigh bed and a heavily carved chest of drawers. The late 19th-century bedroom is garnished with a grain-painted "cottage" bedroom suite. Potter Stephen Nutt, meanwhile, works out of the house's cellar, turning redware on his wheel.

We are lucky that the Guyon-Lake-Tysen House has lasted the centuries considering that Staten Island was occupied by the British during the Revolutionary War, and many of its earliest buildings, including the early Dutch Church where the voorlezer gave his sermons, were destroyed during the occupation.

In summer, craftspeople plying their trades in many of the buildings make this a thriving living history village. In addition to the potter, plan to run into, among others, the tinsmith (in a former store representing the period around 1860), the basket maker (in a ca. 1810-20 Dutch home), the furniture maker (in a 1966 adaptation of an 1835 building), and the printer (in the ca. 1860 print shop), all of them hard at work and eager to talk about it.

Come in the lengthy off-season and you should still find one or two craftspeople going about their daily routine, but since most of the residences and businesses are empty, you will be given a guided tour, usually into five buildings.

In addition to meeting Stephen Nutt and visiting the Guyon-Lake-Tysen House, we were given an inside look at the Bennett House, a Greek Revival residence with a considerable collection of toys, dolls, and games, and the Stephens/Black General Store, a combination mercantile outlet and post office.

What could one buy in a Victorian-era general store? Containers for edible treats like National Biscuit Company Water Crackers and Runkel Brothers Breakfast Cocoa establish the Stephens/Black Store setting to be 1860 to 1875, although there are stocked items that would have been sold into the early 20th century. A well-rounded combination of consumer items—lanterns, oil heater wicks and lamps, dress-making materials, and bird cages—supplement the foods. Off and on, the store also served as a post office, and Staten Island residents' post boxes still line the right side of the store.

Presently, Richmondtown historic village has 26 buildings, 11 of which are on their original sites and 12 of which have interiors regularly open to the public; in time, more will be opened.

Location: Richmondtown Restoration is at the intersection of Richmond Road, Clarke Avenue, and Arthur Kill Road, adjacent to La-Tourette Park in the Greenbelt area in the center of Staten Island. From Brooklyn, take the Verrazano-Narrows Bridge, follow the New Jersey West route and take the Richmond Road/Clove Road exit; at the second light turn left onto Richmond Road and after about five miles, turn left onto St. Patrick's Place and follow the signs. From the Bayonne Bridge, exit at the Goethals Bridge sign, bear right and take the first exit (Richmond Avenue). Turn right onto Richmond Avenue, then left onto Arthur

Kill Road; at the third traffic light, turn right onto Clarke Avenue and follow the signs. From Elizabeth, New Jersey, take the Goethals Bridge onto the Staten Island Expressway (I-278), Richmond Avenue exit; head south and turn left onto Arthur Kill Road; at the third light, turn right onto Clarke Avenue and follow the signs. From the Staten Island Ferry, take Bay Street south about two miles, then turn right onto Vanderbilt Avenue; at the fourth signal, bear left onto Richmond Road and after about five miles, turn left onto St. Patrick's Place and follow the signs. **Admission** is charged. **Hours:** Year round, Wednesday through Friday; Saturday and Sunday, afternoons; the restoration is in full operation in July and August. **Allow** an hour to an hour and a half. **Information:** Staten Island Historical Society, 441 Clarke Avenue, Staten Island, NY 10306; (718) 351-1611.

Events: A few of the many are: Labor Day weekend, Richmond County Fair; mid-October, Old Home Day, 18th- and 19th-century crafts and domestic activities demonstrations; early December, Christmas in Richmondtown.

Note: Tours start in the visitor center in the courthouse. A snack bar and picnic tables are on the grounds.

If you are staying overnight: Holiday Inn, 1415 Richmond Avenue (I-278, Richmond Avenue exit), (718) 698-5000; Cosmopolitan Hotel, 1274 Hyland Boulevard, (718) 979-7000.

BEAUTIFUL
NEW YORK

BEAR MOUNTAIN AND HARRIMAN STATE PARKS

If it wasn't for one person's generosity, this spectacular view would have been reserved for prisoners' eyes only.

T HE STUNNING VIEW FROM THE SUMMIT OF PERKINS MEMORIAL DRIVE, perhaps the best vista of all those in the Hudson River Valley, came very close to becoming hell on a hilltop.

A few years past the turn of the century, the New York State Prison Commission decided that this isolated parcel of knolls and glens would be the perfect spot for a prison—specifically Sing Sing Prison.

The public was outraged and protested vociferously, full of the spirit of then President Theodore Roosevelt, the most dedicated conservationist ever to sit in the Oval Office. To the rescue came Mrs. Mary Williamson, who offered the state 10,000 acres of Orange County and Rockland County land and $1 million for the purchase of other nearby land with the conditions that the Palisades Interstate Park commissioners would become the new proposed park's managers and that the Bear Mountain prison site be scrapped. Both conditions were accepted and, in 1910, Bear Mountain and the adjoining Harriman State Parks were created.

Almost everyone who comes here drives to the summit of Bear Mountain along Perkins Memorial Drive. The summit measures 1,305 feet up from sea level, lilliputian by standards of the Rocky Mountains, for example, but mighty high by New York metropolitan area standards. On a clear day, you may not see forever, but you can see Broadway, or at least the skyline of midtown Manhattan, 45 miles south.

Most of the elevations in the parks range from 1,000 to 1,200 feet above sea level. Many peaks have been named for animals: Catamount Mountain, Panther Mountain, Wildcat Mountain, and, of course, Bear Mountain. Other landmarks have names derived from Indian languages, such as Stahahe Lake ("stones in the water") and Lake Tiorati ("sky-like").

It is inevitable that hikers will want to tackle Bear Mountain, and the 3.3-mile-long Major Welch Trail on the north slope is fitting for all levels. The trail entrance is behind the Bear Mountain Inn, and the climb parallels the western shore of Hessian Lake before taking you up a gentle slope, then a steep slope of 800 feet to the summit. Splendid views abound throughout the trail.

The Popolopen Gorge Trail, another short hike, is 4.3 miles long and follows a brook and a gorge by that name; however, it's not really suited for young children or the elderly. Able-bodied experts should consider the challenging Ramapo-Dunderberg Trail, 20.8 miles long, and the rugged Suffern-Bear Mountain Trail, which stretches 24.3 miles and is recommended for Grizzly Adams types. The Appalachian Trail also passes through the park, stretching 16.3 miles from Bear Mountain to Route 17 and crossing nine summits along the way.

Outdoors people who would rather spend their precious leisure time on the water will be happy to know that rowboats and canoes are allowed on ten park lakes. You can bring your own or rent a rowboat on Hessian Lake. A permit is needed to operate any craft on park waters and can be obtained in the park at Tiorati Circle and at Beaver Pond Campground. No gas-powered motorboats or sailboats are allowed.

Bear Mountain Park, the more developed of the two parks, also offers a potpourri of facilities: a 94 x 224-foot swimming pool, bathhouse and lockers, basketball court, and miniature golfcourse in summer. Winter activities include ice skating and groomed cross-country ski trails, most falling within the easiest category. For those who would rather head out onto, as Robert Frost would have said, "the road not taken," there is ski touring on ungroomed hiking trails.

Regardless of the time of year in which you visit and your hiking adventures, you can arrange to come face to face with bull frogs, catfish, garter snakes, and even copperheads. They are just some of the creatures who make the park lands their natural homes and are also on view at the Bear Mountain Trailside Museum and Zoo.

There has been a museum building here since 1927 and throughout the years facilities have been added, enlarged, and expanded. Three buildings devoted to geology, botany, and history were added in the 1930s and have been given several face lifts over the years, one as recent as 1986 when the small animal museum was renovated. City residents whose experience with the animal world is usually limited to pigeons can learn how the other half of nature lives.

Location: Bear Mountain State Park is reached by taking Route 9W or exit 14 off the Palisades Interstate Parkway. Harriman State Park is reached by taking the New York State Thruway (Interstate 87) to exit 16, then Route 6 (Long Mountain Parkway) to the Palisades Interstate Parkway south; from the parkway, take exit 14A onto Lake Welch Drive into the park. **Admission** is free to enter the grounds and the Bear Mountain Trailside Museum and Zoo. Permits, obtained for a small fee, are required to take boats onto any park lakes, and fees are charged for most activities such as miniature golf, swimming, ski touring, and skating. There is no charge to take your car up Perkins Memorial Drive to the summit of Bear Mountain or to enter the Trailside Museum. **Hours:** Year round, daily. **Allow** an hour to drive to the summit of Bear Mountain. There are enough recreational opportunities in the parks to last a full day or more. **Information:** Palisades Interstate Park Commission, Administration Building, Bear Mountain, NY 10911; (914) 786-2701.

Events: A partial list includes: January, ski-jumping tournaments; February, winter carnival; March through May, "Hudson Valley Life" lecture series; fall, ethnic food festivals and Bear Mountain Crafts Fair; December, Bear Mountain Christmas Festival (Christmas trees, gallery exhibits, outdoor light display, talking bear, Santa in residence).

Note: Several other state parks, including Rockland Lake, High Tor, Nyack Beach, and Tallman Mountain State Park, are in the immediate area. You can request specific information regarding these other parks from the address listed above.

If you are staying overnight: Bear Mountain Inn, Bear Mountain State Park, (914) 786-2731; Palisade Motel, Route 218 at the junction with Route 9W, Highland Falls, (914) 446-9400; West Point Motel, Route 218 east of the junction with Route 9W, Highland Falls, (914) 446-4180; Sebago Cabins, Harriman State Park, (914) 351-2360, late April through mid-October; Iona Island Campground, Bear Mountain State Park, (914) 786-2701, by reservation only; Tiorati Plateau Campground, Harriman State Park, (914) 351-2568, no reservations.

FIRE ISLAND NATIONAL SEASHORE

National Park Service photo by M. Woodbridge Williams

The only federal wilderness area in New York State is less than 40 miles from New York City at Fire Island National Seashore.

Fire Island National Seashore is a stringbean-thin patch of seaside recreation—some of it pure wilderness—within a suburbanite's commute of midtown Manhattan. To its majority of visitors, Fire Island National Seashore is a summertime beach destination.

To those who look a little further, the national seashore is a refuge for a bevy of wild birds, a place to touch a horseshoe crab to see how sharp it really is, an opportunity to walk through an outdoor environment unaffected by human alterations, and a place to explore the life of a lighthouse keeper.

There are four separate areas that make up the 32-mile-long barrier island. Access to the Lighthouse Area in the west and the Smith Point area in the east is by car. The two areas in the heart of Fire Island,

Watch Hill and Sailors Haven, can only be reached by private boat or by ferry from Long Island in season. In between each area of Fire Island are expanses of protected land or clusters of small communities or a combination of both, but no roads.

For the quickest getaway from the city, take the Robert Moses Causeway from West Islip to the Lighthouse Area, which borders Robert Moses State Park. The state park and the national seashore both offer beaches and lighthouses but only the Fire Island national seashore's visitor center has educational programming and exhibits to explain about this land of sun and recreation.

Fire Island has long been a land of shipwrecks, the first occurring on May 8, 1657. A rash of wrecks for well over a century and a half led to the building of the lighthouse, which began operation in 1826. The current brick, striped lighthouse was completed in 1858.

The walk from Field 5, the closest parking lot, is just 0.6 mile to the lighthouse. The visitor center, the stone building next to the light, was formerly the keeper's home, and displays inside tell the tale of a lonely existence. There are 12 rooms in the keeper's building, which, when used regularly, was divided in half by a staircase, splitting it into separate residences for the keeper and the assistant's families.

Fire Island's out-of-the-way locale—in the days before bridges connected it to Long Island—made it a haven for rumrunners during Prohibition. A display about the island's past delves into this illegal era. One captain and former boat builder, Bill McCoy, was known for bringing to the island batches of only high quality liquor. In comparison to other bootleggers who dealt in cut or impure alcohol, his was referred to as "the real McCoy."

Though associated with an easy and carefree beach life, Fire Island has always faced a pretty harsh climate. To see evidence, take the half-mile-long boardwalk trail past mountainous sand dunes and cranberry bogs, along the shore of the Great South Bay, and past patches of pitch pine and bearberry. A trail leaflet explains the various sites. Stop #16 takes you past trees with bald south sides, appearing as if an army with pruning clippers went on a rampage. This is the result of salt winds constantly blowing in from the ocean.

Want to learn more? Take one of the regularly scheduled interpretive walks or sit in on a park service program. Programs range from the history of the Fire Island Lighthouse to a sing-along of old sea chanteys.

Here, as in all areas of the national seashore, it is important to remind visitors to stay on the boardwalks and other designated walkways. Human feet trample fragile plants and dunes, and poison ivy grows in abundance on the island. Also, staying on the boardwalks will help diminish the chances of being bitten by ticks carrying Lyme disease (see note at end of chapter).

One other precaution . . . the national seashore beach at the Lighthouse Area is for all practical purposes a nudist beach. There is also a nudist beach in the vicinity of the Smith Point West area. If you have your children along or if you find nudity offensive, be forewarned.

Sailors Haven area, the next national seashore area heading east is only accessible by boat. Owners of private boats use the 36-slip marina. Other visitors take the ferry from Sayville. Expect to find a party flavor in season when you step off the boat.

Aside from the swimming beach (a lifeguard is on duty in summer), the main draw is the Sunken Forest Trail, a mile-and-a-half-long stroll on a boardwalk that takes you through an unusual maritime forest. In addition to the ever-omnipresent poison ivy, you will encounter more than a dozen other shrubs, trees, and plants, including: sassafras, cattail, inkberry, and black oak.

As usual, there is a trail leaflet marked with stopping points. The Sunken Forest Trail points out 35 sites, the highlight for many being #19, the canopy. Here, tree tops have grown laterally instead of vertically, blocked by high levels of salt concentration in the air above the height of nearby sand dunes. With the trees unable to grow above the level of the dunes, they have formed a thick canopy, keeping this stretch of forest shaded and cool. As you walk through the forest, don't be too surprised if a deer, fox, or rabbit should appear within eyeshot.

The Sailors Haven area is also home to a visitor center with a "do-touch" table, showers, changing rooms, picnic tables, concession stands, and even a dog-walk area. It doesn't, however, have a campground. The only family campground on Fire Island is at the Watch Hill Facility, the next area heading east, also only accessible by ferry or private boat.

The 26-site campground is about one-quarter mile from the ferry terminal, reached by a boardwalk trail. Park service personnel recommend that campers with heavy or large amounts of equipment bring a cart or wagon along to help haul their gear to their campsite.

But don't start packing yet. As you might guess, with a campground this small on such a popular destination, reservations are necessary and are for the most part selected by lottery. There also is a limit of five days and four nights per stay, and there are no sites for RVs.

Watch Hill has a small visitor center, a nature trail, concessions, picnic tables, showers, and a swimming beach with a lifeguard in summer. The marina has 150 slips.

A seven-mile-long wilderness area, the only federal wilderness area in New York State, connects Watch Hill to Smith Point, the most eastern point of Fire Island. You can explore this wilderness area on foot or with a four-wheel drive vehicle, but you can only drive a vehicle there if your intent is to hunt or fish; to do so, you must fill out an application for a permit at the Smith Point visitor center.

Camping is allowed in the wilderness area, but it is true wilderness camping. Campers must hike in and out, check in at the Smith Point visitor center, and be completely self-sufficient. There is no available parking so campers must be dropped off and picked up. (The parking lot near the visitor center has a $3.00 fee for day parking in season.)

Ranger Sharon Kienzle says that fall and spring are the best seasons for camping here, spring a little less popular because of frequent rains. Summer camping is discouraged because of masses of mosquitos.

Fall and spring are also the best seasons for bird-watching since Fire Island is on the Atlantic Flyway, a major migratory route. Kienzle adds that while the entire island is a feast for friends of feathered flyers, Smith Point may be the best place to see rare birds, being less settled than areas west.

There also is a "please-touch" table at the Smith Point visitor center, which is full of surprises both for children as well as their parents. The razor clam is only a little sharp, but you still wouldn't want to step on one. The waved welk egg case is soft, almost spongy. The baleen, which forms the plates of whales' upper jaws, feels almost like a soft wood; its ends are like feathers. Baleen plates have been used throughout the years to make everything from corset stays to buggy springs, and, as a result, whales, like the North Atlantic Right Whale, are now endangered.

All specimens in the visitor center are labeled, but if you can't tell the shells without a scorecard, plan to take part in one of the ranger-led walks. In addition to shells, you can find out about shipwrecks and other human history or just learn about all the edible plants growing wild on the island. Then consider taking time to walk the ¾-mile-long trail here that will take you past beach plums (stop #7), one of Fire Island's best known edible plants. Other edibles? How about sarsaparilla, rose hips, glassworts, juneberries, and blueberries—it's a veritable beachcomber's banquet.

Location: Fire Island National Seashore consists of unsettled portions of Fire Island located between several communities. To reach the Lighthouse Area from the Sunrise Highway (Route 27), take exit 41, then take the Robert Moses Parkway south; cross the Robert Moses Causeway and continue straight to the island. To reach Sailors Haven from Sunrise Highway (Route 27), take Lakeland Avenue south onto Main Street and follow the green and white signs for Fire Island Ferries; the ferry terminal is off River Road. To reach Watch Hill from Sunrise Highway (Route 27), take Waverly Avenue south to the ferry terminal. To reach Smith Point West from the Sunrise Expressway (Route 27), take exit 58, then take the William Floyd Highway south and cross Smith Point Bridge to the island. **Admission** is free to all parts of the national seashore. Parking fees are charged in season for the beaches at Robert Moses State Park and Smith Point County Park. Admission is charged for the ferries from Long Island to Sailors Haven and Watch Hill. **Hours:** Fire Island National Seashore is open year round. Peak season is late June through Labor Day weekend; some visitor centers open earlier and close later depending on staffing. Sailors Haven Marina is open late April to mid-October; Watch Hill Marina is open mid-May to mid-October. Ferries generally run early May through October. **Allow** a half hour to walk the Lighthouse Area Trail, an hour to walk the Sunken Forest Trail, and 45 minutes to walk the Smith Point West Trail. Allow 30 minutes for the ferry ride to Sailors Haven and 25 minutes for the ferry ride to Watch Hill. **Information:** Superintendent, Fire Island National Seashore, 120 Laurel Street, Patchogue, NY 11772; (516) 289-4810.

Note: The William Floyd Estate, home of a signer of the Declaration of Independence, is also part of the national seashore even though it is located on Long Island (20 Washington Avenue, Mastic Beach). It is open April through October, Wednesday through Sunday and holidays; admission is free. Call (516) 399-2030 for more information. Park service personnel emphasize that visitors should take precautions to avoid being bitten by ticks carrying Lyme Disease. The disease, first recognized in 1975 in Old Lyme, Connecticut, is carried by ticks the size of a pinhead, and first symptoms include a rash followed by flu-like symptoms and more severe symptoms if left untreated. Some ways to help prevent contact are to stay on trail boardwalks, avoid walking through wooded and brushy areas, wear long pants with cuffs tucked into socks, and wear light clothing to help spot ticks.

If you are staying overnight: Holiday Inn, 3845 Veterans Memorial Highway (just over four miles southeast of Long Island Expressway, exit 57), Ronkonkoma, (516) 585-9500; Land's End Motel, 70 Brown's River Road, Sayville, (516) 589-2040; Summit Motor Lodge, 50l East Main Street (Route 27A), Bay Shore, (516) 666-6000; Watch Hill Campground, Fire Island National Seashore, (516) 597-6633. (Summer camping applications are accepted in February and March with a drawing taking place in April to assign campsites. For an application for the lottery, write to the Laurel Street address listed above, and be sure to enclose a self-addressed stamped envelope; you won't receive an application without one. Fire Island staff member Katie Vanderveldt says that no-shows are common, even in summer and especially on weekdays. Feel free to call and check on last-minute availabilities if you get the sudden urge to take out your tent). If no space is available on Fire Island, consider Heckscher State Park, one mile south of East Islip off Heckscher Parkway, (516) 581-2100.

ADIRONDACK SAMPLER

The craggy cliffs and rushing waters of Ausable Chasm impress all, but the most memorable part of your visit is the thrilling boat ride over the rapids.

NEW YORK STATE'S ADIRONDACK MOUNTAINS ARE MADE IN PART FROM the oldest rocks on the face of the earth. So it's appropriate that this rugged chunk of northeastern New York State is one of the oldest resorts in the country and contains what is claimed to be the oldest tourist attraction as well.

The Ausable River, flowing for about 50 miles from the slopes of Mount Marcy to Lake Champlain, is responsible for much of this region's beauty. At High Falls Gorge in Wilmington, the river's cold waters drop a total of 600 feet over the course of several waterfalls. Near the river's mouth is Ausable Chasm, with its massive sandstone cliffs sheltering the rushing river and the nature lovers who stroll on walkways high above it and ride in boats inside it.

Ausable Chasm has been open to the public since 1870, and its management claims to be "probably America's oldest organized tourist attraction." Ever since Major John Howe, the chasm's discoverer, first journeyed inside it while suspended on ropes, people have been awestruck by the sights inside this ponderous river-carved gash in solid sandstone.

The walk through Ausable Chasm takes you up and down steps, perhaps 150 total, over a three-quarter-mile-long course. You walk along a stone floor and wooden stairs and now and then cross the chasm on steel bridges. Markers along the path explain a little about the huge gorge and help you identify natural landmarks.

At one, you learn that the rocky cliffs encasing the gorge are made of Potsdam sandstone (named for the northern New York State town), which ranges in texture from a soft, brittle sandstone in some spots to a hard, dense quartzite. Geologists estimate that it took at least 15,000 years for the Ausable River to cut through the rock and carve the chasm; the cliffs, it is estimated, were created by glacial action 500,000 million years ago.

Elephant's Head, across the chasm, looks as much like its name as any rock formation we've ever seen; it was formed when deep cracks occurred in the sandstone cliffs. The "Cathedral," another appropriate name, offers a sheltered refuge in a large open grotto-like sanctuary behind you. Jacob's Well, by a ledge high above the cleft, is a natural pothole—smooth, sleek, deep, and dry, the result of the action of stones repeatedly whirling in an eddy, boring gradually into the stream bottom. To look at the depth of the pothole and think that it was made by so many small stones makes one's mind reel.

You will feel dampness as you walk in the chasm, but you won't feel the spray of water until you reach Table Rock. At this point, you hop in a red, wooden dory—capacity 32 people, including two guides—and take off on a 10- to 15-minute-long ride down a part of the river called the Grand Flume.

It's quiet at first, but a guide will break the silence with a few tales of the long natural and human history inside these sandstone walls. As you ride through the chasm's narrowest point, you'll hear that the cliffs are less than 20 feet apart, and the water there can be as deep as 90 feet.

There is no boat ride at High Falls Gorge, but there are thrills nonetheless. You cross the Ausable River on foot three times and so are given a wide spectrum of views of the natural curiosities which it spawned.

While the most memorable feature of Ausable Chasm is the deep and craggy chasm itself, the highlights of High Falls Gorge are the Ausable River's four gushing waterfalls, each of which you see from varied vantage points, close up, directly above, and far away.

Your view gets bigger and broader as you gradually wind your way along the wooden path, up and down stairs, across bridges, and precipitously perched on the cliff's edge, following the trail outlined in the descriptive brochure and map you are given when you buy tickets. Between stops 4 and 5, you cross the Ausable River and are given a glance at both Main and Mini Falls; at stop 5, you peer directly into torrential Rainbow Falls.

Between stops 7 and 8, you once again cross the Ausable River at a point called the "best view." You will understand why when you get there. Climax Falls has joined the scene, making a quartet of power-packed, gushing cataracts. Take time to stand on the bridge for a while and savor the scene. This is one sight you will remember long after you have left the area.

The brochure explains some of the Ausable River's more subtle alterations of the land, such as the lichens at stop 8 that are really a marriage of algae and fungi cohabiting together as a means of survival.

Then there is the metallic brown tint of the river's waters. At Rainbow Falls, you read that the drab color is a result of dissolved iron ore mineral from the surrounding mountains. As at Ausable Chasm, there are potholes of all sizes here and explanations as to how they came to be.

You don't need to be in top shape to walk through Ausable Chasm and High Falls Gorge but you do need to be able and willing to climb more than 100 steps. To experience a mountain top view, however, you need to be in even better shape, which is why we recommend Whiteface Mountain, the only one of the 46 Adirondack peak summits that can be reached by car.

Here, it is your car which puts forth the effort to reach the way to the top . . . well, most of the way to the top. You travel a distance about five miles in length from the ticket booth at the base of Whiteface Mountain Veterans Memorial Highway to just a few hundred feet short of the

4,867-foot-high peak, the state's fifth highest mountain. From there you have a choice of walking up the Whiteface Mountain Nature Trail, primarily a stone walkway a fifth of a mile long, or taking an elevator to the summit. The nature trail consists mostly of stones rather than steps; wear good sturdy shoes or don't risk the climb. The trail is closed during and just after rainstorms, for good reason.

Even though the star attraction of Whiteface Mountain is the view from the summit, don't close your eyes while on the drive. Notice how the soil grows thinner and rockier as you rise in elevation. The trees, slowly but certainly, become smaller and thinner and are like stunted dwarfs as the auto drive ends. Stop at some of the numerous parking areas on the way up and feel the air getting gradually colder.

If you do walk the short trail from the highway end to the summit, pause a few moments to read the markers along the way. You can tell the direction of the prevailing wind by checking the balsam firs, known as flag trees, along the left side as you climb. At these high altitudes, the trees grow few branches on their windward sides.

As you continue climbing, you will ultimately reach timberline, the point where the climate is so harsh and cold that trees can no longer grow. While you won't see trees in the alpine zone above timberline, you will spot herbs and stubby, small shrubs like the bearberry willow (bearing fuzzy fruits similar to the pussy willow), the alpine goldenrod, and the alpine bilberry (a cousin of the blueberry).

The view from the summit is a lot like pizza. When it's good, it's great. When it isn't so good, it's still pretty good. You can see the Montreal skyline, Lake Champlain, and Vermont's faraway Green Mountains on a sparkling day. If it's hazy or cloudy, you will still have an unobstructed vista of Lake Placid, the village by that name, the entire Ausable River Valley, cars working their way up the same snaking path you just drove, and untold mountain tops in every direction.

A complex housing a gift shop, cafeteria, and rest rooms offers shelter from the chills and winds. The silo standing next to the complex is home to New York State's equipment for the Atmospheric Science Research Center.

Location: Ausable Chasm is reached by taking Interstate 87 (The Northway), exit 34, onto Route 9 north to the chasm. It is 12 miles south of Plattsburgh. **Admission** is charged. **Hours:** Mid-May to early October, daily. **Allow** an hour and a half for the entire tour. **Information:** Ausable Chasm, Box B, Ausable Chasm, NY 12911; (518) 834-7454.

Note: The boat ride will not operate in times of high water. At those times, a reduced rate of admission is charged and visitors are given a free pass for a return trip. Still, the admission rate (even with the boat ride) is expensive for an attraction where the average visitor spends only 90 minutes. In 1987 the charge was $9.95, including the boat ride. A cross-country ski center also operates here in winter.

If you are staying overnight: Holiday Inn, Route 3 (Interstate 87, exit 37), Plattsburgh, (518) 561-5000; Howard Johnson's Lodge, Route 3 (Interstate 87, exit 37), Plattsburgh, (518) 561-7750; Econo Lodge, Route 3 (Interstate 87, exit 37), Plattsburgh, (518) 561-1500; Ausable Chasm KOA, Route 373 (east of Route 9), Ausable Chasm, (518) 834-9990; Holiday Travel Trailer Park, Route 373 (east of Route 9), Ausable Chasm, (518) 834-9216.

Location: High Falls Gorge is on Route 86 and is reached by taking Interstate 87 (The Northway), exit 30, onto Route 73 north; from Lake Placid, take Route 86 north to the gorge. From Ausable Chasm and the Northway heading south, take Route 9N to Jay, then Route 86 south to the gorge. **Admission** is charged. **Hours:** Late May to mid-October, daily. **Allow** 45 minutes to an hour. **Information:** High Falls Gorge, Wilmington, NY 12997; (518) 946-2278 in season; (518) 946-2211 off-season.

Note: Picnic tables are on the grounds.

If you are staying overnight: Lake Placid Hilton, Mirror Lake Drive (Route 86), Lake Placid, (518) 523-4411; Holiday Inn, Olympic Drive (Route 86), Lake Placid, (518) 523-2556; Art Devlin's Olympic Motor Inn, 350 Main Street (Route 86), Lake Placid, (518) 523-3700; Landmark Motor Lodge, Junction Routes 86 and 431, Wilmington, (518) 946-2247; Adirondak Loj Campground, Adirondak Loj Road (3 miles south of town on Route 73, then 5 miles west on Adirondak Loj Road), Lake Placid, (518) 523-3441; Lake Placid-Whiteface Mountain KOA, Fox Farm Road (Route 86), Wilmington, (518) 946-7878; Whiteface Terrace Campsite (Route 86), Wilmington, (518) 946-2576.

Location: Whiteface Mountain Veterans Memorial Highway is reached by taking Route 86 (north from Lake Placid or south from Jay) to Route 431 to the highway toll house. **Admission** is charged. **Hours:** Late May to mid-October, daily. **Allow** one hour. **Information:** Olympic Authority, Olympic Center, Lake Placid, NY 12946; (518) 523-1655; (800) 462-6236 toll free in New York State; (800) 255-5515 toll free in eastern United States.

Note: The highway climbs an average grade of 8 percent. Check your radiator, brakes, oil, and water before taking the drive. The drive is part of a larger tour of the 1980 Winter Olympic facilities, which includes the Olympic Jumping Complex, Olympic Sports Complex (Mount Van Hoevenberg), and Whiteface Mountain Chairlift (to top of smaller Little Whiteface Mountain). Contact the above address for more information.

If you are staying overnight: See High Falls Gorge accommodations.

HOWE CAVERNS

Courtesy: Howe Caverns, Inc.

More than 200 couples have gotten married underground inside Howe Caverns,
but most visitors are satisfied just taking the tour.

Y OU CAN GET MARRIED 16 STORIES UNDERGROUND INSIDE HOWE
Caverns. Why anyone would want to is beyond us. But you can do it.
More than 200 couples have.

You also can ride in a boat, have your picture taken, make a wish, and
see a grown man hum into a rock.

Howe Caverns, in the village of Howes Cave, about 40 miles west of
Albany, is like most caves and caverns in the eastern United States:
privately owned. So unlike those operated as state or national parks,
there are a lot of gimmicks on the tours and commercialization on the
grounds.

Which isn't necessarily all bad. The Howe Caverns complex consists
of, in addition to the tour underground and common tourist conveniences

like a snack bar and gift shop, a 24-room motel complete with swimming pool, especially convenient for the guests at your underground wedding.

On the other hand, it can get a little on the tawdry side when you enter the Bronze Room, named for the color of the ceiling and walls, and the guide takes a group photograph and offers you the opportunity to buy a 5″x7″ black and white glossy.

During most of the tour you are looking at unusual rock formations, stalactites or stalagmites, or examining a remnant of human history. When we reached a landmark called the pipe organ, where stalactites and stalagmites have grown from opposite ends and melded together, our guide, Mike, smiled and said that if he hums into a nearby rock known as the keyboard, the sound resonates and seems to come from the pipe organ.

"Now, it's a bit embarrassing to hum into a rock, but here goes," he said, "hummmmmmm."

As Mike lifted his mouth from the keyboard, his captive audience greeted him with a resounding round of applause.

There were encore performances, not of Mike's singing, but of stalactites and stalagmites growing in bizarre shapes and sizes. Continue and you see one resembling a pint-sized version of the Leaning Tower of Pisa and another called the Great Beehive. You get a geology lesson, too. Stalactites and stalagmites are caused by dripping water that picks up small amounts of limestone and leaves it behind after it evaporates.

Stalactites, which grow from the ceiling downward (they are spelled with a *c*, as in ceiling), form as dripping water deposits limestone particles; the process occurs over millions of years. Stalagmites, which grow from the ground upward (and spelled with a *g*, as in ground), are formed in a similar manner, except that the limestone particles in the water drip all the way to the floor before evaporating. Flowstone, a first cousin to stalactites and stalagmites, is a limestone deposit growing on cavern walls; it looks like sheets of rippling ice. You can feel drops of water falling on your head and shoulders as you wander 200 feet underground. When you touch these limestone landmarks, they feel like glass.

Time in a cavern is measured in eons. Only about one cubic inch of a stalactite, or any other limestone formation, will form in a hundred years. The staff says that the caverns had their start about six million years ago, before the now long-extinct wooly mammoth appeared on earth; at that time, this part of New York State was covered by sea water.

You see where water has left its mark in the caverns, like the witch's profile in solid rock, carved bit by bit by dripping water. You cross under the balancing rock, a ponderous hunk of rock looking precariously lodged in place against the walls. In reality, it has been in this position for millions of years. Mike said that it is estimated that the last rock fell in the caverns

10,000 years ago; another isn't expected to fall for another 30,000 years.

Human history, on the other hand, is measured in years. About a third of the way into the tour, Mike told us the story of Lester Howe, the caverns' eponym, credited with being the first to discover and exploit the cavern. Farmer Howe followed the lead of his cows who liked to stand in one particular sunny spot on his property. On investigation, he discovered a dark hole in the earth through which streams of fresh air blew.

Before long, Lester Howe was operating a bona fide tourist attraction. For 50 cents, Howe would supply visitors with a rain hat, a pair of rubber boots, and an oil lamp or torch and take them on eight-hour-long journeys into his caverns. He also threw in a box lunch. When you get to the bronze room where your picture is taken, your guide will direct your eyes to soot marks on the walls. These were caused by oil lamps at rest while Howe's tourists ate lunch.

There are no oil lamps today. Your way is lit by multi-colored electric lights that lend a festive, if not natural, feel to the caverns. But if you want nature, prefer it completely natural, you will get that, too. In the second part of the tour, your guide will turn off all artificial lights. Chances are you have never been in such complete darkness; the little red light on my camera glowed like a shooting star in the sky.

No need to wait for a real shooting star to make a wish when you're in Howe Caverns. Just toss a coin into the subterranean wishing well. The money is collected every two weeks and given to charity. Mike said, "Most people wish for a safe boat ride," (since that's what happens next).

"Hop into one of our two luxury liners," Mike directed us with a sarcastic smile. Travel by boat is not a common way to explore a cave, but Howe Caverns has two 22-passenger boats to carry you across the Lake of Venus. The lake is fed by the rushing water of the underground River Styx.

"One of our competitors," Mike continued, referring to nearby Secret Caverns, "has a 100-foot waterfall. We have a waterfall, too. Ours is 93 and one-half feet . . . ," he said with a carefully placed pause, "shorter." Just before you reach the six-and-a-half-foot-high waterfall, the boats turn around and retrace their paths.

This is where you stop at the Bridal Altar, where all those weddings occur. Are you single and looking? Don't leave without setting foot on the six-inch-thick calcite heart imbedded in the floor; step on it, a legend says, and you will be married within a year.

Are you married and looking? Sit on the heart, advised Mike, and you will be divorced within a year.

We had no sitters, just a few optimistic romantic standers.

Overindulging in romance is fine, but not so wise for food, since everyone wraps up the tour with a journey through the Winding Way—the most fun part of the trip. It's a curving and twisting 560-foot-long path through the rock, carved over thousands of years by the natural power of water. At its broadest point, Winding Way is six feet wide; at its narrowest, it's just three feet. It makes you wish you had started a diet or worn a tight belt before entering this limestone labyrinth.

Location: Howe Caverns is in Howes Cave, just east of Cobleskill. Take Interstate 88, exit 22, onto Route 7 and follow the yellow arrow-shaped signs and other yellow and black signs. **Admission** is charged. **Hours:** Year round, daily. **Allow** an hour and 20 minutes for the tour. **Information:** Howe Caverns, Howes Cave, NY 12092; (518) 296-8990.

Note: The temperature in the caverns is a constant 52 degrees so wear a light jacket or other warm clothing. Also wear sturdy shoes; the floor can be slippery. There are picnic tables and fireplaces for cooking on the grounds. There is also a snack bar and restaurant. Secret Caverns, another privately owned enterprise, is nearby in Cobleskill.

If you are staying overnight: Howe Caverns Motel, at the caverns site, Howes Cave, (518) 296-8950; Best Western, Campus Drive (Route 7, 3 miles south of town), Cobleskill, (518) 234-4321; Bed and Breakfast Leatherstocking (reservation service), 389 Brockway Road, Frankfort Hill, NY 13340, (518) 733-0040; Hide A-Way Campsites, two miles west of State Route 30A (follow signs from Interstate 88, Central Bridge exit), Central Bridge, (518) 868-9975; Locust Park (campsite), Route 7 (just east of town), Central Bridge, (518) 868-9927.

THE THOUSAND ISLANDS

Some islands in the Thousand Islands region are miles long, while others, like the one above, are barely big enough to support one house.

ACTUALLY, THERE ARE MORE THAN 1,800 ISLANDS IN THE THOUSAND Islands region, that 50-mile stretch of the St. Lawrence River along the state's northern border—separating New York State, U.S.A., from Ontario, Canada. The largest is Wellesley Island, over 20 miles long, while the smallest could fit inside your living room.

From high above, the view of these freckles of greenery on the body of the St. Lawrence is nature's masterpiece of water intermixed with land. This place is as friendly to boaters as it is to sightseers; computer wizards might be tempted to call it "cruiser friendly."

There are two ways to get a good overall look at the islands: from high above or, if you fall into the category of pleasure boater or fisherman, from water level. Let's travel by water first.

Alexandria Bay, the hub and commercial center of the region, pats itself on the back and calls itself the "world capital of bass fishing." That's no idle boast and you will find both small and largemouth bass in the waters. The town has been the setting for fishing tournaments many times, and it once hosted the Bass Anglers Sportsman Society's Bass

Masters Classic, a meaningless title to most of us but to a bass fisherman, equivalent in stature to baseball's World Series.

But Alexandria Bay is not the only place in the Thousand Islands to cast off your boat for a few hours of fishing. Cape Vincent, south of Clayton, is a choice spot for both black bass and muskie. Clayton is good for pike and perch. Chippewa Bay, north of Alexandria Bay, and Wellesley Island are likely places to haul in pike and largemouth bass.

New York State fishing licenses may be obtained at many places, including Department of Energy Conservation offices, tackle-and-bait shops, chambers of commerce, and town clerk offices. You need a Canadian fishing license, however, to fish in Canadian waters. If you are caught without one, you will probably be fined, have your fish confiscated, and be given so many hours to obtain the Canadian license.

If you don't know your bass from your elbow and just want to eyeball the islands, you can set out in your own boat—if you are one of the lucky few that owns one—or hop aboard one of several tour boats that offer sights and river trivia.

Two lines operate out of Alexandria Bay: Uncle Sam Boat Tours and Empire Boat Tours. 1000 Islands Seaway Cruises is based in Clayton, and several Canadian outfits give tours. The best known is Gananoque Boat Lines, operating from the town of Gananoque, Ontario.

The various lines serve up a potpourri of choices. There are dinner cruises, sunset cruises, charter cruises, and express ferry shuttles to Boldt Castle (see pages 208 to 211). All depart several times daily on general tours of the Thousand Islands, weaving amid and among the archipelago and stopping at the most famous of all, Heart Island, home of Boldt Castle, where you have the option of seeing the castle and taking a later boat back.

In addition, each boat line gives a bit of a tour. Uncle Sam and Empire boats have a live tour guide on board, Gananoque, a taped guide. You will learn island tidbits and trivia regardless of which line you take.

What is an island? According to our guide, it is any piece of land sticking at least two feet above water and supporting at least two trees.

"That one to the right barely makes it," the guide called out, and our fellow passengers on the top deck rushed to the right.

"That's the smallest one in the river. It's name is Tom Thumb," he added.

Most of the islands are big enough to support a summer camp or a second or third (or fourth) home. The boat took us past those with mansions once owned by families with names like Astor and Strauss, although, as in Newport, Rhode Island, these 40-room laps of luxury were humbly called cottages.

As for trivia, how about the following food fact: Philadelphia Cream

Cheese and Thousand Islands salad dressing both have links to the Thousand Islands area, while one also has a connection to Philadelphia, Pennsylvania. Which is which?

It's the dressing that connects Philadelphia, PA, to the Thousand Islands. George Boldt, owner of Boldt Castle, was sailing on the St. Lawrence in his yacht when his steward surprised him with a new dressing. Boldt enjoyed the taste so much, he named it for the region and served it in his hotels: the Waldorf Astoria in New York and the Bellevue-Stratford in Philadelphia. His steward later gained fame as Oscar of the Waldorf.

Philadelphia Cream Cheese? It was developed in nearby Philadelphia, New York, in the mid-19th century.

Keep your eyes open while on board and you will see some strange sights to go with strange facts, including two-boat garages; Smugglers' Cove, where rumrunners hid during prohibition; and the world's smallest international bridge, connecting two islands privately owned by one family: one island is in the United States, the other in Canada.

You also will be able to see the 1000 Islands Skydeck from your boat tour, but the more thrilling view is from atop the 400-foot-high observation tower. The skydeck is on Hill Island, just a few hundred feet over the border in Canada, so be sure you have a driver's license, birth certificate, or other form of identification to present at customs. The perspective from the bridge to Canada is itself commanding but you can enjoy just so much scenery from the window of a moving car.

If you want to look down your noses at all those island mansions, take the 40-second elevator ride or climb the spiral staircase to the observation deck. It is enclosed by glass so even those suffering from mild acrophobia should feel secure. If you want a higher view and have the legs and the nerve, you can climb to two upper levels.

Stretch out your legs even more at one of New York's several state parks. Wellesley Island State Park, surrounded by the river northwest of Alexandria Bay, offers the most facilities: nature trails, fishing, summer hiking, and a swimming beach. Keewaydin State Park, on the mainland a mile west of Alexandria Bay, boasts fishing, summer hiking, and a swimming pool. Formerly a private estate belonging to, among others, New York publishing magnate William T. Dewart, Keewaydin accommodates recreation-minded persons looking for both a romantic and aquatic view, with two gazebos overlooking the St. Lawrence.

Other state parks with bathing beaches include, from north to south, Jacques Cartier (about 20 miles northeast of Alexandria Bay), Kring Point, Grass Point, and Cedar Point (about 14 miles southwest of Clayton). Each state park mentioned also includes picnic facilities and, as would be expected in any park along the waters of the St. Lawrence, allows for superb fishing opportunities. In winter, Keewaydin State Park is the place to be for ice fishing, ice skating, cross-country skiing, and snowmobiling, while Wellesley Island State Park accommodates cross-country skiers (with rentals) and snowmobilers.

Also consider stopping at the Thousand Islands Shipyard Museum in Clayton. The museum's collection contains more than 150 boats, thousands of nautical artifacts, and displays on related topics ranging from the evolution of the outboard motor to the life of a prohibition rumrunner.

Location: To reach the Thousand Islands region, from Interstate 81, take exit 50 (last before Canada) onto Route 12, south to Clayton or north to Alexandria Bay. **Admission** is charged for the boat rides, the Skydeck, and to the state parks. **Hours:** The American boat tour lines run generally early May through October; Gananoque Boat Line tours run from mid-May through mid-October. Each company offers up to 10 tours daily in July and August, and as few as two tours daily in May and October. The Skydeck is open daily May through October. Keewaydin and Wellesley Island State Parks are open year round; others vary by season. **Allow** two hours for the Empire boat tours, two and a half hours for the Uncle Sam and 1000 Islands Seaway Cruises tours, and three hours for the Gananoque tour. Allow 45 minutes for the Skydeck.

Information: 1000 Islands International Council, Box 400, Alexandria Bay, NY 13607; (315) 482-2520. Empire Boat Tours, 4 Church Street, Alexandria Bay, NY 13607; (315) 482-9511, (800) 542-2628 in New York State. Uncle Sam Boat Tours, Alexandria Bay, NY 13607; (315) 482-2611, (800) 253-9229 in New York State. 1000 Islands Seaway Cruises, 604 Riverside Drive, Clayton, NY 13624; (315) 686-3511. Gananoque Boat Line; (613) 382-2144. 1000 Islands Skydeck; (613) 659-2335. Thousand Islands State Park, Recreation and Historic Preservation Region, Box 247, Alexandria Bay, NY 13607; (315) 482-2593. Thousand Islands Shipyard Museum, 750 Mary Street, Clayton, NY 13624; (315) 686-4104.

If you are staying overnight: Thousand Islands Club Resort, Wellesley Island (follow signs from Interstate 81, exit 51), (315) 482-2551; Pine Tree Point Resort, Anthony Street (a mile northeast of town), Alexandria Bay, (315) 482-9911, (800) 253-9229 (in New York State); Bertrand's Motel, 229 James Street, Clayton, (315) 686-3641; Fairwind Lodge Motel and Cottages, Route 12E (two and a half miles west of town), Clayton, (315) 686-5251. Just about every state park here offers camping, and reservations are recommended. Write to the Thousand Islands State Park, (address above) for a reservation form. Private campsites include Merryknoll Campground, Route 12E (southwest of town), Clayton, (315) 686-3055, and French Creek Marina (access for cars and boats), 98 Wahl Street (south end of town), Clayton, (315) 686-3621.

WATERFALLS AND GORGES OF THE FINGER LAKES

Photo by Michael Schuman

Watkins Glen State Park is a natural wonderland filled with cliffs, crags, and waterfalls.

F IND LEGENDS FASCINATING? THEN YOU WILL LOVE HEARING HOW AC-
cording to Iroquois Indian lore the Finger Lakes were created.

The Great Spirit, it was said, made the Finger Lakes region for the
use of the Iroquois people, who then asked how they would recognize
their homeland.

In response, the Great Spirit extended his hand to them and said, "You
must have faith and press onward. You should know your lands, for I
have pressed my hand upon them and in my fingerprints rest the blue
waters."

There is another version of the same story, this one told by geologists
and other scientists. A million or so years ago rivers flowed in the Finger
Lakes valleys. During the Ice Age, glaciers carved out deeper valleys
and, when they melted, the depressions filled with water.

Those who come to this part of west-central New York, whether pur-
posely or serendipitously, can't help but admire the sheer beauty of the
entire region. The glens and valleys and lakes combine to form vistas
that remind many observers of the Scottish highlands or the Irish countryside. Come here looking for sights for sore eyes and you will not leave
disappointed.

The same principle applies to the recreation-minded; boating, camping,
swimming and hiking, and, in winter, cross-country skiing, are found
throughout the region.

The area has a total of 11 deep lakes—Seneca is the deepest at 632
feet—and 18 parks. Watkins Glen State Park, at the south end of Seneca
Lake, is the most famous of all the Finger Lakes parks. It is also the
oldest regional state park and the most spectacular. Its gorge is so awe-
inspiring it can make one giddy.

There are 19 waterfalls and 300-foot-high cliffs in Watkins Glen, as
well as a mile-and-a-half-long trail that takes visitors up and down stairs
and over and under waterfalls, all the while skirting the gorge's edge.
Look down and you see a multileveled wonderland of cliffs and crags,
mosses and pools, and powerful, plunging rockets of water. At the very
bottom is Glen Creek. The creek started forming the gorge 10,000 years
ago and the process still continues.

Before you walk the trail, be sure to get a copy of the park leaflet. Ten
posted numbers along the trail denote landmarks, all explained in the
brochure. The trail walk is fairly easy, but there are a total of 814 stone
steps. To avoid the mass of steps near the trail's start, you can take a
shuttle bus to a further entrance. Regardless, you should wear good
shoes; footing can be slick.

While all the stops are worthwhile, Cavern Cascade at number 3 and the Cathedral at number 6 are two of our favorites. You can actually walk behind the high falls at Cavern Cascade thanks to the force of the water that has worn away a thin layer of shale in the cliff wall.

Step on the stone slab with the rippled surface at the Cathedral and you are standing on the floor of an ancient sea. These ripples were once in sand at the bottom of an inland ocean hundreds of millions of years ago.

After you have walked the gorge, try a second or third hiking trail, or relax reading by pool side that paperback you brought along; the park is graced with a 50-meter pool as well as a children's pool.

Nighttime at Watkins Glen brings you back eons. An outdoor sound and light spectacular, called Timespell, utilizes lasers and music to take you to the beginnings of the earth and, specifically, to the formation of Watkins Glen gorge.

Says the stirring voice of the narrator, " . . . we are about to leave human time altogether and go far, far back into the geologic past—almost a million times 5,000 years. We are going back to a time when the earth was young—over four and one half **billion** years ago."

The bare features of the gorge blackened in the night serve as the stage on which the vivid laser lights are cast, while the resounding narrator's voice bridges the time from the dawn of the gorge's creation to the ice age to the thriving Seneca Indian communities here a few hundreds of years ago to the glen's first tourists in the mid-19th century. Lights, all the while, dance off waterfalls and cliffs; sound imitate erupting volcanos, crackling ice, and the rhythmic, steady beating of the Senecas' drums.

Indian legends also played a role in the naming of the major feature in another park, Taughannock Falls State Park, by Cayuga Lake. One says that Chief Taughannock, a Delaware Indian, was slain in battle against the Cayugas and the Senecas, and his body was thrown over the falls. Another says simply that "taughannock" is an Iroquois or Algonquin word which translates to "the great falls in the woods."

Taughannock Falls, 215 feet high, is the highest vertical waterfall in the eastern United States. A ¾-mile-long trail extends from the park office by the lake shore through a gorge to the base of the falls. As at Watkins Glen State Park, a leaflet corresponds to posted numbers at nature trail stopping points.

Stop at the little waterfall at marker number 2 and you see evidence of a waterfall's power; the constant pouring of water has gradually eaten away at rock supporting it. The same principle applies to super-sized Taughannock Falls, which in 10,000 years has sculpted the ¾-mile-long gorge you must walk through to reach its base. 10,000 years ago, the falls were right at Cayuga Lake's shore.

In addition to hiking trails, there is a swimming beach, a bathhouse, playgrounds, and playing fields in the park. Fishing is available in nearby Taughannock Creek and Cayuga Lake.

Buttermilk Falls State Park, just south of Ithaca, has falls that refresh rather than overwhelm. A natural pool forms at the base, and park spokesmen don't exaggerate when they compare the atmosphere to that of an old fashioned swimming hole. Stretching out by pool's edge and taking a dip can invigorate even the most jaded and worn-out traveler.

Cool and shaded trails take hikers uphill and alongside Buttermilk Creek, which drops more than 500 feet in a series of cascades and rapids. All together, there are ten waterfalls and two glens. The potential danger to those acting carelessly caught the attention of filmmakers when the movie industry was young. "The Perils of Pauline," filmdom's first successful serial, was shot in Buttermilk Glen.

A few words about some other Finger Lakes region parks:

Keuka Lake State Park, another hilly and wooded refuge, is in the heart of wine country. Stunning views combining vineyards and the lake are commonplace. Lake swimming is available and trails take hikers among the trees and hills.

Swimming and fishing are favored activities at Cayuga Lake State Park near Seneca Falls, while swimming and boating enthusiasts should consider making Seneca Lake State Park near Geneva their base of operations.

There are two more gorges worth noting. On the southwest fringes of the region is Stony Brook State Park near Dansville. The trail bordering Stony Brook Glen extends ¾ of a mile, climbs about 250 steps, and passes three waterfalls. Stony Brook does Buttermilk Falls one better by providing swimming in two stream-fed pools.

Finally, while it is technically out of the Finger Lakes region, Letchworth State Park near Portageville, about 25 miles west of Dansville and home of the Genesee River Gorge, deserves mention. The walls of the 17-mile-long gorge are at points over 600 feet high. Three waterfalls, the highest of which plunges over 100 feet, highlight this creation, crafted on one of Mother Nature's best days. Swimming, hiking, fishing, white water rafting, and white water canoeing are recreational options.

Location: Watkins Glen State Park's main entrance is on Route 14 (Franklin Street) in the village of Watkins Glen. Taughannock Falls State Park's entrance is on Route 89, eight miles north of Ithaca, near Trumansburg. The main entrance to Buttermilk Falls State Park is along Route 13, two miles south of Ithaca. **Admission** is charged to enter all parks and an additional fee is charged for Timespell. Parking fees at

Taughannock Falls and Buttermilk Falls State Parks are waived in winter. **Hours:** Watkins Glen, Taughannock Falls, and Buttermilk Falls State Parks are open year round, although gorge trails are closed at all three parks in winter. Watkins Glen State Park is open in winter for hiking, cross-country skiing, and snowmobiling. Taughannock Falls State Park is open in winter for beginners' downhill skiing, skating, some hiking, and cross-country skiing. Buttermilk Falls State Park is open in winter for hiking and cross-country skiing. Timespell is presented twice each evening early May through October. **Allow** one to two hours to walk the gorge trail at Watkins Glen State Park and an hour to 90 minutes to walk the gorge trails at Taughannock Falls and Buttermilk Falls State Parks. Allow 45 minutes for the Timespell presentation. **Information:** Watkins Glen State Park, P.O. Box 304, Watkins Glen, NY 14891; (607) 535-4511. Taughannock Falls State Park, Box 283, R.D. 3, Trumansburg, NY 14886; (607) 387-6739. Buttermilk Falls State Park, R.D. 5, Ithaca, NY 14850; (607) 273-5761. Timespell, White Water Development Corp., Inc., Franklin Street, Watkins Glen, NY 14891; (607) 535-4960 or (607) 535-2466. For information on other parks, contact Taughannock Falls State Park.

If you are staying overnight: Holiday Inn, 2310 N. Triphammer Road (at junction with Route 13), Ithaca; (607) 257-3100. Taughannock Farms Inn, Route 89, Trumansburg; (607) 387-7711. Falls Motel, 239 N. Genesee Street (two block south of Route 14), Montour Falls; (607) 535-7262. Chieftain Motel, at junction of Routes 14 and 14A, Watkins Glen; (607) 535-4759. Watkins Glen State Park, 302 campsites; Taughannock Falls State Park, 76 campsites; and Buttermilk Falls State Park, 60 campsites; contact these campgrounds at addresses and phones listed above. Watkins Glen-Corning KOA Kampground, Route 414 (four and a half miles south of junction with Route 14); (607) 535-7404. Willowood Campsites, Route 13 (four miles south of Ithaca); (607) 272-6087.

ALLEGANY STATE PARK

Photo by Michael Schuman

It is easy to be humbled by the sheer beauty of western New York's Allegany State Park.

STAND AT THE TOP OF STONE TOWER AND LOOK OUT OVER THE RANGES upon ranges of blue and grey hills in the distance. The view is humbling; human beings are insignificant in relation to the miles of untamed outdoors.

It is easy to be humbled at Allegany State Park, its 65,000 acres in western New York State bumping against the Pennsylvania border. This is the Empire State's largest state park and likely its wildest.

The mountains are dominating, the lakes calming. Drive the curving park roads and you might be reminded of vacations in other places: the Blue Ridge Parkway in North Carolina and Virginia or the White Mountains of New Hampshire.

This is wildlife territory. Hardy hikers on any of the 75 miles of trails can have a chance encounter with deer and beaver, salamanders and snakes. (Don't expect to find the park's only poisonous snake, the timber rattler, as a dinner guest at a park campground; they are very uncommon.)

Nature is generous though. There is plenty of room for humans and much to do in all seasons. There are even activities for people who just want to relax and collect views. For one of the best, take the gravel road from Park Route 1 to Stone Tower, elevation 2,200 feet.

Also try the junction of Ridge Run Road and Park Route 2 and the scenic point at the 4.0 mile marker on Park Route 1 south of Red House Lake for other all-encompassing looks at the world below.

For equally savorous scenes from the valley looking up, pull your car over at any of the roads that surround either Red House Lake or Quaker Lake. You won't need to walk more than a few steps in any direction to have varied views of green trees forming a buffer between dark blue water and faint hills. There may be wildflowers of yellow and red at your feet and little white houses tucked in valleys sandwiched in by sturdy blue slopes and ridges.

Continue your nature show at Thunder Rocks, accessible by France Brook Road or Ridge Run Road, both gravel drives off Park Route 2. Thunder Rocks are house-size conglomerate boulders, heavy sandstone with quartzite pebbles imbedded, that were not carried here by glaciers, as many believe, but remain where they were formed 180 million years ago. Recreation Specialist Grace P. Christy says it is possible to climb the rocks without equipment and there have been relatively few accidents, but there is an element of danger.

Want less risky exercise? The network of hiking trails is vast, ranging from easy ones like the Sweetwater Ski Trail in Red House and the Three Sisters Hiking Trail in Quaker to the rugged Conservation Loop and Osgood trails in Red House. Experts will want to tackle the North Country Trail, by far the longest, covering 18 miles and bisecting the park for much of its run before paralleling the New York–Pennsylvania State line.

If you plan to hike, especially on the longer trails, bring along a canteen of water, food for energy, proper hiking shoes, and insect repellent; a small first aid kit isn't a bad idea, although serious injuries are rare.

The shortest jaunt is Bear Springs Trail, a leisurely half-mile walk off Park Route 1. Most park trails range from two and a half to five miles.

We recommend Bear Caves-Mount Seneca Hiking Trail, which curves off Park Route 3 in the park's southern tier. Four miles long, it is somewhat difficult, taking hikers up some steep slopes and by rocky ledges, but it offers scenic rewards as one climbs from point to point. Hikers can explore the three small caves along the trail on their own or venture into them as part of naturalist-led nature walks.

Looking to cool down? Lifeguards are on duty weekends from Memorial Day to the third Saturday in June and daily through Labor Day at beaches on Red House and Quaker lakes. Stretch out on the sand with a tube of sun screen and that paperback you have been planning on reading, and when you need a break from the printed page, awe yourself by taking in the pines, aspens, maples, and beeches surrounding the lakes.

Active recreation is in the form of boating, fishing, and hunting. Fishing is permitted year round on Quaker and Red House lakes and during trout season (April through September) in the many streams. You must have a valid New York State fishing license and a permit from the Allegany Park Police. Likewise, hunting for small game, turkey, and deer is allowed in season for those who have the proper permits and licenses.

The centers of summer family activity are three recreational areas, two of which are at Red House and Quaker lakes. The third, Cain Hollow area, near Quaker Lake, is the newest, opening in 1971.

G-rated entertainment is provided at Quaker Lake all summer long in its open-air amphitheater. Past films presented include the classic comedy "The Great Chase" with Charlie Chaplin or the more recent "Popeye" starring Robin Williams. Also regularly scheduled are nature films such as "Yellowstone Cubs" and "The World of Jacques-Yves Costeau" and Disney's magic such as "Dumbo" and "The Black Hole." You may also find a folk concert, puppet show, or sing-along on any given evening.

There are 230 cabins and a dozen-odd campsites at Quaker Lake, open early April through mid-December. At the newer Cain Hollow Campground, 164 tent and trailer sites are available through Labor Day.

Red House, named for a nearby Indian community which itself was named after an Indian who painted the door of his cabin red, has 144 cabins, of which 80 are winterized for year-round occupancy, and 134 campsites for tents and trailers.

Nature aside, the most eye-opening feature of the park is the English Tudor-style administration building. It has a gift shop, a restaurant, and a museum devoted primarily to the park's natural history; learn about its birds, its mammals, and its geology.

Western New York winters may close historic homes or even businesses but not Allegany State Park. Ice skating takes place on Red House Lake and ice fishing on Quaker Lake. As in warm weather, a New York State fishing license and a park permit are required.

Three designated areas are set aside for tobogganing and sledding, one at the Summit area off Park Route 1 about 6.4 miles north of Red House Lake, another near the Beehunter Picnic Grounds off Park Route 2 near Camp Allegany, and the third on Park Route 2, two miles south of Red House Lake.

Utilizing Yankee ingenuity to the fullest, the park staff grooms 24 miles of cross-country ski trails on old logging roads and on the track bed of an 1890s narrow gauge railroad. Skiers of all levels will find trails to match their skills. Those who want even more challenges are invited to try the more than 50 miles of ungroomed snow-covered hiking trails. Ski rentals are available and there is a warming hut.

Snowmobiles are permitted on some park roadways and on 15 miles of off-road trails, but owners should check in with the park police before hitting the snow; certain areas are off-limits and park and state rules are in effect.

Rainy day activities? The nearest sizable community is Salamanca, in the adjoining Allegany Indian reservation. Trivia fans will be interested to know that it's the only city in the world located on an Indian reservation. It's also home to the Salamanca Rail Museum and the Seneca-Iroquois National Museum.

A passenger depot built in 1912 has been restored and made into the railroad museum. Step inside an old caboose, examine the handsome red oak wainscoting, or take a summer or fall train excursion along the route of the old New York and Lake Erie Railroad.

To learn about the people on whose land the city sits, step inside the Seneca-Iroquois National Museum for a look at authentic crafts (as opposed to the tomahawks with Day-Glo feathers found at tourist traps). Wampum belts, beadwork, huskwork, paintings, and bone carvings are exhibited in displays telling the tail of the Seneca Nation's history and culture.

Or just walk and browse in the restored downtown area of the city called Salamanca Cityscape. There are more than 40 shops and restaurants, and there is a self-guided walking tour focusing on Salamanca's background as a lumber and rail center.

Location: Allegany State Park is south of Route 17, west of Olean, and east of Jamestown. You can enter the park from Route 17, exits 18 or 19, or from Route 219 in Salamanca. A less-traveled entrance is in Limestone in the southeast corner of the park. **Admission** is charged from Memorial Day weekend to Labor Day. **Hours:** Year round. **Allow** two to four hours for the park. **Information:** Allegany State Park, RD #1, Salamanca, NY 14779; (716) 354-2545.

Location: The Salamanca Rail Museum is at 170 Main Street, between East and Wildwood Streets, in Salamanca. The Seneca-Iroquois National Museum is on the Allegany Indian Reservation, Broad Street Extension west of Salamanca; from Route 17, take exit 20. **Admission** is free to both museums, donations accepted. **Hours:** Rail Museum: year round, Tuesday through Saturday and Sunday afternoons. Seneca-Iroquois Museum: year round, daily except off-season Mondays and holidays. **Allow**

one to two hours in each museum. **Information:** Salamanca Rail Museum, 170 Main Street, Salamanca, NY 14779; (716) 945-3133. Seneca-Iroquois National Museum, P.O. Box 422, Salamanca, NY 14779; (716) 945-3895.

If you are staying overnight: Quality Inn, 2711 West State Street (just under two miles west of town on Route 417), Olean, (716) 373-1500; Castle Inn Motel, 3220 West State Street (just over two miles west of town on Route 417), Olean, (716) 372-1050; Colony Motel, 620 Fairmount Avenue (a mile and a half west of town on Route 394), Jamestown, (716) 488-1904. Reservations for campsites and cabins in Allegany State Park are needed and requests must be in writing. For the summer season, March 15 through December 15, applications must be postmarked no earlier than January 1; for the winter season, December 16 through March 14, applications must be postmarked no earlier than October 1. Applications are available from the park office. Kinzua Lake Campground, West Perimeter Road (just under 10 miles south of Route 17, exit 17), Steamburg; (716) 354-5855. Bailey's Pope Haven Campground, Pope Road (Route 17, exit 16, head north on Route 394, then just over three miles north on Route 241), Randolph; (716) 358-4900.

NIAGARA FALLS

Courtesy: Niagara Falls Convention & Visitors Bureau, Inc.

Nobody should go through life without visiting Niagara Falls at least once.

T O LIVE IN THE UNITED STATES AND NEVER VISIT NIAGARA FALLS IS a shame.

To live within a day's drive and never visit Niagara Falls is a crime.

Like the Grand Canyon and Old Faithful, Niagara Falls is a work of nature that has become a symbol of the United States and is a must-see for tourists from all nations. Area brochures are printed in French, Spanish, German, and Japanese, and you will hear plenty of foreign tongues spoken here.

According to Ray Wigle, director of communications for the Niagara Falls Convention & Visitors Bureau, approximately 10 million people—the equivalent of about 40% of the population of Canada—visit the falls each year. About 6 million visitors are from the U.S., 3 million from Canada, and some 1 million from other countries.

Suffice it to say nobody will ever be lonely at Niagara Falls, especially in peak season. Most observers say the Canadian side, known as the

Horseshoe Falls, is the prettier of the falls—and they are right. The Canadian falls are over twice as wide as the American falls and curve dramatically, whereas the American falls cascade over a straight brink.

Niagara Falls, Canada, also has what some have called the tackiest street in the country, with wax museums and other tourist magnets exposing the sordid and the sensational. Although neither city is at a loss at telling visitors how to spend their money, Niagara Falls, New York, is the more sincere.

If all you want to do is to see the falls, you can do so from several vantage points. Whirlpool State Park, on the Robert Moses Parkway, is one of the best, permitting a view overlooking the whirlpool that forms as a result of the Niagara River's 90-degree bend.

Other superb vistas are yours from Goat Island, reached by either pedestrian or vehicular bridges, and from 242-foot-high Prospect Point Observation Tower in Niagara Reservation State Park. The state park visitor center, opened in 1987, may be the best place to begin your visit. Displays on water power and a 70-millimeter film on the majesty and potency of the falls set the mood.

It is the sheer power of Niagara Falls that impresses the most. There are higher waterfalls; Taughannock Falls near Ithaca is 215 feet high. Yet though Niagara Falls is only 184 feet high on the American side and 176 feet high on the Canadian, the falls are dramatically wide. The curved brink of the Canadian falls is about 2,200 feet long; the American brink covers about half that width, still formidable. The water flow over the falls is about 700,000 gallons per second, and when you feel the mist at Prospect Point, the falls at Niagara will earn your respect.

To see the falls from a distance is one thing. To meet the falls head on is another. There are two ways from the American side to experience Niagara Falls at their own level, to confront the spray face to face, and to expose your ears to its perpetual roar. To many, the *Maid of the Mist* and the Cave of the Winds are the only methods of fully experiencing the beauty and raw force of Niagara Falls. Short of going over the falls in barrel, you can't get any closer.

The first *Maid of the Mist* set sail in 1846, when James K. Polk was president, and it was a president who, some 60 years later, gave the boat ride its mightiest endorsement. Theodore Roosevelt called it "the only way to fully realize the Grandeur of the Great Falls of Niagara."

Since then, world leaders and other VIPs have donned black rubber raincoats and faced the falls from the deck; actress Marilyn Monroe, Indian statesman Jawaharlal Nehru, and Soviet Premier Alexei Kosygin are a few. Kosygin, it is said, refused to protect his head with his rain hood until the *Maid* was virtually on top of the Horseshoe Falls, telling an aide he enjoyed the feel of the mist on his face.

You may not want to be as brave as Kosygin. The *Maid* trip climaxes by taking passengers to the base of the American Falls and into the basin of the Horseshoe Falls. The half-hour-long ride starts out at the dock at the Prospect Point Observation Tower's base, and for the first ten-odd minutes feels no different than any other river cruise. As you approach the falls, mist starts to dance off your face, the boat bounces to the rhythm of the river and the fortissimo of the falling water quickly becomes a thunderous drone.

If you bring your camera aboard—and we recommend you do—your prize shot will probably be the one of the inevitable rainbow. However, we want to caution you not to expect too much from photos taken in the basin; water will spray your lens, likely fogging close-up pictures. Rely on your memories, which will truly be made of the mist.

Your memories also will be made of tales and legends about the falls that the captain imparts on the way up and back. The most memorable is about Roger Woodward, a seven-year-old boy who was swept over the falls in a boating mishap on July 9, 1960. Roger unbelievably survived the fall and was rescued by the *Maid of the Mist* crew, becoming the fourth person to survive the fall and the only one to go over and live wearing just a bathing suit and life preserver.

In 1980, at age 27, Roger Woodward returned with his wife, Susan, to take a more conventional look at the falls.

We don't know whether Roger embarked on the forty-minute-long Cave of the Winds trip but it, too, is an institution and is highly recommended to compliment the *Maid*. Here, your perspective is from land—Goat Island.

After buying tickets, visitors change into felt booties and yellow rain-coats, then take an elevator down 180 feet and prepare to be hit by another misting.

Walk through a small tunnel and you are at the base of Bridal Veil Falls, the rushing cataract of the American falls sandwiched between Luna and Goat Islands. A web of wooden catwalks and staircases takes visitors to numerous points on the cliff side from which views of the American and Bridal Veil Falls are astounding. The ever present rainbow is seen best at the tour point called Rock of Ages, while the climax is at the last stop, Hurricane Deck, just 25 feet from Bridal Veil Falls. Prepare, once again, to get wet.

Cave of the Winds guides also relate the stories of Niagara past, and you shouldn't be surprised to hear some of those you also heard on the *Maid of the Mist*. Other interesting bits of falls trivia relate solely to Cave of the Winds. The two elevators taking raincoat wearers up and down were open to the public in 1925. Prior to that, a 279-step staircase was used. Imagine the trip back up after the soaking look at the falls was finished. And as at Howe Caverns, two young lovers felt this was a perfect place for their wedding; a Pennsylvania couple was married here in 1893, and they didn't have to travel far for everyone's favorite honeymoon destination.

The most romantic view of Niagara Falls can be seen up to three hours after dark—starting at 7 P.M. in the dead of winter and 9:15 P.M. in the heat of summer—when the falls are illuminated. One look and you'll know why honeymooners still come to Niagara Falls for the most romantic vacation of their lives.

Location: From Interstate 90, take Interstate 290 (Youngmann Expressway) in Buffalo to Interstate 190, towards Niagara Falls; take the first exit after crossing the North Grand Island Bridge onto the Robert Moses Parkway and follow the parkway to Niagara Reservation State Park. *Maid of the Mist* departs from the base of the Observation Tower at Prospect Point in the park. The Cave of the Winds trip departs from Terrapin Point on Goat Island, connected to the state park by a pedestrian bridge and to the Robert Moses Parkway by a vehicular bridge. **Admission** is charged for the *Maid of the Mist* and the Cave of the Winds. A nominal admission is charged for the observation tower. **Hours:** *Maid of the Mist* trips take place mid-May to late October, daily. Cave of the Winds trips are offered Memorial Day to mid-October, daily. The Prospect Point Observation Tower is open year round, daily. **Allow** a half hour for the *Maid of the Mist* ride; four boats are in operation and they depart every 15 minutes in summer and every half hour in spring and fall; there is rarely more than a 20- to 30-minute wait for a boat. Allow 40 minutes for the Cave of the Winds trip. **Information:** Maid of the Mist Corp., 151 Buffalo Avenue, Niagara Falls, NY 14303; (716) 284-8897. Cave of the Winds; (716) 282-8979. Niagara Falls Convention and Visitors Bureau, 345 Third Street, Suite 101, Niagara Falls, NY 14303; (716) 278-8010.

Events: Thanksgiving through early January, A Festival of Lights, holiday lights illuminate the falls; parades, fireworks, entertainment.

If you are staying overnight: Niagara Hilton, 3rd and Mall Streets, (716) 285-3361; Best Western Red Jacket Inn, 7001 Buffalo Avenue, (716) 283-7612; Beacon Motel, 9900 Niagara Falls Boulevard, (716) 297-3647; Driftwood Motel, 2754 Niagara Falls Boulevard, (716) 692-6650; Plaza Court Campground, 7680 Niagara Falls Boulevard, (716) 283-2638; Niagara Falls North KOA, 1250 Pletcher Road (off Robert Moses Parkway, four miles north of Interstate 190, exit 25B), Lewiston, (716) 754-8013; Niagara Falls KOA, 2570 Grand Island Boulevard (Route 324, north of Interstate 190, exit 19), Grand Island, (716) 773-7583.

WORKING IN NEW YORK

ERIE CANAL VILLAGE

Photo by Michael Schuman

The main drag in 19th-century Erie Canal Village.

"**Y**OU TALK OF MAKING A CANAL 350 MILES LONG THROUGH THE WILderness. It is little short of madness to think of it at this day."

Thomas Jefferson in a speech to New York State representatives just prior to the start of construction on the Erie Canal.

"I've got an old mule and her name is Sal
Fifteen miles on the Erie Canal.
She's a good ol' worker and a good ol' pal,
Fifteen miles on the Erie Canal."

A Tin Pan Alley song written by Thomas S. Allen.

Even Thomas Jefferson was fooled. But he was in good company. Few people thought the building of a canal across upstate New York was even remotely possible.

For one thing, the canal would have been the longest in the world. For another, there was no machine power in 1816, just muscles in arms and legs. Trees had to be cut, stumps pulled, brush burned, and the canal bed dug with only shovels, scoops, and human strength.

But Dewitt Clinton campaigned for governor in 1816 on one issue: the building of the canal he hoped would connect the Hudson River to Lake Erie. He knew of the potential commerce made up of freight and passengers itching to move west. The voters agreed with him.

It was just six months into his term, on July 4, 1817, that the first shovel of dirt was turned. That spot is now occupied by a re-created village composed mainly of authentic buildings transported from within a 50-mile radius of its location.

Not long ago we took a ride on the *Independence*, a canal-style packet boat, near that same spot. As in the early 1800s, a team of mules trudged along a towpath pulling us as we sang songs like "Low Bridge, Everybody Down," "Buffalo Gals," and "Jimmy Crack Corn."

It was a slow ride as we toddled rather than cruised, but we were intrigued as we heard the tale of the canal they said couldn't be built.

The packet boat ride is one of the many ways to pass your time while visiting Rome's Erie Canal Village. The re-created community is similar to many that grew up around the dawdling canal during its early years of shuffling people and freight to Buffalo.

On any given day in peak season, you will see a couple dozen staff persons in period dress on the grounds and inside the Wood Creek School, Bennett's Tavern, the women's clothing shop, the blacksmith shop, aboard the *Independence*, or on the Prairie, a steam locomotive symbolic of state of the art transportation in early America.

Before you enter the living history section of the village, you are ushered into a building where an introductory slide show is presented. The sequence of slides begins with a melange of cars and sounds of honking horns followed by the words, "What if all this hadn't been invented yet?"

You learn that local Indians carried their boats from the Mohawk River to Wood Creek, actually little more than a trickle, and by following natural though barely passable waterways, could navigate themselves to the Great Lakes. The Indians called this stretch the Great Carry.

Four artificial waterways would eventually be constructed on this site. The first, built in 1794, simply connected the Mohawk River and Wood Creek, a total of three miles, removing forever the inconvenience of the Great Carry.

The Erie Canal was next, built in shifts over the course of eight years. But the acrid Erie's waters were only four feet deep and, except for one site near its terminus, the canal was equipped only with single locks. In many locations along its 363-mile route, the canal was obsolete soon after it was completed.

So it was widened and deepened in the 1840s and served the people of New York until the 1910s when it was gradually replaced by the bigger New York State Barge Canal System.

The barge system is still in use today. In fact, many travelers on the

New York State Thruway, especially those from other states, mistakenly assume the barge system paralleling the interstate is a remnant of the original Erie Canal.

The barge system actually bypasses the historic waterway. But visitors to Erie Canal Village can see what remains of the original Erie Canal, referred to as Clinton's Ditch, which runs through the village, though is not used for rides. When you ride on the *Independence*, you are on the bed of the enlarged canal that came through Rome in the 1840s.

Off the water, 19th-century village life goes on as usual. The teacher in Wood Creek School takes a pointer in hand to show us, as she would her students, the Erie's location on an 1845 map. A McGuffey's Reader sits on each harsh, grey desk, and the chalkboard is covered with platitudes extolling the virtues of humility and generosity: "People who think big of themselves make small packages" and "Man is sometimes more generous when he has little money than when he has plenty."

In addition to the classroom, respectable women would have been found in the home and the marketplace. So you shouldn't be surprised to find the lady of the house in any of the three village residences, each presenting a look at life in different periods when canal commerce was booming.

She will likely be baking cookies or perhaps a loaf of bread in the ca. 1840 Crosby House. If you have the knack of being in the right place at the right time, you will be able to sample such a treat hot from the wood stove.

There was no luxury like a wood stove for the residents in the little Cape next door, built 20 years earlier in another part of Rome; they relied on a fireplace for heat and had to get water from an outside well.

The third house, the Shull House, representing Victorian Rome, was built in 1869 by a farmer and cattle dealer in Little Falls. It actually faced the canal in its original location, and the Shull family was one of many that prospered because of the waterway.

When not at home, Mrs. Shull would have been in a store like the women's apparel shop, offering a look at lifestyles during later years along the Erie. Thanks to both the canal and the railroad, fashionable items like hoop skirts and mourning veils were available upstate as well as in big cities to the south. This Victorian-era shop would have been filled with women who had nothing to mourn but wanted to dress in black as Queen Victoria did after the death of her husband, Prince Albert.

Men, on the other hand, gathered in the blacksmith shop; all who lived here needed animals for work and all animals needed shoes. Visit in peak season and you will hear the clanging of the hammer and iron from a blacksmith in residence.

Any person of either sex who needed to catch a train would be found in Bennett's Tavern. Proper ladies, however, relaxed in the parlor, since the taproom was off limits. Then as now, salesmen took to the road to earn a living and the second floor guest room serves as a showcase for peddler's wares as he might have displayed them for potential buyers. Enter a smaller guest room and you see a suitcase, top hat, and frock coat, giving the room the appearance that someone just stepped out for a pint.

Downstairs in the tavern, you can cool off with a brisk drink of less potent potables than 19th-century guests would have sampled. The choice is usually root beer, iced tea, or lemonade. You also can indulge in a light snack such as pickled eggs or cheese made right at the village, for a small charge.

Location: Erie Canal Village is on Routes 49 and 46 west of Rome. From the New York State Thruway heading west, take exit 32 (Westmoreland/Rome) onto Route 233W to Route 365 to Route 69 to the village. From the New York State Thruway heading east, take exit 33 (Verona) onto Route 365 to Route 69 to the village. **Admission** is charged. **Hours:** Daily, mid-May through September. **Allow** three to five hours. **Information:** Erie Canal Village, 5789 New London Road, Rome, NY 13440; (315) 336-6000, ext. 250.

Events: Late summer, Cheese festival, cow milking, samples and demonstrations of cheese making, including New York Cheddar, Colby, and Muenster; December, Christmas carol sing, music, decorations, sleigh rides, food.

Note: Picnic tables are on the grounds. There is a snack bar, but you also can bring your own picnic.

If you are staying overnight: Quality Inn, 200 S. James Street (in the center of Rome on Routes 46, 49, and 69), (315) 336-4300; Paul Revere Motor Lodge, 7900 Turin Road (three miles north of Rome on Route 26), (315) 336-1776; Family Inns of America, 145 E. Whitesboro (in the center of Rome off Route 49), (315) 337-9400; Esquire Motor Lodge, 1801 Black River Road, Rome, (315) 336-5320.

NEW YORK STOCK EXCHANGE

From the visitor's gallery, the heartbeat of the nation's economy resembles an anthill on a parched summer lawn.

F IX IN YOUR MIND AN IMAGE OF AN ANT HILL ON A DRY PATCH OF YOUR backyard lawn on a hot, parched summer day and you will be prepared for a view of the trading floor from the visitors' gallery at the New York Stock Exchange.

Standing high above the floor where all the action takes place, it is at first hard to follow the mesmerizing movements in the human jungle below. But a visit to the stock exchange is well arranged so visitors get to the gallery as the last stop on their journey into the heartbeat of the nation's economy.

Prior to stepping onto the gallery, you will see a slide presentation, scour wall and push button displays, and listen to a brief but efficient primer on the basic technique of reading that tape that flows like an endless river of dots and numbers, telling you how your favorite stock is doing.

So even if you think Dow Jones and the Industrials was a mid-'60s rock group, don't hesitate to step inside the pillared building at 11 Wall Street. You won't leave with the expertise of a Louis Rukeyser, but you will exit with considerably more knowledge than you had when you came in.

The history of the traders' mecca, known familiarly as Wall Street, had its beginnings on a pleasant May day in 1792 when George Washington was in his first term as president and the new country was still crawling.

At the time, securities like bales of cotton or casks of sugar were bought and sold at auctions through competitive bidding. The two dozen traders and brokers most involved in the securities market met on May 17, 1792, under an old buttonwood tree in the middle of that busy district, near 70 Wall Street, with the intention of preventing a monopoly of sales by the auctioneers.

They agreed to avoid public auctions, to collect a minimum commission on all sales of public stock, and to "give preference to each other" in their negotiations. This eventually would become known as "the Buttonwood Agreement."

They continued to meet by the buttonwood tree. And when chilly air moved in towards the end of the year, they gathered in the cozy confines of the Tontine Coffee House at the corner of Wall and Water Streets. Said a visitor from Sweden in the early 1790s, "In the neighborhood of the Tontine all public auctions are held. Large packages, bundles and barrels cover the sidewalks." And this is how it all started.

Further quotations, some more insightful than others, accompany more facts in the fascinating exhibit on the stock exchange's background.

Could women ever find a place in the world of economics? The exhibit shows that in 1899, a financial writer named John McKenzie said, "Women make poor speculators. When thrown upon their own resources they are comparatively helpless. Excelling in certain lines, they are forced to take back seats in speculation. Without the assistance of a man, a woman on Wall Street is like a ship without a rudder."

It took decades to prove McKenzie incorrect. The first woman was not admitted to the trading floor until 1967.

In "Your Questions Answered," you will find at the touch of a button easily comprehensible explanations of all those terms you always felt were two obvious to ask about. Think about all the dinner parties where conversation turned to money and investments and you seemed to be the only one who didn't speak the language.

Select a question like, "What is meant by bulls and bears?"

The answer will appear: "Bulls believe stock prices will rise. Bears say they will decline."

Or this one: "What is meant by price-earnings ratio?"

Answer: "It is the price of a share of stock divided by earnings per share for a 12-month period. It is a convenient way to compare stocks of varying prices and earnings."

Then there is, "What are the major market indicators?"

By the time you leave you'll know the answer is the New York Stock Exchange, the Dow Jones Industrial Average (which is composed of 30 of the most widely held common stocks), and Standard and Poor's index of 500 stocks.

And you will be well on your way to accomplishing perhaps the most challenging feat here, learning that elusive technique that many otherwise intelligent people can't seem to master: how to read a stock table.

There are two ways to learn. First, there is a wall display explaining all in language for the layperson. There is also a regularly scheduled 12-minute talk by a New York Stock Exchange staff member, also in terms that are easy to understand. Those already familiar with the stock table can spend the time at any of three computer terminals, checking on the latest reports of his or her stocks.

The tour ends with a guide to the trading floor. Learning that all stock exchange employees on the floor are dressed in distinct colors identifying their duties will help you see some semblance of order in what seems, to the uninitiated, to be the epitome of disorderliness.

Because of space limitations, only a certain number of people are allowed in the visitors' gallery at one time, so you will likely have to wait a few minutes before entering. New York Stock Exchange spokesperson Martha Cid says that the longest wait is usually 15 minutes and rarely more than half an hour.

There is undeniable excitement in seeing the trading floor for the first time, similar to the experience of first laying eyes on famous Washington sites like the Capitol or the White House or any other locale you see almost every night on television. Switch on the network news the evening after your visit and as you hear the anchorperson say, "Today on Wall Street, the Dow Jones Industrials were . . ." you won't be able to help feeling a bit of a thrill knowing you were right there.

When you look down onto the floor, you'll see masses of people, mostly men, rushing from telephones to counters and back again amid an ocean of discarded paperwork covering the floor. Relax if you can't recall all you had heard during the earlier talk. A taped explanation about six minutes long plays automatically. Watch the people in the green jackets—they are supervisors. Those with orange shoulder straps on blue jackets are messengers, while brokers have oval or square numbers on their jackets.

Reporters wear dark blue jackets; their job is to take information on computer cards and insert it into light sensitive machines to distribute it. In years past when tickers were used, information was put in pneumatic tubes and transported from sending to receiving stations. A model of a classic, but now obsolete, brass and oak trading post is on display just outside the visitors' gallery entrance.

The original old posts are now relics in museums and universities across the country; one is in the New York State Museum in Albany. They have gone the way of the stock ticker, which hasn't been seen here for over two decades. Transmission of stock and quote data from the floor has been fully automated for more than 20 years.

Location: The New York Stock Exchange visitors' center is at 20 Broad Street, near the intersection with Wall Street. **Admission** is free. **Hours:** Year round, weekdays except for most holidays. **Allow** 45 minutes to an hour and a half depending on your interest and the time you visit. **Information:** New York Stock Exchange, 11 Wall Street, New York, NY 10005; (212) 623-5167.

Note: As with most attractions, summer and school vacations are traditionally the busiest times here. If you make your trip during those periods, plan to come before 11:30 a.m., or expect a short wait.

If you are staying overnight: Get information on conventional lodging and tour packages from the New York Convention and Visitors Bureau, Inc., 2 Columbus Circle, New York, NY 10019; (212) 397-8222. For information on alternative lodging, contact City Lights Bed & Breakfast, Ltd., P.O. Box 20355, Cherokee Station, New York, NY 10028; (212) 737-7049. Another bed and breakfast service is Urban Ventures, P.O. Box 426, New York, NY 10024; (212) 594-5650.

OLD BETHPAGE VILLAGE RESTORATION

Time to go to work on Long Island, 19th-century style, at Old Bethpage Village.

Courtesy: Old Bethpage Village

T HERE WAS A TIME WHEN A SHOPPING SPREE ON LONG ISLAND MEANT the purchase of a bundle of rags and linseed oil from John B. Luyster's general store and an order for a felt hat from hatmaker Lewis Ritch.

Long before the development of plastic, Long Islanders were already shopping on credit. In fact, almost all business at Luyster's store was conducted on a credit basis, and the desk on which the accountant kept the books can still be seen when you visit the store at Old Bethpage Village in Old Bethpage.

Luyster's store and Ritch's hatmaking shop join 16 other structures relocated to the re-created 19th-century village. When you leave the modern reception center and walk along the dusty road of clamshells and dirt, you enter Long Island, a generation before the Civil War.

You can buy something to eat in the village but you can't use 20th-century currency; you exchange that in the reception center for 19th-century paper scrip. The going rate when we last visited was 50 cents from the 20th century for four Old Bethpage cents. But the trade-off is just fine; four cents bought then what 50 cents buys today.

Your shopping spree at Old Bethpage Village will be limited to old-time goodies like birch beer, apple cider, pretzels, and penny candy, which you can buy at the store of Luyster's closest competitor, John M. Layton, or at the center of Old Bethpage social activity, the Noon Tavern. Most of us wouldn't have any use for rags and linseed oil anyway.

As we paid for our snacks—wintergreen and cherry candy sticks for a penny each—we learned that the money we were using was legal tender in Old Bethpage only; each town printed its own paper money.

What else is found on Layton's shelves? His stock runs the gamut from school slates to sausage grinders and everything a farmer would need. Long Island's economy was still primarily agricultural during this period.

The Powell Farm, a residence and working farm, is the only original part of Old Bethpage Village. Even though the industrial revolution was finding its way into Long Island in the 1840s, farming was still the bread and butter, so to speak, for most families' existence.

Pumpkin pies were baking and batter for a pound cake was being mixed when we entered the Powell kitchen. In 1850 the Powell clan included children, grandparents, and hired hands for a total of 15 persons under one roof—food preparation was an endless job.

There were also hungry animals to feed. A hired hand using a bulky wooden implement was slicing beets and greens, from one of the four major kitchen gardens, to be fed to the resident cows in the Powell family barn. Nearby are a smokehouse and an outhouse and apple and pear orchards. Many of the meals are made from products grown or raised at the farm, and the women working in the kitchen stick to 19th-century recipes.

When you leave the farm, walk, as the Powells did, down the main road to the village center to see signs of other commerce that made Old Bethpage thrive. Enter the Lewis Ritch hat shop where, with a hefty supply of felt, a set of wooden crown molds, and about four days of labor, Ritch could fashion a stylish felt hat for village farmers.

A handmade hat lasted ten to 15 years and since hatmakers could rush out no more than two hats a week, craftsmen like Ritch ran other businesses on the side to supplement their income. Ritch, for instance, also had a woodwork business.

For another example of time-consuming work, visit the broom maker.

In the 1840s, some broom parts like dowels and strings were manufactured in factories. But brooms were still handmade and we were told by the resident artisan that a good worker could turn up to 30 brooms a day; at six cents a broom, he would sweep up with $1.80 for a day's work, not a bad income at that time. But little did he know he would be an obsolete man in 10 years when brooms would be routinely made in factories.

An innkeeper, however, never needed to worry about becoming useless. His job will continue as long as people need places to eat and rest. The Noon Inn, conveniently situated at the main crossroads in Old Bethpage Village, was constructed about 1840 and restored about ten years later. It provided sustenance and sleep to weary Long Islanders for many years at the crossroads of Newbridge and Prospect Avenues in East Meadow, ten miles west.

It also served as a meeting place for locals. The barroom, with its bottles and decanters stacked behind the wooden counter and its patriotic prints posted on the walls, was the center of action. It is here that you can buy cider and pretzels with your 19th-century scrip, and there are tables and benches where you can relax.

Upstairs is the ballroom where townwide social activities took place. There are also two guest bedrooms, since local law mandated that any establishment serving alcohol must provide sleeping quarters.

Most families, like the Noons, lived in the building in which they did business. And as the private homes at Bethpage reveal their owners' professions, they also give hints to their backgrounds.

The Powell homestead, with its few contemporary furnishings mixed with modest colonial furniture handed down through generations, is typical of the Quaker heritage.

The Dutch roots of wealthy farmers Roeloff and Minne Schenck are symbolized by the hidden bed box, the huge stone jambless fireplace, and the split Dutch door, effects more commonly seen in the Hudson Valley.

The Schenck House, the first restored building visitors approach from the reception center, is considered the oldest Dutch farmhouse in Nassau County, and one of the oldest in the country. The home was in the Schenck family for more than 200 years.

Farmers such as the Schencks made their living from the land but other Long Islanders thrived on different natural commodities. Joseph Conklin's small one-and-a-half-story home is filled with fishing, eeling, crabbing, and clamming implements, reminders of his life's work at sea. The tiny kitchen with its rough-hewn table is representative of his moderate income.

John Layton, on the other hand, did splendidly with his general store, as demonstrated by his residence in the same building. It is decorated in early Victorian style with due respect to the fads of the day, including flowers dipped in beeswax and a framed newspaper print chronicling "The Life and Age of Woman, Stages of a Woman's Life from Infancy to the Brink of the Grave."

It is at age 30, the print says, that "Woman may be considered at the zenith of her intellectual and physical powers."

But don't think on that too long. Not everything written 130 years ago was accurate, for this was also a time when any well-read Bethpage resident would urge you to stay home at night, fearing that night air caused tuberculosis.

Location: From the Long Island Expressway, take exit 48 or from the Northern State Parkway, exit 39; head south from either onto Round Swamp Road and follow the signs to the village entrance. **Admission** is charged. **Hours:** Year round; March through November, Tuesday through Sunday; rest of year, Tuesday through Friday and Sunday. **Allow** three to five hours for the village. **Information:** Old Bethpage Village Restoration, Round Swamp Road, Old Bethpage, NY 11804; (516) 420-5288.

Events: There are many and they are celebrated at all times of the year. The biggest is the Long Island Fair in mid-fall. A brief sampling of others includes: spring planting, 19th-century-style baseball in summer, early food preparation demonstrations in fall, military musters in September, an early Bethpage cooking contest in November, and a celebration of St. Nicholas Day at the Schenck House in December.

Note: Before leaving the visitor center, be sure to see the 20-minute film which sets the tone for your visit. Picnic tables are on the grounds.

If you are staying overnight: Holiday Inn, 215 Sunnyside Boulevard (north of Long Island Expressway, exit 46), Plainview, (516) 349-7400; Pickwick Motor Inn, Round Swamp Road (off Long Island Expressway, exit 48), Plainview, (516) 694-6500; Plainview Plaza Hotel, 150 Sunnyside Boulevard (off Long Island Expressway, exit 46), Plainview, (516) 349-9100. Note that lodging is extremely expensive in Long Island. It is very difficult to find a double room priced less than $80 per night. If you are en route to another location, consider staying elsewhere.

CORNING GLASS CENTER

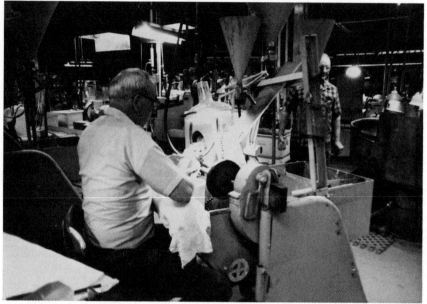

Look over the shoulders of Steuben Glass workers at the Corning Glass Center as they engrave complex designs on crystal by hand, rarely done in these days of automation.

W HEN PRINCE CHARLES AND LADY DI MARRIED IN 1981, THEY DIDN'T receive any Corningware as a wedding gift.

They are probably the only couple in the world that didn't.

Or so it seems.

Think of Corning and you think of Corningware. Make a visit to the Corning Glass Center and you will be able to see one of the most complete museum complexes anywhere devoted to one theme.

It's a place where glassworkers with cat-like patience speak in their own cryptic tongue, where the museum maintains twice as many pieces as there are people in Corning, and where you will see glass stronger than Arnold Schwarzeneger's fist. To make things easier for visitors, the center is divided into three parts: the Corning Museum of Glass, the Hall of Science, and the Steuben Glass Factory.

Although the Steuben factory is the final segment of the Corning showplace trilogy, we'll discuss it first since it is here that you actually see New Yorkers hard at work.

A videotape introduces you to the factory by offering an overview of the glassmaking process. Sit near the front benches to best hear the presentation, since the background noise of machinery is deafening—despite the glass partition separating workers from onlookers.

Corning Glass spokespersons proudly point out that the Steuben factory is one of the few that still makes hand-crafted glass. It is also a place where workers speak a curious language; watch the shop working at a glory hole with the gaffer putting the final touches on a piece of glass before it is placed in a lehr and afterwards, sent to the finishing lines.

Translated from glassmakers' lingo into English, it means this. A small team of workers is called a shop; they work around a reheating oven called a glory hole, where molten glass is shaped. (You see plenty of these from where you sit.) The gaffer, another name for the master blower, forms the finished product as the artist intended it. The piece is then moved to the lehr, an annealing oven, where the glass cools and solidifies. The last stop is the finishing lines, where the piece is ground and polished to enable its natural luster to shine.

Some of the Steuben glass is engraved, and you will be able to see engravers plying their craft close up. Patience is a needed virtue to engrave Steuben glass. In addition to responsibility for performing an exacting job, they execute it with countless visitors literally looking over their shoulders. Although it's hard to fathom anyone of us taking a job permitting outsiders to watch us intently at work, Steuben workers expect it. Study them as they engrave the most complex designs on crystal using rotating copper wheels.

Humanity has been working with and decorating glass for thousands of years, and we have been using it even longer. At the Corning Museum of Glass, you can take a look at the items made by the Steuben workers' counterparts more than 3,000 years ago. Glass vessels made in Mesopotamia (present day Iraq) by coating a clay and animal dung core with molten glass are some of the oldest pieces here; they have been dated to 1,400 B.C.

The museum has more than 24,000 objects, and most visitors are overwhelmed once they see the size of the collection. Casual visitors tend to study the first few galleries and then suffer from what one museum director elsewhere once called "visual indigestion," seeing too much of a good thing at one stretch.

As you tour the museum, keep in mind that it is arranged with a time tunnel effect. You start off with ancient and Islamic glass, such as an 800-year-old perfume bottle engraved with images of animals. A magnifying glass lets you look closely; how many different animals can you find?

Gradually, you approach the Middle Ages and the Renaissance, with Venetian goblets and German flasks, before reaching colonial America and the modern day world. There's a handy time line comparing glass developments with major historical events.

You see three English goblets coupled with the year 1776, when the Declaration of Independence was signed. When the Erie Canal was completed in 1824, mass production of American tableware was fully underway, thanks to the development of mechanical pressing. Two ornately patterned compotes, probably made in Sandwich, Massachusetts, an early glass manufacturing center, illustrate these earliest days of mechanization.

Save time for the detailed collections near museum's end, such as the dazzling display featuring hundreds of different paperweights. Encased in glass are likenesses of everything from the purple finch to the quizzical face of Ulysses S. Grant.

You will probably wear a quizzical expression, too, when you step inside the Hall of Science and Industry and see glass do some pretty remarkable feats. It is almost as if glass were the star performer at a carnival side show where a barker would lure you inside with tempting calls of, "See a glass pipe as strong as any hammer. See a slab of glass withstand a bath in corrosive acids. See the world's largest light bulb, 75,000 watts of power. See a man take rods of glass and transform them into shapes of animals as easy as if he was molding clay." If you have never seen these types of demonstrations before, you will truly be amazed and surprised.

Location: From New York City and the east, take the Southern Tier Expressway (Route 17) to the Cedar Street exit in Corning and follow it to the Corning Glass Center. From the New York State Thruway (Interstate 90), take either exit 41 or 42 and follow either Route 414 (or 14 to 414 in Watkins Glen) into Corning. At the end of Route 414, take a left onto Pulteney Street, then the next right onto Greenway; the glass center is on the right. **Admission** is charged. **Hours:** Year round, daily. **Allow** two to three hours. **Information:** Corning Glass Center, Corning, NY 14831; (607) 974-8271.

Events: Special exhibits are scheduled annually. When we last attended, there was one focusing on glass from the Roman Empire, including glassware from the collections of museums disparate as the Romanisch-Germanisches Museum in Cologne, West Germany and the J. Paul Getty Museum in Malibu, California.

Note: Glassware in all forms is sold in several different shops in the complex. The Designer Shop sells glassware from a number of domestic and international glass firms, including Steuben pieces. The Collector's Shop features work by contemporary glass artists. The Consumer Shop has various Corning products including closeouts and discontinued items. The Gift Shop stocks glass jewelry and Corning sunglasses as well as T-shirts and traditional gifts. There are also two light eateries, closed, however, in winter months. In summer, a free bus takes visitors from the parking lot to the glass center and other popular sites in town. Many visitors enjoy following a visit to the glass center with a walk down Market Street in downtown Corning; it has been refurbished to represent a turn-of-the-century appearance, with dozens of specialty and gift shops, eateries, and outlets. The shops carry everything from glass (naturally) to quality Christmas ornaments to ceramics to New York State wine.

If you are staying overnight: Corning Hilton Inn, Route 17 (east of town), Corning, (607) 962-5000; Stiles Motel, Route 415 (Route 17, exit 42, then a half mile west), Painted Post, (607) 962-5221; Cecce Guest House (bed and breakfast), 166 Chemung Street, Corning, (607) 962-5682; Rosewood Inn (bed and breakfast), 134 E. First Street, Corning, (607) 962-3253.

FARMERS' MUSEUM

It's not the Fourth of July. These sparks are from blacksmith Paul Spaulding's hammer at The Farmers' Museum's Village Crossroads.

Courtesy: New York State Historical Association

THE FARMERS' MUSEUM AND VILLAGE CROSSROADS IN COOPERSTOWN presents, in a nutshell, how life was conducted in 19th-century small town New York State.

There was a country doctor, but he was trained to deal only with simple ills, not major sicknesses or catastrophes. He would send his patients next door to the pharmacy where they would be introduced to all sorts of cures: dandelion root for menstrual irregularities or liver problems, lettuce for use as a sedative or to tone down nymphomania, or leeches for bloodletting.

Even though malpractice suits weren't the talk of the town then, the lawyer's office is conveniently close to the doctor's office, while at the end of the lane, for those who could not find healing from any mortal source, is the rural church.

After a hard day of work, citizens could be found unwinding at the Ephraim Bump Tavern, a place for leisure for all but the tavern keeper, who was kept busy entertaining both the rowdy and the reserved.

The tavern was an early American combination of Joe's Corner Bar and Grille and a modern Holiday Inn. Some of the rougher patrons sat in the taproom, indulging in lively spirits or spitting a chaw of tobacco onto the sawdust-covered floor as they played checkers or dominoes. Gentlemen and ladies, on the other hand, withdrew to the sitting room, where they would wait quietly for the next stagecoach.

A handful of other buildings where workers earned their livelihood are in the village crossroads, but the crossroads in total amounts to only about one-third of the sights to see in the museum's massive complex.

Pass through the small town center, and step onto a real working farm, the Lippitt Farmstead, thick with pungent odors of straw, hay, and livestock, where 20th-century visitors meet 19th-century agriculture.

You'll be met in a gritty, hands-on manner, as you are cordially invited to become a hired hand for a few moments. Try your luck at milking a cow or churning butter.

If you are in the farm kitchen at the right time, you may be offered a sampling of bread, pudding, vegetable pie, or fresh meat. When we last savored the scents inside, catsup (in the days before "ketchup") was simmering in one cast-iron pot, and pork and beans were cooking in another. Farm wife Andre Dougherty was heating up the beehive oven, planning to make a loaf of wheat bread; highly desired white bread was a luxury out of reach for all but the wealthiest citizens.

A typical farm wife would have likely spent six hours in the morning making dinner, the major meal, served at midday; she would then spend about six additional hours preparing supper, the evening and smaller meal. While the condiments and main courses were cooking, Andre sat to one side weaving straw into a work hat for a farm hand to wear while laboring in a hot field. Using one free hour every day, she estimated that completion of the hat would take two to two-and-a-half months.

The Farmers' Museum staff encourages visitors to ask about any implement or curiosity that's within your view. That's how we discovered that the formal and fancy room in the Bump Tavern was for the convenience of proper gentlemen and ladies who were permitted, but did not prefer, to sit with the more earthy locals who relaxed in the taproom, where liquor flowed like the nearby Susquehanna River.

Tavern keeper Karen Kremer told us that many visitors aren't familiar with the function of an early American tavern. The Bump Tavern, ca. 1795, was constructed in the tiny hamlet of Ashland in Greene County. It served many purposes: an inn for weary travelers, a gathering place for social events, and a home for craftsmen and tradesmen.

One would see a broad range of persons inside, from the upper crust to the working class. You can sit at a taproom table and play checkers or dominoes or exercise your creativity with the innumerable formations of a clapping Jacob's Ladder.

If you're looking for practical items and basic goods, try the general store or, surprisingly, the pharmacy.

Offered village druggist Craig Haney, "Customers could come here to find paint, soap, bootblack, and other household items, which the pharmacist sold mainly out of economic necessity." This proud, pillared drug store, built in 1832, has leeches in a jar and pillboxes for sale at $17.50 to $18.50.

Major competition would have come from the 1828 general store, fully packed with many village-made crafts and other commonly stocked items for sale; they range from nutmeg for five cents (who says you can't buy anything for a nickel anymore?) to a woolen shawl for $65.

Here the wares made by the blacksmith, printer, cabinet maker, and broom maker are on sale. Until you step inside the store you won't believe brooms could come in so many varieties; one staff member says they are the most popular gift that visitors purchase. There are hand-crafted hearth brooms with straggly bristles that hang like whiskers of a beard for $9.50, whiskbrooms for $9.25, and house brooms for $12.75. It was common in the early 1800s to barter, and village residents would bring in cordwood or raw textiles to trade, but today only cash and credit cards are accepted.

You will meet the broom maker and other tradepersons like the weaver and a turn-of-the-century photographer in the main barn, which could easily serve as a museum on its own. The barn's displays and collections interpret the lot of farmers in 19th-century central New York State.

Examine the tools and machinery, such as a garden seeder, corn shellers, plows, and carts, and then round out your view of farm life by visiting a farmer's home and the nearby amusement center, where you are offered a peek at life's diversions before the advent of arcades and movies.

"Happy Times" is the name of the museum's hypothetical amusement center. There are carousel horses and rocking horses, and there is the Museum of Wonders like those which toured from town to town, village to village.

Here the curious would see the oddities of nature like the two-headed calf and the paintings by George "Grandpa" Martin on bed ticking and burlap; Martin brought these paintings with him when he took to the road giving dramatic performances. As is done today, tragedies were exploited for profit, evidenced by the painting of the murder of the Van Nest family in Cayuga County. Look closely; can you see the murderer peering through the window?

But there is one exhibit in this amusement collection that is not typical.

Imagine yourself as a small-time farmer digging for a well and coming across—buried six feet down in the hard, cold ground—the petrified body of a huge giant of a man.

That is what happened in 1869, and the report of this discovery in Cardiff, New York, was immediately news. The giant was soon exhibited to the public for an admission of 50 cents per person. The giant was even taken on the road as part of a tour to some of the Northeast's biggest cities, including New York City, Boston, Syracuse, and Albany.

It was on this tour that a paleontologist from Yale University named Othniel C. Marsh saw what he considered to be a sculptor's marks on the giant, and that's when the real story of the Cardiff Giant surfaced.

A man named George Hull from Binghamton had, in 1868, commissioned several artisans to sculpt the giant and, upon completion, it was buried on Hull's cousin's farm. After a year it was uncovered, and after it had been on display for a while, Hull sold three quarters interest in the giant to a syndicate of prominent area businessmen.

But the exposure of the hoax didn't detract from the giant's appeal, and it would remain on exhibit through most of the 1870s. It was finally placed in storage in 1880 and in 1947, it was purchased by the museum and moved into its current home.

Location: From the west, take the New York State Thruway (Interstate 90), exit 30 (Herkimer), and follow Route 28 south to Cooperstown. From the east, take the Thruway (Interstate 90) to exit 25A and follow Route 20 west and then Route 80 south. From the south, take Interstate 88 to exit 17 (Oneonta), and follow Route 28 north. From New York City and the southeast, take the Thruway (Interstate 90) to exit 21 (Catskill) and follow Route 145 either to Interstate 88 west to exit 17 (see above) or take Route 20 west to Route 80 south. The museum is on Route 80 (Lake Road), one mile north of the center of town. **Admission** is charged. **Hours:** May through October, daily; April, November and December, Tuesday through Sunday. **Allow** two to four hours. **Information:** The Farmers' Museum, P.O. Box 800, Cooperstown, NY 13326; (607) 547-2533.

Events: Late spring, Draft Horse day (wagon rides and multiple horse hitches), Working Animals on the Farm (demonstrations of animal power in early America); summer, Livestock Show; early fall, Autumn Harvest (20-25 craftpersons, performers, music and dancers).

If you are staying overnight: Deer Run Motel, Route 80 (9 miles east of center of Cooperstown), Cooperstown, (607) 547-8600. The Inn at Cooperstown, 16 Chestnut Street, Cooperstown, (607) 547-5756; The Otesaga Hotel, Lake Street (Route 80 on lake shore), Cooperstown, (607) 547-9931; Bed & Breakfast Leatherstocking (reservation service), 389 Brockway Road, Frankfort Hill, NY 13340, (315) 733-0040.

AMERICAN MUSEUM OF FIRE FIGHTING

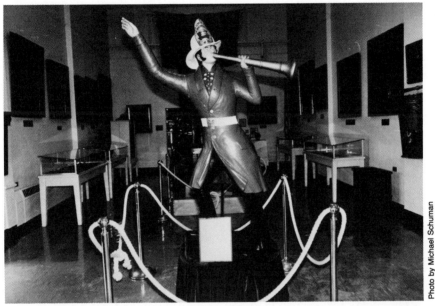

This 19th-century wooden fire chief was modeled after a real man who might have ridden one of the dozens of old fire engines at the American Museum of Fire Fighting.

BILL RHOADES, 67 YEARS OLD, IS A FORMER FIRE FIGHTER FROM BAY Shore, Long Island, who proudly declares, "I've been a student of fire engines since I was 14 and a volunteer fireman since I was 30."

Some say experience is the best teacher. That being the case, there is no better person to lead us on a tour of the American Museum of Fire Fighting in Hudson.

You may not have Bill Rhoades to show you round, but it's likely that you will have somebody like him. All guides are residents of the Volunteer Firemen's Home of the state of New York on whose grounds this museum sits.

Like many an old-timer, Bill feels that modern methods can't match the quality of the past.

"They don't make them like they used to," he says on more than one occasion on our visit.

But Bill isn't even talking about his youth. He is referring to a time long past, long before his days of manning the red engines. We look at a brilliantly carved, high carriage, piano-style fire engine built in 1851. Rhoades told us that it actually was crafted by a piano maker so it is no coincidence that the chassis looks like a baby grand.

He points out its four panels, each adorned with a hand-painted portrait done by Joseph H. Johnson, an artisan known among fire-fighting buffs for decorating many fire engines. The likenesses depict Chief Engineer of New York Alfred Carson and three better-known American statesmen: Henry Clay, George Washington, and Thomas Jefferson; this engine was owned by New York's Jefferson Engine Company.

Rhoades then says that despite the beauty in these depictions, one of them is flawed. We look closely at Jefferson's image, and, sure enough, we see the third president is wearing two left shoes. Other than a reference to possible poor dancing ability, it is not known why that is. But if your guide should try to catch you on that painting, you'll be ready for him.

The piano-style fire engine is displayed in a hall devoted solely to fire-fighting apparatus built prior to the 20th century. The museum also has equipment from the steam and motorized ages, through the late 1920s.

One of the most modern acquisitions is a long, lanky hook-and-ladder made by Elmira's La France Fire Engine Company, which churned out fire-fighting vehicles for decades; this one served from 1916 to 1956 in Oyster Bay, Long Island.

But Bill Rhoades's claim that "they don't make them like they used to" holds true when you spot an earlier hook-and-ladder, another New York State product, built by Rumsey & Company in Seneca Falls. It's lengthy body belies its light weight—so light in fact that it was meant to be pulled by manpower and only later was altered so it could be pulled by horses. Hand-painted floral patterns on the chassis, ladders, and tools make this another beauty.

The oldest vehicles are usually the most ornate. A double deck end-stroke machine built in 1846 in Philadelphia resembles a circus calliope more than a fire machine. The sides of the panel box serve as canvasses for more of Joseph H. Johnson's works: George Washington crossing the Delaware, the rescue of Captain John Smith by Pocahontas, and a female allegorical figure, the Genius of Freedom. There are painted depictions of eagles on the ornate wooden carvings on the machine's sides and classy brass sunbursts on its wheel hubs.

It is surprising that this much art exists in such an unlikely place, and we see how Rhoades is understandably proud of it. But if there is any one fire-fighting machine that makes him beam the most, it is one you will see when you first set foot inside the museum.

The Newsham Engine was built in London in 1725, when good King George I was ruling England and George Washington hadn't been born. The Newsham is the oldest piece of fire-fighting machinery in the museum and claimed to be the oldest in existence anywhere in the United States. This contraption of wooden wheels and leather pipes was one of two carried across the Atlantic on the ship *Beaver*, arriving in New York in 1731; it would enjoy a long active life, serving the people of Manhattan for 154 years.

Engineer Richard Newsham's invention is now regarded as America's first successful mobile fire-fighting machine. But its mobility came with limitations; because both axles were fixed, it was necessary to lift the machine, solid wooden wheels and all, to make any turns.

While comprising the bulk of the museum collection, fire-fighting machines are not all you can see. As soon as you open the museum door, your eyes are accosted by a wooden statue freezing in time the most thrilling yet threatening moment in a fire fighter's life. It depicts a fire chief, circa 1850, in blue coat and white hat, raising a trumpet to his mouth with one hand and thrusting the other into the air as if to urge on his cohorts.

This hand-carved relic of folk art is proof that beauty among design in the fireman's sphere was not limited to machinery. Rhoades tells us that the statue stood atop a firemen's association building in the Coney Island section of Brooklyn for more than 75 years before being brought here for eternal protection and rest. The figure was modeled after a real person, Jameson Cox, chief engineer of the New York Fire Department in the 1820s.

Rhoades concludes the tour by letting us know of one case where equipment changed for the worse only to return to its original design. As we look over the collection of old leather hats, Rhoades says that they were initially designed to protect the wearer from head injury, guard the face from torrid heat, and shed water from the back of the neck. Leather eventually was replaced by inexpensive plastic, but in time it was shown that plastic didn't protect the head or resist heat like leather. So in some cases, they have gone back to leather and, Bill smiles, are once more making them like they used to.

Location: From the New York State Thruway (Interstate 87), exit 21, take Route 23 east, cross the Rip Van Winkle Bridge, and turn left onto Route 9G (South Third Street) heading north into Hudson; turn right onto State Street, then left onto Carroll Street, which leads into

Harry Howard Avenue; bear right after Underhill Pond and the museum will be on the left, less than a mile away. From the Taconic State Parkway, take the Route 23B exit and head west into Hudson on Route 23; turn right onto Route 9, left onto Joslen Boulevard, left again onto Harry Howard Avenue and follow to the museum. **Admission** is free. **Hours:** April through October, daily except Monday. **Allow** 45 minutes to an hour and a half. **Information:** American Museum of Fire Fighting, Harry Howard Avenue, Hudson, NY 12534; (518) 828-7695.

Note: Enter through the arched gateway facing Harry Howard Avenue, follow the driveway and bear to the left. The museum is in the brick building furthest to the left, separate from the rest of the Volunteer Firemen's Home complex.

If you are staying overnight: Howard Johnson's Motor Lodge, Route 32 (off Thruway exit 20), Saugerties, (914) 246-9511; Carl's Rip Van Winkle Motor Lodge, Route 23B (off Thruway exit 21), Catskill, (518) 943-3303; Catskill Motor Lodge, Route 23B (off Thruway exit 21), Catskill, (518) 943-5800.

GENESEE COUNTRY MUSEUM

Photo by Michael Schuman

Rumor had it that when the spiritualist owners of this eight-sided house died, their spirits came back to haunt it. Will you meet them when you visit Genesee Country Museum?

ENTER GENESEE COUNTRY MUSEUM IN MUMFORD AND YOU ENTER A world where white bread was like caviar to village residents, and families advertised for hired help in this manner:

"Wanted, by a respectable family, a smart girl 12 to 14 years of age whose parents or guardians would wish to bind out to do housework until she is of age."

Enter the village and you enter the 19th century in western New York State in an area once known as the Genesee Frontier.

"Building a church then was like building a shopping mall today," said Cele Mills, costumed staff member at the Brooks Grove Methodist Church. "It brought people to the area."

Today it's the village that brings modern-day visitors to this parcel of land about 20 miles southwest of Rochester. In the more than 50 authentic buildings, most moved from within a 90-mile radius and dating from the turn of the 19th century to 1870, you get a peek at the lifestyle of early New Yorkers.

As in most re-created villages, you get more out of your visit by talking to the craftspersons and others inside the buildings than by just breezing through them.

It was Lorraine Dudley at the Jones Farm who shed light on the question of their daily bread. The warm and homey scents of baking drifted out the windows of the farmhouse as we approached it.

Dudley, in puffed sleeves, apron, and mop hat, stated that white flour was a rarity on the frontier, as was refined white sugar, even for a wealthy 1830s family of dairy farmers like the Joneses.

Dudley bent over and took a fresh-from-the-oven rhubarb pie from the fresh-from-the-factory cast-iron wood stove, which itself was an emblem of family wealth in these early days. Having a cast iron stove in the 1830s was a rarity, sort of like being the first family on the block to have a microwave oven in the 1970s.

We asked Dudley what families like the Joneses would have used instead of white sugar and flour so familiar today.

"Molasses or brown sugar," she answered, "maybe honey," and added that she and other staff members cook whatever is in season when you visit.

"And they would have cooked anything they could hunt, as well as salt pork, chicken, venison, but very little beef."

Step inside the Jones Farm kitchen on certain days and you are likely to see 19th-century culinary arts in progress, such as cheese making and butter churning. On the other hand, enter the pioneer farmstead, representing the earliest period portrayed here, or the elegant Livingston-Backus House, built in portions from 1827 to 1840, and you will see cooking of different sorts.

Since the village interprets a span of 70 years, life is depicted in various periods. Cooking in the pioneer farmstead is done in a floor hearth, while in the Livingston-Backus House, it's either over an open hearth or inside a brick oven.

It's easy to see changes in fashion and lifestyle over the years. Clothing is altered in ten-year increments, and the lavish Victorian homes in the far southeastern corner of the village offer a look at plush living of which the wealthy Jones family could only dream.

There's the Hamilton House, an Italianate villa, with its rigid tower and mansard roof, relocated here from the town of Campbell, north of Corning. Next to it is the exotic Octagon House, whose porch extends around its perimeter and whose inside is filled with ostentatious Rococo Revival furniture and bric-a-brac.

Eight-sided houses weren't uncommon in Victorian times, but they didn't spring up like weeds either. Their residents would have had slightly off-center tastes and may have leaned towards the eccentric. The owners of this one, the Hyde family, were members of a spiritualist group. When Corporal and Mrs. Hyde died within two days of each other, rumors arose that their spirits often came back to haunt their old house. We came across neither when we visited.

We did, however, meet several adept craftspersons from earlier periods throughout the village: a yarn spinner, a weaver, a tinsmith, a blacksmith, a potter, a printer, a broom maker, and a basket maker.

The blacksmith was banging out nails when we walked in. The basket maker, Betty Lennox, was plying her craft in Kieffer's Place, a two-story log home dating from 1814. She had already finished the tedious tasks of carving out splints from a white ash log and shaving them to make them smooth and was in the process of making a cat-head basket. Why that name? Betty showed us the bottom of the basket, on which the splints took on the shape of a cat's ears and face.

We also toured other period buildings, including the school, the general store, the country inn, and the various churches. We also visited some that we've seen in few other re-created villages, such as the insurance office, the dressmaker's shop, the tackle shop, and the brewery and hop house. (The presence of the brewery is not surprising once you learn that the founder of the museum is John L. Wehle, chairman of the board of the Genesee Brewing Company.)

There is even a plot of hops growing in the back, one of many historically accurate gardens on the village grounds. In the brewery we discovered that beer, Archie Bunker's favorite beverage, has roots back to the Mayflower. The ship's log says that Massachusetts was chosen as the Pilgrims' destination instead of Virginia because "we could not now take time for further research of consideration, our victuals having been much spent, especially our beer."

The collection of old buildings is embellished by two more specific collections inside it. There is the carriage barn, filled with 40 horse-drawn vehicles including coaches, cutters, sleighs, and fire-fighting equipment.

There is also the Gallery of Sporting Art, which could stand by itself as a fine arts museum devoted to a single subject. The term "sporting art" here refers not to sports played with a ball or stick but to wildlife and hunting and fishing. There are statuary, oils, and watercolors, including those by Batavia, New York native Roy Mason; his oil, *Duck Hunters at Sunset* is haunting.

A sculpture garden, featuring eight bronze works commissioned specially for the museum by artists like Kent Ulberg, Richard Greeves, and Kenneth Bunn, decorates the grounds near the museum.

Finally, after a visit you should be able to answer the question, "What is the derivation of the word "Genesee?" It's a word often heard in upstate New York, the name of everything from a river to streets to businesses.

It comes from the name "Gen-nis-he-y," which the Seneca Indians gave to the northward flowing river nearby. It means "pleasant valley," and it was only a matter of time until the entire region would become known as Genesee Country.

Location: Westbound: from the New York State Thruway (Interstate 90), exit 46, take Interstate 390 south to exit 11 onto Route 251 west to Route 383 into Mumford and follow the signs. Eastbound: from the New York State Thruway (Interstate 90), exit 47 (Leroy), take Route 19 south to Route 5 east, then left onto Flint Lime Road and right onto Flint Hill Road into Mumford and follow the signs. Northbound on Interstate 390; take exit 10 (Avon) onto Route 20 west to Route 5 west into Mumford and follow the signs. **Admission** is charged. **Hours:** Early May through mid-October, daily. **Allow** four hours to a full day; if you can't spend at least three hours here, save your visit for another day. **Information:** Genesee Country Museum, P.O. Box 1819, Rochester, NY 14603; (716) 538-2887 or (716) 538-6822.

Events: There are many, nearly one every weekend. A partial list includes: Memorial Day weekend, Homecoming, gardening clinics, sheep shearing demonstrations, traditional holiday ceremony; early June, Highland Gathering, bagpipe bands, genealogical displays; July 4, Independence Day celebration, old-fashioned observance with parades, patriotic music, cannon firings; early August, Firemen's Muster, hand-and-horse-drawn fire equipment, mock firemen's competitions, band concerts; August, Old Time Fiddler's Fair, 19th-century music with fiddles, dulcimers, banjos, mandolins; Labor Day Weekend, Salute to Autumn, farming and other chores needed to prepare for fall harvest; early October, Agricultural Society Fair, antique farm equipment, produce, farmers' market, poultry show, draft horse exhibition.

Note: Two restaurants are on the grounds. One is open all season, the other only in summer. Picnic tables are on the grounds and you are welcome to bring your own picnic. The village can be overrun by schoolchildren on field trips in spring, but most school groups are usually gone by 1:30. When your feet get tired on those hot summer days, consider taking the free village trolley from one spot to another; it runs daily in July and August and on weekends the rest of the season.

If you are staying overnight: Marriott Thruway, Route 15 (one mile south of Thruway exit 46), W. Henrietta, (716) 359-1800; Red Roof Inn, Route 15 (at junction with Thruway exit 46), W. Henrietta, (716) 359-1100; Genesee Country Inn, 948 George Street, (716) 538-2500. Also contact Bed & Breakfast Rochester, P.O. Box 444, Fairport, NY 14450, (716) 223-8510 for bed & breakfast listings.

HANFORD MILLS MUSEUM

It's man versus log as local resident Dan Kosier tries to stay afloat during one of the Hanford Mills Museum's frequent festivals.

S TAND AND LOOK AT THE TRICKLING CREEK, JUST A LITTLE BURBLING stream seemingly more refreshing than rushing. You will wonder how it packs its power, enough to run the massive machines inside the Hanford Mills Museum in East Meredith.

But Kortright Creek indeed provides the power to turn the maze of belts and wheels and lathes and pulleys inside the country shop and mill complex that grew from a single sawmill, when much of this area was wilderness, to become the virtual lifeblood of the hamlet.

The museum incorporates eight original buildings, but the central fixture was the first structure, a sawmill turned major manufacturing operation, built some time between 1820 and 1840. Numerous additions expanded the mill throughout the 19th century, the last one taking place in the 1890s.

The guided tour takes you downstairs, where in the damp chill you can watch the 10 x 12-foot Fitz Steel Overshot water wheel churn the waters of Kortright Creek, creating the massive power needed to operate the whirring blur of belts and shafts that makes the machinery upstairs work. After setting your eyes on the entire complex, you will think that a gushing river and not the tiny creek would be behind it.

The mill has never been shut down, even in the coldest months. Because the flume that brings in the water is eight feet underground and below the frost line, it doesn't freeze in winter.

Upstairs, where the air is warmer most of the year, visitors are shown a melange of machines on which demonstrations are offered. Craftspersons can be witnessed at any given time churning out gingerbread door trim for a nearby resident, legs and arms for early American-style chairs, or milk crate inserts for an area dairy. Even though this complex is a museum, it is still actively used to produce specialty items. On our tour, a young journeyman was busy at a Whitney lathe, putting smooth final touches on wooden chair legs for a man who sells Hitchcock chairs.

Some machines were built for single purposes that seem trivial, like shaping barrel tops or carving wide holes in milk crates. Then there are more all-purpose machines: a 50-inch circular saw, a Chase hardhole cutter, five lathes, three band saws, and seven table saws.

Step a few feet away from the wood-making operation and you will be at a point where chaff was separated from grain and the grain was ultimately ground. You can look through the window of a grain elevator where grain was placed in a large hopper and stored in a warehouse. There is still the chalkboard where shipments of grain were logged in and a wooden shovel, used because metal ones could touch a nail and ignite a spark.

The grain mill connects to the sawmill—it is not known if this has been the case since it was built—but it's a symbolic union, since feed grinding was to become a major portion of the business here until the early 1960s.

The man who began this business was David Josiah Hanford. D. J., as he was known, bought the sawmill in 1860 and built the gristmill in 1869. He passed the business onto his two sons, Will and Horace, in 1890, who sold it to three brothers by the appetizing name of Pizza in 1945. The Pizzas continued running the complex until 1967.

It was Hanford's mill that planted the seed of livelihood for East Meredith. It started with D. J. Hanford's mill building and grew in time to include three or four farmhouses that sprang up near the mill, standing as the pride of this place that was then known as Brier Street.

Additional farms, tradesmen, and small businesses gradually took root around Hanford's operation and by the turn of the century, the village was made up of two general stores, two blacksmiths, a meat market, and a furniture factory, among other businesses. But over the years the mill was the keystone of the village's economy and greatly molded the direction in which it would grow.

Courtesy: Hanford Mills Museum

Reflect on your visit to the Hanford Mills Museum at the museum's water-powered sawmill.

By the early 20th century when D. J. Hanford's sons were running the show, the combined saw and gristmill operation formed just one part of the business. At one time or another, Will and Horace and their employees also produced such novelties as butter tub covers, cheese and milk boxes, broom handles, and bob-sled and buggy parts.

The Hanford family installed an electric dynamo run by water power in the 1890s and soon generated electricity for both the mill and the village and continued to provide electric service—including even the East Meredith street lights—until the arrival of the electrical grid in 1926.

It also is believed the family-run mill was instrumental in bringing telephone service to this remote area and that the Hanfords possibly had the first switchboard. During all those years that the Hanford mill business was the heartbeat of the village, it also served as the daily gathering place for most of the residents. The Hanfords ran a supply store here where locals could buy a grab bag of goods from a gasoline engine to a washing machine; in time, this became the place for neighbors to meet other neighbors and catch up on local gossip.

And then, with the coming of the Ulster and Delaware Railroad in 1899, the mill seemingly served another purpose. Because the railroad right-of-way ran behind the Hanford property, it is believed the Hanfords also maintained the first freight office in East Meredith until the passenger station and depot was completed.

D. J. Hanford had fought for a decade to bring the railroad to the mill, knowing he would need it to expand his business. He died before it arrived, but sons Will and Horace reaped the many benefits it brought. Before the railroad came to them, goods had to be hauled three miles; now they just needed to be wheeled out the back door and loaded onto boxcars. The mill added more markets from greater distances, and it is believed that the railroad kept the business going well into the 20th century.

While the sawmill constitutes the major portion of your visit to the Hanford Mills Museum, there are additional buildings on the grounds (either restored or in the process of being restored) worthy of a glance, not the least of which is the business office, frozen in time, with its early 20th-century adding machine and old Dayton fan.

Location: From the east on Interstate 88, take the Emmons-West Davenport exit; then take a left, heading east on Route 23 towards West Davenport. At Davenport Center, turn right and follow the signs to the museum. From the west on Interstate 88, take the third Oneonta exit and follow Route 23 into Davenport Center; follow the signs to the museum. The museum is 10 miles from Oneonta. **Admission** is charged. **Hours:** May through October, daily. **Allow** 90 minutes for the tour. **Information:** Hanford Mills Museum, East Meredith, NY 13757; (607) 278-5744.

Events: June, Trout Fishing Clinic, seminar in trout fishing; Traditional Fourth of July, brass bands, speakers, jugglers, clowns, children's games; late July, Concert and Picnic, light classical or chamber music; mid-August, Children's Fair, jugglers, entertainment; late September, Antique Engine Jamboree, engines on view, barbecue, country western music.

Note: Picnic tables are on the grounds.

If you are staying overnight: Holiday Inn, Route 23 (one mile east of junction with I-88), Oneonta, (607) 433-2250; Town House Motor Inn, 318 Main Street (Routes 7 and 23), (607) 432-1313; Celtic Motel, 112 Oneida Street, Oneonta, (607) 432-0860.

SUFFOLK MARINE MUSEUM

Photo by Mitch Carucci

*In 1888, oysters for your dinner would have been unloaded from a schooner such
as the* Priscilla, *pictured here at the Suffolk Marine Museum.*

IN THE EARLY 1900S, THE *SUFFOLK COUNTY NEWS* REPORTED A MAJOR
local story: Captain Joseph Weeks set a regional record of opening 75
gallons of oysters in just three work days, while employed in William
Rudolph's oyster house.

That oyster house is still in Suffolk County, on display at the Suffolk
Marine Museum in West Sayville, and it looks as if Captain Weeks or
some other hard-handed oyster handler just walked out.

The purpose of this museum, says Associate Curator of Small Craft
Ralph A. Notaristefano, "is to protect and preserve the maritime heritage
of Long Island—all of Long Island, the North Shore, the South Shore,
the East End."

The museum's main building, once the carriage house of a large estate,
harbors seafarers' artifacts on a variety of subjects. In the Penney Boat-
house, craftsmen restore old and build new boats, usually on weekends,
and they are pleased to talk with onlookers, whether you are a veteran
mariner or a novice who can't tell a sloop from a schooner. The oyster-

man's home, decorated in 1890s style, shows where a typical worker returned after a long day's work culling oysters.

And, of course, there are the boats. About 50 small craft are sheltered in outdoor pavilions—a small boat house to be their new home is under construction and completion is a few years away. Two larger ships, the Long Island-built schooner *Priscilla* and the sloop *Modesty*, are docked next to the William Rudolph Oyster House.

When you enter the little, but practical, oyster house, you get a close look at the gritty world of the Great South Bay oystermen who, from the late 1800s to the 1940s, culled and packed oysters in structures like this. The 30-mile-long bay, with its warm waters and suitable salt content was regarded as the best oyster-breeding ground north of Chesapeake Bay, and it produced renowned blue point oysters.

The workbench is covered with mountains of oyster shells and a few other isolated sea creatures that snuck in the last load, including whelk eggs and a starfish, the oyster's mortal enemy.

The bench also displays the tools of the oystermen: opening knives, culling iron, crackling block and hammer, and rubber mitts, or finger stalls. It was a neat trick to speedily open an oyster while at the same time not damage its meat or cut one's hands. Look above the bench and you will see skylights which provided workers with their only illumination. The pay in 1910? A dollar a day.

Displays inside afford vital information about the Long Island oyster industry and the lot of its workers, from the tools they used to the boats they sailed (and later motorized).

"Nostalgia for sail had little influence on bay men," one exhibit reads. "When the small gasoline engine was perfected for small boats before World War I, most bay men eagerly installed them in their sailboats."

Tucked in the corner of the oyster house is the oyster shipper's office, a semblance of order in a cluttered building. The oak desk is filled with lots of slots and pecks of pigeon holes, and the wooden filing cabinet next to it has brass fittings. Also seen in the oyster house—at least on most days—are Adrian Daane and Ollie Locker, two of the last surviving oystermen of the Dutch community who worked this part of the bay for decades. They are on hand to chat with visitors about a way of life now gone.

You also can see evidence of other past ways of life when eyeing the small craft collection. Several craft were the work of Gil Smith who was born on Long Island in 1843 and who built boats well into his 90s. A museum brochure says Smith was to boats what Chippendale was to furniture—"the finest craftsman of his day."

Ralph Notaristefano pointed out some of Smith's original catboats, narrower and shallower than similar New England fishing boats. In New England's rougher waters, boats were big and tubby. Since the waters

Photo by Mitch Carucci

The Rudolph Oyster House bench, where Long Island oystermen worked for a dollar a day.

of the Great South Bay are generally about six feet deep, Smith designed his catboats to skim across the water.

In time, wealthy boat owners learned that Gil Smith's catboats, built for subsistence farmers and fishermen, were speedier than existing similar-sized vessels built specifically for sport. They then asked him to make catboats for racing, and examples of both working and racing catboats are in the collection, the working catboats being bigger in the beam and deeper to hold as many shellfish as one could stuff in them

Smith made several types of boats and a beautiful Gil Smith duck boat is displayed in the main building, along with the accoutrements of a pike pole, used to push or pull the duck boat over ice, and an ash pushing oar, which propelled the boat through the shallows of a salt marsh. A sharpie, a wood canvas canoe, and a St. Lawrence River skiff are also proudly displayed. The skiff was once sailed by Commodore Frederick G. Bourne, on whose former estate the museum sits.

There is another beauty exhibited in the main building. With so much idle time at sea, sailors became handy with crafts, and the scale model of the 120-gun *Man-of-War* sculpted from bone is one result. The minute detail indicates that the artist, a mariner who was a prisoner of war in Britain, had plenty of free time on his hands.

Extra time gave ocean-bound men the chance to practice their knot-tying, too, and the intricate strand braids, knob knots, and decorative rope work on view are some of the results. Mounted on the wall nearby are ships' figureheads, additional examples of seamen's art, from vessels that ran aground on or near Long Island.

In fact, shipwrecks and groundings dating from 1657 are memorialized here in the form of several files filled with photographs and descriptions of accidents along Long Island's shore; a corresponding map designates their locations. You don't need to be a maritime historian to be impressed by nature's raw power.

An 18th-century flintlock pistol and a once-sunken chest are further artifacts taken from downed ships, while a megaphone straight from the days of Rudy Vallee (though intended for more serious purposes than Vallee's crooning), and a handsome blue uniform, symbols of the United States Lifesaving Service, also fill the space in the main building.

Location: The Suffolk Marine Museum is on Route 27A (Montauk Highway), east of the town center of West Sayville on the grounds of Suffolk County Park. Follow the main park road until it ends, where you will circle the museum. **Admission** is free; donation suggested. **Hours:** Year round, daily; afternoons only on Sunday. **Allow** one to two hours. **Information:** Suffolk Marine Museum, Box 144, West Sayville, NY 11796; (516) 567-1733.

Events: Mid-September, Old Timers Regatta, regatta race, small craft show, demonstrations; winter months, Lecture Series, topics include small craft construction and canoe restoration.

If you are staying overnight: Holiday Inn, 3845 Veterans Memorial Highway (just over four miles southeast of Long Island Expressway, exit 57), Ronkonkoma, (516) 585-9500; Land's End Motel, 70 Brown's River Road, Sayville, (516) 589-2040; Summit Motor Lodge, 501 East Main Street (Route 27A), Bay Shore, (516) 666-6000. Note that lodging is extremely expensive on Long Island. Even here in central Long Island, you will be hard pressed to find a double room priced under $80 a night. If you are en route to another location, consider staying elsewhere.

AT LEISURE
IN NEW YORK

NATIONAL BASEBALL HALL OF FAME

"Armour in the Combat Zone" is an appropriate label for the catcher's equipment in Cooperstown's Baseball Hall of Fame.

L IKE THE EARTH AND HUMANITY, NOBODY KNOWS FOR SURE HOW BASE-ball got here. There is the creationist theory that the almighty Abner Doubleday invented the game on a slow day in a Cooperstown pasture in 1839. Then there is the evolutionist idea that the game slowly developed from similar British games such as rounders and one o'cat.

But this is not the time to think of such metaphysical mysteries as God and Baseball. Or with respect to diehards, Baseball and God.

America's pastime has been here for well over a century and despite strikes, contract disputes, and drug scandals, it endures. There is something about the game, something that draws thousands to watch men hitting and catching baseballs on any given summer day and to make year-round pilgrimages to the Baseball Hall of Fame and Museum in Cooperstown.

Opened in 1939, the centennial year of Doubleday's supposed invention, the hall of fame and museum (two separate entities housed under one roof) combine to form America's only major sports museum not located within site of a major interstate highway.

That's the bad news for anyone who dislikes driving. The good news is that the maze of back roads on which one has to drive to get here is among some of the most beautiful countryside in the state. The view is no less lovely in Cooperstown itself where verdant hills border shining Otsego Lake, immortalized in the works of author James Fenimore Cooper, whose father settled the town and lent his name to it, as Glimmerglass.

Appropriately, Main Street, with its geranium-bedecked street lamps, is home to the shrine of America's pastime. Its aged exterior belies the modern interior which was extensively renovated in 1980. If you last visited the hall and museum prior to that, then you might find the old adage to be true—you won't even recognize the place.

The bare floors and dime store displays are gone, replaced by carpeting and state of the art exhibits. There is much more here than just old baseballs and plaques.

Not that we want to minimize the significance of the Hall of Fame's plaques, which are to many the main draw. Nearly 200 players, managers, founders, and executives have their likenesses immortalized in bronze. The Hall of Fame Gallery is imposing; it's spacious; it has high ceilings and marble columns; and it commands respect as does a cathedral. To a serious baseball fan, that is not a far-fetched statement. This is where the greats are enshrined for eternity, from Cobb to Cronin to Clemente.

Throughout the remaining four floors, it is the game rather than any single individual that is eulogized. A tattered glove with a pocket the size of a toddler's palm, once used by the legendary Ty Cobb, is on view. Keeping it company are the bat swung for career home run number 521 by Ted Williams, a jersey worn by Casey Stengel, and Babe Ruth's Yankee locker, as well as hundreds of other samples of baseball equipment and uniforms that belonged to the greats.

However, most are not placed in singular exhibits. They are on view in larger displays relating to specific themes. You may find some in the Great Moments Room where, through personal items, original art, and photographs, you recall just where you were when Roger Maris hit his 61st home run in 1961 or when Sandy Koufax pitched his fourth no-hitter. Other balls and bats and gloves are parts of sizable presentations devoted to diamond legends like Ruth or Stengel.

And still others are in the History of Baseball section, which boasts nearly 1,000 such artifacts and which occupies most of the second floor. Arranged in a time tunnel effect, it starts by discussing baseball's primeval ancestors and concludes with a look at modern effects on the game.

It is here that you dive into confusion about baseball's origins. A reproduced page in a British children's book includes notes about a game called "Base-ball"; the book was published in 1744, 75 years before Abner Doubleday was born.

Dynasties are glorified and rule changes are interpreted in the History of Baseball section, but some of the most appealing exhibits are in the area called Evolution of Equipment. Most visitors find they laugh in amazement and amusement when inspecting baseball gloves with no finger and catcher's masks resembling wire chicken cages. Early bats and balls and heavy flannel uniforms from the days when players wore handlebar mustaches and the word "strike" meant only a good pitch are here for your pleasure, too.

So are baseball cards. There's a colorful arrangement on 100 years of them, starting with tobacco cards of the late 19th and early 20th centuries. (Yes, baseball cards came with cigarettes long before they accompanied gum.) But baby boomers will have their memories jogged by the classic Bowman baseball cards, sold from 1948 to 1955, and Topps cards sold continually since 1951. As neither a current collector nor the father of one, I was surprised to see that in the 1980s, Topps has major competition from the old Fleer and new Donruss companies, showing that this old childhood pastime is still as popular as when Mantle and Mays made headlines.

Other parts of the museum? There are sections devoted to every subheading regarding baseball that one can imagine. The list includes: the World Series, the early Negro Leagues that barnstormed the country when major league baseball was segregated, the mid-summer classic known as the All-Star game, the minor leagues, and some of the grand old American ballparks—Yankee Stadium, Ebbetts Field, and the horseshoe-shaped Polo Grounds, among them—guaranteed to bring out the sentimentalist in every fan.

Then there's the Records Room in the basement, which keeps you up-to-date on leaders in major league categories among active players; it's sort of like the old stock ticker, changing moment by moment, as you keep your eyes on the performances of your personal favorites. You will see who leads the majors in strikeouts, home runs, runs batted in, and more as you visit. You will leave here with only one question unanswered. Just how was baseball invented? Cooperstown doesn't say.

Location: From the west, take the New York State Thruway (Interstate 90), exit 30 (Herkimer), and follow Route 28 south to Cooperstown. From the east, take the Thruway (Interstate 90) to exit 25A, and follow

Route 20 west, then Route 80 south. From the south, take Interstate 88, exit 17 (Oneonta), and follow Route 28 north. From New York City and the southeast, take the Thruway to exit 21 (Catskill) and follow Route 145 either to Interstate 88 west to exit 17 (see above) or take Route 20 west to Route 80 south. The Hall of Fame is on Main Street in the center of town. **Admission** is charged. **Hours:** Year round, daily. **Allow** an hour and a half if you are a casual fan, from two to four hours if you are a diehard. **Information:** Baseball Hall of Fame and Museum, P. O. Box 590, Cooperstown, NY 13326.

Events: Mid-summer, induction ceremony and major-league exhibition game.

If you are staying overnight: Deer Run Motel, Route 80 (9 miles east of center of Cooperstown), Cooperstown, (607) 547-8600; The Inn at Cooperstown, 16 Chestnut Street, Cooperstown, (607) 547-5756; The Otesaga Hotel, Lake Street (Route 80 on lake shore), Cooperstown, (607) 547-9931; Bed & Breakfast Leatherstocking (reservation service), 389 Brockway Road, Frankfort Hill, NY 13340, (315) 733-0040.

MUSEUM OF CARTOON ART

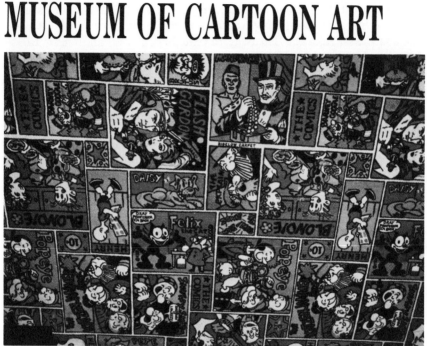

Even a glance at the floor can be entertaining at the Museum of Cartoon Art.
This Bigelow carpet covers the museum's second floor.

Y OU HAVE TO BE A SUPERMAN NOT TO NEED A SECURITY BLANKET today. Crime, evil doers, bad guys. Good grief! Isn't there anyone who can make the world safe for democracy?

Relax. Just make yourself a fat Dagwood sandwich and take a look at the funnies. Otherwise, you just might want to shout, "#@!!*#*."

The funnies. Aside from making us smile and giving us relief from headlines about world hunger, AIDS, and nuclear arms, they are a written account of our American culture and society.

They have spawned new words in our language and they reflect our times; they are records of social history. Milton Caniff mirrored our spirit during World War II with his proud and patriotic "Terry and The Pirates." Murat "Chic" Young gave the world his famed flapper in "Blondie." And Cathy Guisewhite has graced the eighties with "Cathy," about an insecure, affection-starved single woman coming to terms with liberation.

A comic strip is many things. Yet as Lucy once asked Charlie Brown after watching Snoopy do his paw-pounding suppertime shuffle, "But is it art?"

Some folks who work in a castle fit for Prince Valiant answer an enthusiastic yes. The castle is Ward's Castle, built as the home of a millionaire industrialist in 1876 and now the Museum of Cartoon Art in Rye Brook, hugging the Connecticut border.

Is it art? Just look at Milton Caniff's "Terry and the Pirates" and "Steve Canyon." His painstaking brush work, fine lighting, and sense of perspective have influenced many cartoonists and filmmakers; his admirers included novelist John Steinbeck and "Doonesbury" creator Garry Trudeau, who sent fan letters to Caniff.

Trudeau's work, like Caniff's, is exhibited here, too, representing the wide scope of cartoonists on view. You will also come across the master of animation, Walt Disney; the half-pint philosophers of "Peanuts"; and the efforts of Charles Dana Gibson, who drew sports fans and bums but is best known for the haughty and high class beauty, the Gibson Girl. Then there are Willard Mullin and Bill Gallo, known more for their bums— the Brooklyn Dodgers type—than girls, that is unless you consider Gallo's symbolic 1962 New York Mets fan, Basement Bertha.

In total, there are hundreds of types to be seen on the gallery walls and television monitors. We walked in once and saw Betty Boop bopping on videotape to the sound of scratchy jazz from the days of Paul Whiteman. And you'll find more, on the floors, on a child's school desk, and even in the restrooms!

The main museum floors are covered with a full-color carpet depicting classic funnies from the days of "Barney Google" and "Felix the Cat." The school desk at the top of the second floor stairs is adorned with the pen points of Mell Lazarus, creator of spinster teacher "Miss Peach." Those who make a visit to the men's room or, to a lesser extent, the women's room will find graffiti like none you've seen in any other public rest room.

Chuck Jones, a cartoonist for Warner Brothers, paid a visit to the men's room after giving a talk and left his mark on the wall—a likeness of the widely respected Road (Beep Beep!!) Runner. Other comic artists followed Jones's lead and a tradition started. Today, Hägar the Horrible, the monstrous Grog from "B.C.," and the markings of Jules Feiffer are also eternized on the rest room walls. (Management requests that amateurs abstain from leaving their marks.)

But most of what you want to see is out in the open. Papier mâché sculptures of some of the world's most famous fictional characters set the museum's mood. Mischievous towhead Dennis the Menace slides down a bannister, while across the hall a papier mâché version of the bumbling

Everyman, Dagwood Bumstead, savors a warm bath; you just can't help feeling that the phone will ring any minute.

Many don't know that Dagwood actually began his comic strip existence in 1930 as a well-to-do tycoon's son who chased bubble-headed Blondie, flirting with both her and disaster. As soon as he married her, he was disinherited and condemned to a life of mortgage payments, belaboring bosses, and nosy neighbors.

Dagwood's beginnings aren't the only ones chronicled here. Charlie Brown came into this world as an average American suburban youth in the post-war world on October 2, 1950; only later did he become every-one's favorite loser. But what a loser! "Peanuts" appears in more than 1,600 newspapers worldwide, and "Peanuts" products gross more than $250 million annually.

The beginnings of Mickey Mouse are exhibited in a more literal sense as a series of Walt Disney sketches present the method by which he drew his best-known character. The mouse that made Disney roar starts off with a simple round head, similar to Charlie Brown's, connected to a lima bean body.

Disney belongs to a select group, the museum's hall of fame. There are only 24 members and elections are held every other year. You won't find the names of active cartoonists like Charles Schulz and Garry Trudeau there, but you will find Disney, Chic Young, Charles Dana Gibson, and Rube Goldberg.

Joining them is Richard Outcault, a name unfamiliar to most visitors, who is credited with being the first modern cartoonist. Outcault gave the world "The Yellow Kid," a jug-eared, toothy street kid who 90 years ago wore a yellow nightshirt and commented on burning issues of the day. The kid was the first comic-strip character to appear in color, and his importance is emphasized by a massive painting of him on the museum parking lot pavement.

Intrigued by trivia? The term "yellow journalism" is a legacy left by the kid; it came into being because the sensationalist *New York World* carried "The Yellow Kid."

But there is much more in the trivia department. To test your comic knowledge, try this brief quiz and see if you have been spending too much time reading the editorial pages.

1. What was the real name of the character Jeff in the comic strip "Mutt and Jeff"?

2. What has been recorded as the fastest rising comic strip in cartoon history? It began in 1973 and is now in more than 1,200 newspapers?

3. What was the setting of Walt Kelly's classic comic strip, "Pogo"?

4. What is the name of the cartoonists' version of the Oscar and Emmy?

5. What is the only major comic strip in which its characters have aged along with its readers?

Answers: 1. James Jeffries, an escapee from a lunatic asylum. 2. "Hager the Horrible" by Dik Browne. 3. The Okeefenokee Swamp. 4. The Reuben, designed and named after Rube Goldberg. 5. "Gasoline Alley"; Walt Wallet started as a young man adopting baby Skeezix. Skeezix grew up during the depression, matured during World War II, and is now an aging grandfather.

Location: The Museum of Cartoon Art is on Comly Avenue in Rye Brook just over the Connecticut border. From the Hutchinson River Parkway, take exit 30 and turn right onto King Street. After about a mile, turn left at St. Paul's Lutheran Church onto Comly Avenue, then left onto Magnolia Street to the parking lot. From the Merritt Parkway, take exit 27 onto King Street and follow above directions. Rye Brook was formerly a part of Port Chester and was incorporated in 1982 and, therefore, is not listed on older maps. **Admission** is charged. **Hours:** Year round, Tuesday through Friday and Sunday afternoons; closed major holidays. **Allow** an hour to 90 minutes. **Information:** The Museum of Cartoon Art, Comly Avenue, Rye Brook, New York 10573; (914) 939-0234.

Events: Speakers are scheduled the first Sunday of each month and occasionally at other times. The list has included: Johnny Hart and Brant Parker, creators of "The Wizard of Id"; Tony Auth, editorial cartoonist for the *Philadelphia Inquirer;* and Lynn Johnston, who draws the family comic strip "For Better or Worse."

Note: Ask to see the museum's videotape list. Special showings are given if convenient.

If you are staying overnight: Ryetown Hilton, 699 Westchester Avenue (Route 120A), Rye Brook, (914) 939-6300; Coachman Hotel, 123 E. Post Road (Route 22), White Plains, (914) 949-1000; County Center Motel, 20 County Center Road (off Bronx River Parkway, exit 22), White Plains, (914) 948-2400.

BULLY HILL VINEYARDS

A barrel of fun is on tap at Bully Hill Winery in Hammondsport.

Photo by Michael Schuman

IN SPITE OF PUBLICITY IN STATE AND OUT, MANY PEOPLE STILL DON'T realize New York State's stature as a major wine producer.

The fact is that New York is ranked number two in total wine production in the nation (California is number one). There are more than 80 active wineries in the state, and, regardless of where you live, you are no further than a Sunday afternoon drive from fertile land where vines sport grapes like dandelions on a suburban front lawn.

The best-known region for wine making is the Finger Lakes and for good reason; nearly half of New York State's wineries are found along these shores. When it comes to Finger Lakes wine the most famous name is Taylor. That's what drew us to Hammondsport and to Bully Hill Vineyards, founded by Walter S. Taylor, grandson of the man who started a family fortune more than 100 years ago.

Funny thing though is that Walter S. Taylor's family name is mentioned nowhere on the property of his own winery. In places where it has appeared in print, it is blotted out as if it were an obscene word. Whenever he is quoted, he is duly noted as Walter S. Blank or Walter S. XXXXXX or Saint Walter de Bully. You hear the story behind the man with no name as you start the winery tour at Bully Hill.

You don't have to take the tour to taste the wine; sampling is yours for the asking. If you have the time though, follow your tour guide—or your nose— as you walk through the wine-making process into the vineyard, the fermenting rooms, champagne cellar, aging cellar, and other points where the pungent scents of alcohol hang in the air like a low valley fog.

Our favorite stops were the vineyard's views and the aging cellar's massive wooden barrels, a wine connoisseur's paradise. In mid-May the grapes were in tiny clusters and the vines looked bare, but they would soon grow plump in the warm summer sun, even here in upstate New York.

In fact, it's the presence of the lakes and the chilly spring air that makes the Finger Lakes such prime wine country. Because the lakes are so deep (Keuka Lake, within walking distance, is 187 feet deep), it takes a long time for the air to warm, keeping the grapes from coming out too soon; in fall, the lakes help the air stay warm longer. The longer the grapes stay on the vine, the sweeter they taste.

The barrels in the aging cellar, each seemingly big enough to hold a Toyota, are capable of holding 6,800 gallons of wine each. With good care each barrel can last a century. The room smells like vinegar, but the scent numbs after a while. Guide Mary Wahlig told us that aging is basically a form of oxidation and explained a basic difference between red and white wine; red is usually aged longer, up to two years, while white commonly ages in less than one.

Wahlig was the source from which we heard about Walter S. Taylor, who himself has been aging gracefully as company head since the early 1970s. He was once a part of Taylor wines, like many members of his family, but he broke a branch off the family tree and was booted out of the company after publicly criticizing New York State wines; he soon started his own company.

In 1976, Taylor Wines, Walter's new competition, was purchased by Coca-Cola, who in turn sued him over the use of the Taylor name on his Bully Hill Wine products. The court ruled that Walter S. Taylor could no longer put his name on his wine labels unless it was accompanied with "Not connected with or a successor to the Taylor Wine Company," in sizable print.

Taylor took the decision to a visible extreme, referring to himself with no last name or with the phony ones mentioned earlier. He had his name crossed off every label of his wine and even put masks on drawings of ancestors on labels, making them look a bit like the Lone Ranger.

As if to affirm the adage, "Nobody likes a wise guy," Coca-Cola took him to court again, suing him for contempt. And again, Taylor lost. He was fined $11,000 and forced to turn over labels and other "offensive materials" to Coca-Cola for destruction. He did so, delivering them in a manure spreader.

Walter, meanwhile, began to wallow in all the publicity, becoming to many a folk hero, the proverbial little man clobbered by a behemoth corporation. A slogan for Bully Hill Wines grew out of it: "They have my name and heritage but they didn't get my goat." (Epilogue: Several years later, Coca-Cola sold Taylor Wines).

Taylor actually does own a pet goat and the goat's face is depicted often on his wine labels. The labels that he designs and illustrates are unlike those of you will see on conventional winery products. Most are scruffy illustrations of goats and spacecraft or even his self-portrait identifying wines with non-conventional names like "Love My Goat Red," "Space Shuttle Rose," "Rural Walter White," and "Mother Ship Over Paris Rouge."

While Walter S. XXXXXX no longer has his grandfather's name, he does have much of his grandfather's old wine-making equipment, which is stored in three buildings known collectively as the Wine Museum of Greyton H. Taylor (Walter's father, not grandfather).

It's grandfather's green and bulky 1883 wine press that you first see when stepping into the museum's champagne room. The archaic and crude equipment from his era gives visitors a peek into the day when the clarity of each bottle of champagne was checked by candlelight. A candle still sits at the end of an old riddling rack where champagne bottles were stacked so sediment could settle.

It was a time when wine corks were soaked in warm water for pliability and then placed on a corking machine on which a person could cork about 120 bottles per hour. One corking machine on view dates to the late 1700s. Bottles were reused after they were cleaned in the bottle washer, such as one on display, circa 1897, that is little more than a keg fitted with pipes and faucets.

Other machines used for clearing sediment from champagne, adding dosage (wine and sugar syrup used to sweeten champagne), and attaching wire hoods to bottle tops offer a complete look at wine and champagne making, turn-of-the-century style.

Another part of the museum is decked with tools a cooper would use, such as planes, adzes, and drawknives. There is also a 1917 Studebaker grape wagon once drawn by horses to carry boxes of grapes from vineyards to the winery.

The view from Bully Hill, overlooking Keuka Lake and the hills in the distance, is as inspiring as any hilltop view you will ever see. There couldn't be a better setting for sipping wine on a summer day.

There are literally dozens of wineries open for tastings and/or tours in the Finger Lakes region. The following is a partial list: Americana Vineyards, Interlaken, (607) 387-6801; Casa Larga Vineyards, Fairport, (716) 223-4210; Eagle Crest Vineyards, Conesus, (716) 346-2321; Finger Lakes Wine Cellars, Branchport, (315) 595-2812; Glenora Wine Cellars, Dundee, (607) 243-5511; Hazlitt 1852 Vineyards, Hector, (607) 546-5812; Plane's Cayuga Vineyard, Ovid, (607) 869-5158; Taylor Great Western Gold Seal Winery, Hammondsport, (607) 569-2111; Wickham Vineyards, Hector, (607) 546-8415; Widmer's Wine Cellars, Naples, (716) 374-6303.

To receive a list of New York State wineries you can visit, write to: The New York Wine and Grape Foundation, Elm and Liberty Streets, Penn Yan, NY 14527.

Location: Bully Hill Vineyards is one mile north of Hammondsport. From Route 17, take Route 54 in Bath to Route 54A in Hammondsport; after about a mile, turn left onto Middle Road and follow signs (shaped like fish) to the winery. **Admission** is free. **Hours:** Winery: Year round, daily, closed Sunday morning. Museum: May through October, daily. **Allow** an hour for the tour (30 to 40 minutes) and tasting (15 to 20 minutes) and a half hour to see the museum. **Information:** Bully Hill Wine Company, RD #2, Hammondsport, NY 14840; (607) 868-3210, winery tours; (607) 868-4814, museum.

Events: Early and late summer, goat shows; periodically in summer and fall, lectures on wine and wine making.

Note: The winery maintains its own restaurant and cafe. However, you are welcome to bring your own picnic and use the picnic tables on the grounds. October is by far the busiest month. Retail Sales Manager Diane Stratton reported 3,000 visitors in two days on a recent Columbus Day weekend; come early in October!

If you are staying overnight: Hammondsport Motel, William Street (two blocks north of Route 54A on Keuka Lake), (607) 569-2600 (in season only); Days Inn, 330 W. Morris (one quarter mile east of Route 17, exit 38), (607) 776-7644; Bully Hill Bed & Breakfast, owned by the winery on winery grounds, open May through October only, (607) 868-3226; Finger Lakes Bed & Breakfast Association, P.O. Box 862, Canandaigua, NY 14424.

SOUTH STREET SEAPORT

Barbecued ribs, potato knishes, tostadas, sweet and sour chicken, Irish coffee, Cajun rice, Greek gyros. An epicurian mosaic awaits at South Street Seaport.

Courtesy: South Street Seaport

READ THE FOLLOWING LETTERS HOME FROM A HYPOTHETICAL VISITOR to lower Manhattan's South Street Seaport and see if you can tell what's wrong with them.

Letter #1

Dear Folks,

My three-day weekend in New York City has finally arrived, and I'm spending my first day at South Street Seaport. So far I've seen the two levels at Fulton Marketplace and have sampled a Greek gyro, a south Philly steak sandwich, a potato knish, and, for dessert, a helping of gourmet chocolate. I will see the rest of Manhattan over the next two days, but I'm off to see more of South Street Seaport today. There's just one problem—I keep hearing about the South Street Seaport Museum, but I haven't found it anywhere.

Letter #2

Greetings from Gotham,

It's a day later, but I'm still at South Street Seaport. There is so much I haven't done yet. I walked through lots of specialty shops in different buildings and it seems that I bought something in each. I'm coming home with, among other things, a pith helmet, a plush penguin, and some computerized gadget to measure how much in debt I am. Pigged out at a couple of bakeries for breakfast, had an Irish coffee at an old-fashioned Irish pub, a pastrami on rye for lunch, and a shrimp roll for a mid-afternoon snack. Tonight it's Italian or Cajun or maybe down home bar-becued ribs. They've got the greatest multimedia show called *The Seaport Experience*. I saw it today, then toured a couple of grand old ships docked here. Still haven't found the museum yet.

Letter #3

Hello from the Big Apple,

Let me get right to the core of the matter. I'm back at South Street Seaport. My three-day weekend is almost over and I still haven't seen it all. I glanced in all the shops, but I would have loved more time—barely got the chance to browse through the gourmet kitchenware, marine brass store, and cat menagerie. Got a suntan on a noontime harbor cruise on a reproduced side-wheeler. Wolfed down a tostada, a slice of New York pizza, a dish of sweet and sour chicken and fried rice, a falafel, and a hot fudge sundae with real ice cream and a ton of toppings. (I was going to watch the calories, but you only live once.) Saw a printer's shop from the 1870s and an exhibition about Norwegian immigrants. The rest of Manhattan will have to wait for another trip, but not until I have seen the rest of what's here—the other ships, the exhibitions, and the food; there's so much I haven't sampled. Oh yes—I never found the South Street Seaport Museum. That will have to wait, too.

Now, pick one answer from the list below and tell us what's wrong with these letters.

1. No one can really spend three days at South Street Seaport and not be bored.

2. No one eats a Greek gyro together with a potato knish.

3. No one who eats Mexican, Chinese, Italian, and Middle Eastern food in one day has room enough left over for a hot fudge sundae with a ton of toppings.

4. No one could walk around South Street Seaport for three days and still miss the museum.

Let's go over the answers.

1. Yes, one could. Whether one would want to bypass the rest of Manhattan is another thing. But spending a trio of days at South Street Seaport could be done without great difficulty. You've got a complex of shopping and dining malls, historic ships and boats, museum galleries and exhibit buildings, guided historic tours, harbor excursions, and an eye dazzling multimedia show.

2. Incorrect. I did it myself.

3. I've done this on several occasions, too. (Oink!)

4. Correct. If you don't understand what you're looking for, you could easily miss it. If you ask for help, you will get an enigmatic answer. The conversation usually sounds like this:

Q—But where's the museum?

A—All over the seaport.

The South Street Seaport Museum is called "a museum without walls." It's an alternative concept. There are several museum galleries and displays. But instead of being housed under one roof, they are in numerous buildings throughout the entire complex.

Yet, the museum is not just indoors. Vintage ships and boats docked at the waterfront are also part of the South Street Seaport Museum. So is a reconstructed 19th-century printer's office and a diverse handful of first-class museum shops.

Our letter-writing friend, while he never knew it, was touring this special museum without walls on all three days of his visit.

Many like him, including those who work and live in Manhattan, have discovered South Street Seaport to be the Big Apple's newest plum. They have discovered that midtown is not the only place to amble down the streets alternately window shopping, dining, and picking up a bit of culture on the side.

However, the museum hardly comprises the limit of what one can see and do here. *The Seaport Experience* is an hour-long multimedia show acquainting visitors with the history and heritage of South Street Seaport. The overused word, "blockbuster," truly applies here. More than

Masts from the Peking *frame skyscrapers at South Street Seaport. The ship, built in Germany in 1911, has guided tours that take you back to the days of turn-of-the-century sailors.*

100 slide and film projectors are used. Sound is carried on 33 multichannel speakers. The main screen, 45 feet long, has nine distinct sections; it is supplemented by 31 auxiliary screens. And hang on to your seats; they swivel so you can face side screens.

Harbor cruises are another inviting option, especially for the sore of foot. The 125-foot-long *Andrew Fletcher* is a double side-wheeler. Keeping it company is the *DeWitt Clinton*, the type of steamship that replaced side-wheelers in the 1890s. Then there is the century-old schooner, *Pioneer*, on which you can literally sail off into the sunset.

And for those who admit that when the going gets tough, the tough go shopping—and eating—there are more than 120 stores and eateries in the five-building complex. They extend from the common—Mexican food and fashions—to the exotic—MGM film memorabilia and pickles of every kind. Our letter writer discussed only a fraction of what exists.

There is a purpose behind all this food, frolic, and fun, and much of it is historic. New York City was first settled near the point where the seaport sits and the city grew from there. When the Erie Canal opened in 1825, the city became connected to the Midwest by way of water. Products made and grown in the country's heartland were shipped and unloaded here. Thanks to its harbor, New York City flourished. South Street Seaport—the museum, the buildings, the food, and the merchandise—is a tribute to more than three centuries of commerce by way of water.

The South Street seaport suffered a long period of decline after steam power replaced sail power and the city's ports shifted from downtown to Manhattan's west side. But in the 1970s a revitalization program was put into effect with much credit going to the Rouse Company, developers extraordinaire, responsible for similar urban centers like Faneuil Hall Marketplace in Boston and Harborplace in Baltimore. As is the case in these other complexes, automobile traffic is banned through the seaport center.

If you only have one day—not three like our friend—and you want to make the most of South Street Seaport, you might want to follow this example. Here's what we did in six hours.

Hours 1 through 2: Explored Fulton Market (filled with food stalls) and Museum Block, with its food and retail emporia, from top to bottom. Had lunch for two comprised of selections from five different food sellers (including the noted combination knish and gyro plate).

Hour 3: Watched *The Seaport Experience*. Recognized actress Colleen Dewhurst as the narrator while actor Stephen D. Newman (*Network*, *Skokie*) served as guide. We saw fog and heard cannon fire without leaving our seats.

Hours 4 and first half of 5: Walked to waterfront, enjoying views of

Brooklyn Bridge and harbor. Took guided tour of two ships, the *Peking* (a four-masted bark built in Germany in 1911) and the *Ambrose* (a lightship built in 1907). You can walk on your own in certain seasons but the tour affords one deeper understanding. On the *Peking*, men raised the anchor by hand; on the *Ambrose*, it was lifted by hydraulic means. Meals on the *Peking* usually consisted of a chunk of hardtack, often accompanied by roaches and bugs.

Hours 5 (second half) and 6: Went on a browsing expedition through Pier 17 Pavilion, all three levels of it. Saw stores specializing in candles, stuffed animals, safari clothing, German cutlery, designer sunglasses, hats, leather, perfumes, handmade pottery, movie mementoes, and exotic chocolates. And more.

We left after six full hours with a hearty feel for the place. But you can design your own day. And don't miss the museum!

Location: South Street Seaport is roughly surrounded by Water Street, John Street, Beekman Street, and the East River. By car from the east side, take FDR Drive's Brooklyn Bridge and Civic Center exit, which will take you onto Water/Pearl Streets three blocks north of the seaport area. From the west side, take Fulton Street or drive around the tip of Manhattan through the Battery underpass to South Street. From Brooklyn, the Brooklyn Bridge, Manhattan Bridge, and Brooklyn Battery Tunnel all provide access to lower Manhattan. From New Jersey, take the Holland Tunnel. The following subway lines stop at either Fulton Street and Broadway or Fulton and Nassau Streets: 7th Avenue IRT Line (2 or 3); Lexington Avenue IRT Line (4 or 5); 8th Avenue IND Line (A or CC) IND and BMT Lines (J, M or RR). The M15 bus lines along Water Street make several stops near South Street Seaport. Other bus lines, including M9, M10, M101 and M102, also provide access to the seaport. **Admission** is charged to most museum properties, including all ships and guided tours. Admission is also charged to *The Seaport Experience* and the harbor excursions. Admission is free to all the shopping and dining complexes. **Hours:** Year round, daily. **Allow** one hour for a guided museum tour of any ships and one hour for *The Seaport Experience*. One can spend as little as a half hour at South Street Seaport to grab a quick bite to eat or days to see everything and take a harbor cruise. To get a sufficient taste of South Street Seaport, allow a minimum of four hours, preferably about six. **Information:** South Street Seaport, 19 Fulton Street, New York, NY 10038; (212) 732-7678. South Street Seaport Museum, 207 Front Street, New York, NY 10038; (212) 669-9400. *The Seaport Experience*, (212) 608-7888. Harbor tours on the *Andrew Fletcher* or *Dewitt Clinton*, (212) 406-3434. The schooner *Pioneer*, (212) 669-9416.

Events: There are events taking place constantly. A partial list includes: late winter, Jazz Festival, free local performers and big name paid concerts; September, Street Performer Festival, jugglers, mimes, comedians, puppeteers, musicians; fall, Seafood Festival, food, sea chanteys, sea stories, crafts, chowder cook-off; late October Pumpkin Festival, pumpkin-flavored food, pumpkin sculpture competition, hay rides, folk concerts, children's activities; late November and December, Chorus Tree, huge living Christmas tree, singing Christmas and Chanukah songs, decorations, Santa Claus.

Note: The best place to get museum tickets or information is the pilothouse on the waterfront. Other places for tickets and information are the visitors center at 207 Water Street and the A. A. Low Building, 171 John Street.

If you are staying overnight: Get information on conventional lodging and tour packages from the New York Convention and Visitors' Bureau, Inc., 2 Columbus Circle, New York, NY 10019, (212) 397-8222. For information on alternative lodging, contact City Lights Bed & Breakfast, Ltd., P.O. Box 20355, Cherokee Station, New York, NY 10028, (212) 737-7049. Another bed and breakfast service is Urban Ventures, P.O. Box 426, New York, NY 10024, (212) 594-5650.

HALL OF FAME OF THE TROTTER

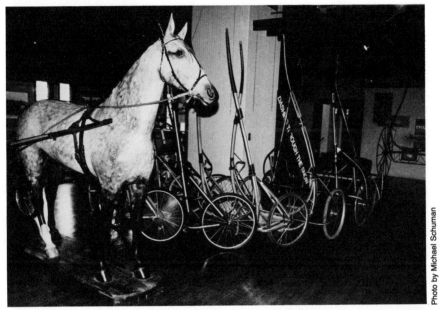

Photo by Michael Schuman

The Hall of Fame of the Trotter—a good place to spend your vacation just horsing around.

F OR SOME, THE DRAW IS THE ABUNDANT COLLECTION OF CURRIER AND Ives lithographs.

Others, especially those with kids in tow, are here to see the horses.

And, of course, there are those who have followed the sport of harness racing for years.

But many just want to get away from the city for a day and have found no better escape than the village of Goshen, population: 4,900, on the fringes of the Catskill Mountains.

These are the people to whom the names of Howard Beissinger, Robert Farrington, and Max Hempt may well be members of a certified accounting firm in Milwaukee. These daytrippers know as much about harness racing as they do about Australian rules football. Mention the name Lindy's Pride and they will think of an airplane that crossed the Atlantic Ocean in 1927.

But you don't have to be a harness racing aficionado to enjoy a visit to the Hall of Fame of the Trotter at the Trotting Horse Museum. Although it is just an hour and a quarter's drive from the cavernous Meadowlands race track in East Rutherford, New Jersey (site of the Hambletonian, the sport's premier race), it may as well be a million light years away.

This is truly small town America, and it was here, in 1838, that trotters first raced on a stretch of land now known as Historic Track. In front of Historic Track was the Good Time Stable, a Tudor-style building with genuine half timbers and angled roof lines; ultimately the stable would become the Hall of Fame of the Trotter, and Historic Track would be the first—and thus far the only—sporting site to be designated a Registered National Historic Landmark.

Despite the museum's historical significance, the people at the hall of fame recognize that the rest of the world is not as familiar with harness racing as they are with baseball and football. Step inside and you can read about the basics in various displays.

Most important is the distinction between trotters and pacers. Both are standardbred horses, as opposed to thoroughbreds, and are raced with a driver (not a jockey) in a two-wheeled vehicle called a sulky.

Trotters move with a diagonal gait; their left front and right rear legs move in unison. Pacers go with left front and left rear in tandem. One thing standardbreds don't do is run; any horse that is caught running, called going "off-stride," must return to the specified gait or be disqualified.

That in mind, head to the gallery called the Living Hall of Fame where a dozen or so persons (still alive) who have contributed greatly to the sport of trotting are enshrined. Or step inside the Peter D. Haughton Room of Immortals, named for a young driver whose career was cut short in an automobile accident, where more than 100 men and women and more than 130 horses are immortalized. The names, like those of Beissinger, Farrington, and Hempt mentioned earlier, will mean nothing to many visitors, but each is accompanied by a capsule summary of his or her accomplishments.

Unlike plaques or medallions seen in many other sports halls of fame, each honoree is immortalized by a miniature statuette crafted by Beverly Lopez, a Weston, Connecticut, artisan who collaborated on such projects as the United States buffalo nickel and the statue of George Patton at West Point.

The statuette of trainer and driver Howard Beissinger, for example, freezes a typical moment in his career: Beissinger sitting on a fence post with a sandwich in one hand, a cup in the other, and a sponge, tape, and brush at his feet. Max Hempt, a driver, horse farm owner, and executive, is dressed in a tie and jacket and sits at an office desk, cigar in hand. Driver Robert Farrington stands at an outdoor faucet, waiting for a red bucket to be filled. Each one is worth a study for the detail and expression alone.

You will likewise admire the Currier and Ives prints. The two famed 19th-century lithographers were avid fans of trotters and depicted them many times in their work. It's not unusual to find lovers of lithography and nostalgia admiring these depictions of the golden age of trotters.

There is room in the building to display only one quarter of the lithograph collection at one time, says Museum Administrator Gail Cunard, so the works are rotated about every six months. Expect to see some as varied as *Hambletonian*, a figure study of the famous horse, *A Spill in the Snow*, in which two sleighs, red as Rudolph's nose, have collided among other sleighs in the snowy back roads of 19th-century America, or *Mr. William H. Vanderbilt's Celebrated Team*, with the distinguished Mr. V. donning grey coat and top hat with massive sideburns exposed, sitting smartly behind a four-wheeled sulky.

Sulky—now there's a funny word. Who in the world of horses gave that vehicle that odd name? The museum staff admits there's no positive answer. But there are legends. In an upper-floor exhibit on the evolution of the sulky, it is written that since this contraption could only be ridden alone, some said that "only a sulky man would ride it."

The sulky first appeared when riders of saddled trotting horses reached middle age, and their ample weight became too much of a racing handicap. The exhibit reads, "it placed a strain on a gentleman's dignity." In addition, sulkies originally had four wheels instead of two, and examples of these dinosaurs are displayed.

The building's original stables have been cleverly transformed into galleries, showcasing aspects of the sport from horse ownership to what the well-dressed horse wears. (Be prepared to shell out an average of $900 a month for grooming and training alone if you want to own a trotter.)

Ready for some trivia? In one gallery that discusses horse colors, we learned what illustrious American composer Stephen Foster was singing about in his immortal "Camptown Races." When Foster said, "I'll bet my money on the bob-tail mare," he was referring to Flora Temple, a champion trotter of the day and a bay horse. The term bay horse refers to her color, somewhere between reddish tan and rich mahogany brown, a common shade for harness racing horses in that day. You'll recall the line, "Somebody bet on the bay."

The bay continued to dominate harness racing well into the 20th century, so says the exhibit. A computer study in 1966 uncovered the following details: a total of 53% of trotters were bays, while the next most common color, at 25%, was brown. Of the 25,347 horses in the study, only four were pinto. Now that, truly, is a horse of a different color.

Location: The Hall of Fame of the Trotter is at 240 Main Street in Goshen. From Interstate 84, take exit 121 onto Route 17 west, then take exit 124B onto Route 207 east; head straight through the traffic lights to the museum on the right. From the New York State Thruway (Interstate 87), take exit 16 onto Route 17 west and follow the directions above. **Admission** is charged. **Hours:** Year round, daily; afternoons only on Sunday. **Allow** at least 45 minutes if you are a casual visitor. Those who would like to pore over the many exhibits should allow up to an hour and a half, while trotter buffs should plan a half a day. **Information:** Hall of Fame of the Trotter, P.O. Box 590, 240 Main Street, Goshen, NY 10924, (914) 294-6330.

Events: Early July, Hall of Fame Day, induction ceremonies, in-person guests; mid-December, Classic Choral Society's Christmas Concert; education series throughout the year.

Note: Films on harness racing are shown daily during race season. The museum gift shop is a utopia for those interested in either the sport or fine reproductions of Currier and Ives lithographs. For information on the racing program at the adjacent track, contact Historic Track, Box 192, Goshen, NY 10924; (914) 294-5333.

If you are staying overnight: Howard Johnson's Motor Lodge, 551 Route 211 East (off Interstate 84, exit 4W, or Route 17, exit 120), Middletown, (914) 342-5822; Gasho of Japan, Route 32 (two miles off Thruway exit 16), Central Valley, (914) 928-2387; Super 8 Lodge, 563 Route 211 East (off Interstate 84, exit 4W, or Route 17, exit 120), Middletown, (914) 692-5828; Dobbin's Stagecoach Inn, 1740 former stagecoach inn with four rooms (bed & breakfast), 268 Main Street, Goshen, (914) 294-5526.

OLD RHINEBECK AERODROME

It's World War I all over again on weekends in the air over Old Rhinebeck Aerodrome.

IT IS WORLD WAR 1 ALL OVER AGAIN IN THE AIR OVER RHINEBECK ON summer and fall Sundays. On Saturdays, a time machine takes you back to a period a bit earlier. And later.

Weekend air shows are high points at the Old Rhinebeck Aerodrome. Using only original aircraft or accurate reproductions with original engines, Aerodrome founder Cole Palen and his staff stage a World War I dogfight on Sundays and a show featuring pre- and post-World War I aircraft on Saturdays. On weekdays there is no air show, but the aerodrome museum collection is open for viewing.

A Sunday visit introduces you to Sir Percy Goodfellow, a pilot on the side of the allies, and his foe, German flying ace Der Black Baron, as they compete in the air for the heart of heroine Trudy Truelove.

Jim Marks, who plays Goodfellow, calls the 90-minute-long show "a classic confrontation between good and evil" and describes Percy as a bumbling pilot with only the best intentions. Der Black Baron, played by curator Palen in a Fokker Triplane, manages to outwit Percy, intoxicating him at one point, kidnapping Trudy, and forcing her to walk out on the plane's wings. Fortunately, good conquers evil and the hero gets the girl in the end.

Claiming it's hard to "get human volunteers," Palen says the young woman you see on the wings is an accurately dressed dummy. However, you do see actual flying stunts performed by Marks, Palen, and other professional pilots.

The Saturday show doesn't tell a story but does have its fill of aerial dramatics performed by pilots in numerous airplanes from the years before and after World War I, which Palen has categorized as the "pioneer" and "Lindbergh" eras.

These include the famous Curtis Jenney; the cumbersome Curtis Fledgling, called an "aeronautical dinosaur" by the show's announcer; the Nieuport 10, a French plane dating to 1915, used after the war for flight school training; and the Hariot, a 1910 French creation tagged by Palen as "a racing skiff with wings"—it will only fly under certain wind conditions.

In both shows, Palen spins and rolls in the air, executing stunts guaranteed to inflict the rest of us with vertigo. He does quick spins called snap rolls; wider, barrel-shaped spins called barrel rolls; spins in which the plane's nose falls downward and the plane appears about to crash; and classic barnstormer's loops. At the end of his performance he is right side up and on the ground and ready to answer your questions.

Palen is most proud of the aerodrome's accuracy. The duplicate planes are exact copies. The stunts performed are those one would have seen in an aerial barnstorming show 60 years ago. The hangars are copied from early photos and even the benches on which the audience sits are historically accurate reproductions.

Cole Palen's own history with aircraft goes way back, though not as far as his earliest aircraft. A Hudson Valley native, Palen grew up in Red Oak Mills, next to the old Poughkeepsie airport. His father ultimately bought the farm property next to the airport, and young Cole became acquainted with several pilots. "They were my heroes," he says.

After serving in World War II (in which he stayed on the ground), Palen, bit with what he calls "aeromania," purchased six aircraft from Roosevelt Field in Long Island as it was about to be closed. In time, he bought some property to use as an airport for his antique planes and began doing air shows in 1960.

Photo by Kai Hulleberg, courtesy Old Rhinebeck Aerodrome, Inc.

Aerodrome founder Cole Palen performs several loops and spins during each air show. Here he is right side up at the controls of a 1918 Curtiss Jenney JN4D trainer.

The museum consists of three hangars, each devoted to different periods in aviation. Airplane enthusiasts will be euphoric when walking through the museum, admiring aircraft that kept people and their dreams aloft. The 1918 Sopwith Snipe, made in Britain, was used near the end of World War I by such successful fighter pilots as Canadian ace Billy Barker. The plane is in the World War I era hanger and is one of Palen's originals. The completely original French 1911 Bleriot, powered by a 71-horsepower rotary engine, had a long-range gas tank and was commonly used in the great circuit races of Europe.

What some might call the Model T of American airplanes is the original Waco 10, an open cockpit biplane with a Curtiss X-5 engine, dating from 1927 and typical of many American aircraft during the Lindbergh era. Lindbergh's Atlantic crossing inspired many to learn to fly, and with the Waco and a World War I surplus engine, it was affordable.

Those who don't know the difference between Waco aircraft and Waco, Texas, will still enjoy looking at some of the earliest flying machines. A reproduction of the Wright Brothers' famous glider, the first heavier than air machine with a mechanical control system, will vie for your attention with a reproduced Chanute glider with two wings and no engine, both in the pioneer era hangar.

The wreckage of a reproduced World War I era Fokker triplane has a jarring effect; the plane crashed on May 2, 1987, and the twisted shell is there to see. The red Monocoupe 90, a 1930 American propellor-driven plane in the Lindbergh era hangar, was flown in several cross-country and pylon races. One flying racer, Phoebe Omlie, had winnings of $3,250 in 1930, a time when the national hourly wage was 50 cents.

If you have the urge to be more than a bystander, flights lasting 15 minutes are offered before and after the weekend shows. You get to be a passenger in a rebuilt 1929 open cockpit biplane called a New Standard D-25. Those even more brave can model clothes that were the latest styles from 1903 to 1920 in a fashion show before the air show; so far it is only women's apparel that is on parade.

Location: From the junction of Routes 9 and 199 in Red Hook, take Route 9 south one and a half miles to Stone Church Road, turn left and follow to the aerodrome; the old stone church is on the right. From the New York State Thruway (Interstate 87), take exit 19 (Route 199), and follow directions above. From the Taconic Parkway, take the exit for Route 199. **Admission** is charged. **Hours:** Museum open mid-May through October, daily; air shows held Saturday and Sunday afternoons. **Allow** 45 minutes to an hour and a half to tour the museum. On weekends allow four hours to see the fashion show, the air show, and the museum. **Information:** Old Rhinebeck Aerodrome, P.O. Box 89, Rhinebeck, NY 12572.

Events: Air and early 1900s fashion shows Saturday and Sunday through season.

Note: Passenger flights are first come, first serve; no advance reservations are taken although you can sign up as early as 10 a.m. on Saturday or Sunday. The museum is closed while the air show is taking place. Picnic tables are on the grounds.

If you are staying overnight: Holiday Inn, 503 Washington Avenue (east of New York State Thruway, exit 19), Kingston, (914) 338-0400; Howard Johnson's Motor Lodge, Route 28 (west of New York State Thruway, exit 19), Kingston, (914) 338-4200; Super 8 Lodge, 487 Washington Avenue (east of New York State Thruway, exit 19), Kingston, (914) 338-3078; Beekman Arms Hotel, 4 Mill Street (junction Routes 9 and 308), Rhinebeck, (914) 876-7077.

THE CANFIELD CASINO

Victoriana at its grandest is on view in a building once called "Morrissey's Elegant Hell" in Saratoga Springs.

F OR DECADES, THE BIGGEST TOURIST ATTRACTION IN SARATOGA SPRINGS was called "Morrissey's Elegant Hell," and people came from all parts of New York, the Midwest, the South—especially the South—to partake in the delights of this three-story gambling casino facing Congress Park in the center of the city.

Despite its sordid nickname, however, it operated with the full knowledge of the good people of Saratoga Springs. Sure, Deity-inspired reformers like Anthony Comstock spoke ill of Morrissey's Hell, and Comstock even tried to raid it once, but the den of roulette wheels and playing cards was permitted to flourish.

Any why not? The gaming table trade brought in money, lots of it, and these mid-Victorian-era years are viewed as Saratoga's glory years. Fabled hotels like the Grand Union and Congress Hall were built, and the city drew big-name entertainers like Victor Herbert and Chauncey Olcott to perform in concert. For those whose wagering preferences ran towards horses, gambling at the race track was as popular as at Morrissey's casino.

Enter the casino today and you will still see poker chips and dice. But they sit silently in a display case next to 100-year-old opera glasses, a pair of white gloves, and the register from a prominent Victorian Saratoga Springs hotel. They are all part of the collection of the Historical Society of Saratoga Springs, housed in the casino.

Most every town larger than a football field maintains a historical society museum. But this one differs from most; few places can claim that their historical society has its home in a gambling casino. (Actually, the casino building houses three separate museums, but where one ends and the other picks up is an invisible line and doesn't really matter to most visitors.)

Few towns have access to such a large and lavish building. Enter the Italianate-style structure and you can still see the large domed windows and brass chandeliers that greeted visitors 100 years ago when they came to play, not realizing they were making history.

The first people to make special trips to this corner of the state came for the curative waters, and it did not take long for the waters to be exploited. In the days of primeval medical knowledge, long before any government regulations, every unscrupulous opportunist sold bottled spring water. One brochure on view, dated 1885, challenged a false business; it reads, "The Story of a Disreputable Transaction. A Fraud Exposed!"

In the spirit of reform that swept the country during and following Theodore Roosevelt's years in the White House, the state of New York took control of more than 160 springs in 1911 and created the spa reservation to preserve them.

In time, those who ventured far from home to take the Saratoga waters wanted social activities to occupy their time, and innkeepers complied by adding frills like billiard tables and musical instruments. The arrival of the railroad increased accessibility and with it came more people, followed by bigger hotels and more frills. And so on.

Walk the streets of Saratoga Springs today and you'll see stunning Victorian houses. Most are privately owned and closed to the public. However, one of the benefits of visiting the casino is the opportunity to see Victorian interiors in the form of complete period rooms re-creating Pine Grove, the home of a prominent local family.

Standing out in the Pine Grove parlor is the Haines piano, inlaid with mother of pearl, that came into the family as a wedding gift. A portrait of a baby who died in infancy is displayed, while a velvet love seat rests on wall-to-wall carpeting, a major Victorian-era status symbol.

Down the hall, a bedroom is filled with furnishings of an earlier time:

an Empire sleigh bed, a Duncan Phyfe window bench, and a white Hepplewhite washstand.

Compare it to the typically heavy and dark Victorian bedroom next to it. Most notable is the "Saratoga Trunk," also known as a "camel-back trunk," for its rounded top; they were immensely popular here in the late 1800s and were hated by porters in the classy hotels because they couldn't be stacked one atop the other.

And what about the exteriors? A display on Victorian architecture explains the standardized patterns of band-sawed boards used to give the sculptured effect we all recognize as ornate and showy gingerbread. Stained glass and front porches, also common Victorian trademarks, are also discussed: "From the shade of the front stoop, one could observe the passing scene, socialize with neighbors, or accept a marriage proposal," reads the posted commentary.

While the casino affords one of the most complete looks at life in Victorian Saratoga, it also delves into the building's most famous purpose for being here. In the 19th-century casino room is a roulette table, a faro table, and an old desk filled with pigeon holes and drawers, used by casino owner John Morrissey. Look closely and you can see that the set of drawers on the right is actually a safe.

Morrissey ran an honest casino, and his rules were few and to the point: no gambling on Sunday, no women in the gaming rooms, no Saratogans in gaming rooms, and no credit.

When did the casino stop serving its intended purpose? Local objections forced gambling to cease in 1907, and Richard Canfield, who succeeded Morrissey as owner, sold the casino in 1911. Gambling returned to Saratoga Springs in the 1920s, but only in lake houses outside the city limits; it was permanently halted following Senate hearings on gambling and organized crime in 1951.

Should you be visiting on a nice day, plan to take a walk through Congress Park, in front of the casino. Congress Spring, the one that started it all, is under a Greek Revival pavilion, and sculptor Daniel Chester French's *Spirit of Life* never fails to impress. (French sculpted the *Seated Lincoln* in the Lincoln Memorial in Washington, D.C., among other notable works.)

Location: To reach Saratoga Springs from the south, take Interstate 87, exit 13N, onto Route 9, which becomes Broadway, the main thoroughfare in the city. Congress Park is off Broadway in the center of Saratoga Springs, opposite Congress Street. **Admission** is charged. **Hours:** July and August, daily; May, June, September, and October, Monday through Saturday, afternoons only on Sunday; Remaining months, Wednesday through Sunday afternoons. **Allow** 45 minutes to an hour and a half to see the museum and a half hour to see the park. **Information:** Historical Society of Saratoga Springs, P.O. Box 216, Saratoga Springs, NY 12866; (518) 584-6920.

Events: August, antique show; December, Christmas Capers, formal party; slide shows, talks and special presentations are scheduled regularly.

Note: There are no guided tours in the museum. The main portion of the museum is on the second and third floors. A small but quality gift shop and the Ann Grey Gallery, which hosts changing local art and history exhibits, is on the first floor.

If you are staying overnight: Holiday Inn, corner Broadway and Circular Streets, Saratoga Springs, (518) 584-4550; Turf & Spa Motel, 140 Broadway, Saratoga Springs, (518) 584-2550; The Springs Motel, 165 Broadway, Saratoga Springs, (518) 584-6336; Saratoga Bed and Breakfast, Church Street, Saratoga Springs, (518) 584-0920. Graycourt Motel, Lake George Road (Route 9, north of Interstate 87, exit 19), Glens Falls, (518) 792-0223; Landmark Motor Lodge, Route 9 (one mile north of Interstate 87, exit 17N), Glens Falls, (518) 793-3441. In-season rates in Saratoga Springs are extremely expensive; it's not unusual for a room that rents for $30 in the off-season to rent for $100 in August. You will find more reasonable rates in surrounding towns like Glens Falls to the north.

FAMOUS
NEW YORKERS

THE STATUE OF LIBERTY

Photo by Michael Schuman

The most famous symbol of the United States overlooks the most famous city's skyline.

T HE LADY CERTAINLY NEEDS NO MORE PUBLICITY. CHIEF RANGER BILL DeHart says that attendance in the months following the reopening of the statue in summer 1986 reached 20,000 visitors a day, more than some attractions draw in a year.

DeHart says the best information we can give you about the Statue of Liberty is advice on the most efficient ways to spend your time on Liberty Island so that lengthy waits and huge crowds don't force you to miss attractions you had your heart set on seeing.

1. Plan your visit in the winter when crowds are at their thinnest. Free guided tours inside the museum are available in the off-season. After mid-March, says DeHart, tours are rarely offered due to unmanageable numbers. You'll also get more individual attention in the off-season, even if you do not take a guided tour. Rangers have more information in their heads than you can read on a marker, and it is worthwhile to spend some time chatting with them when there are few people around.

2. Make the statue your first sightseeing stop in the day and come as early as possible. We rode on a 10:30 A.M. ferry from Battery Park on the Saturday of a winter holiday weekend, and there were few other tourists on board. By the time we were nearing the end of our visit at about 2 P.M., there was a one-hour wait to climb to the statue's crown and a sizable wait to enter the museum.

3. Take the New Jersey ferry whenever possible. It runs as needed— always in summer and early fall and at other times when demand calls. There are significantly fewer people on it than the Manhattan ferry and little if any wait even on busy days. There is also free and unlimited parking. The ferry leaves from Liberty State Park in Jersey City, reached by taking exit 14B off the New Jersey Turnpike extension.

4. If your main desire at the statue is to climb to the crown, think twice about it and then think again. Chief Ranger DeHart says, "The worst thing the average visitor can do is go to the crown."

Why? The view, says DeHart, is often disappointing. From the crown you get a view of Brooklyn and little else; most people, DeHart reports, spend about 20 seconds in the crown.

The alternative is to take the elevator to the top of the pedestal, not as high as the crown but complete with an unencumbered 360-degree view that includes the skyscrapers of lower Manhattan.

If you are dying to climb to the crown just to say you did, make it your first stop once inside the statue and make sure you have strong leg muscles. There is no elevator, and there is no connection between the stairway that leads to the crown and the elevator that stops at the pedestal. You must walk all 354 steps each way. If you have a heart condition, forget the climb. Surprisingly, the climb down will be more taxing than the one up; depending on your condition, your calves are likely to feel like vats of Welch's Grape Jelly by the time you reach bottom.

5. Allow at least three hours for a visit, including time to park your car and 40 minutes total aboard either ferry. And that is cutting it close. To really relax and enjoy yourself, consider allowing five to six hours. Long lines can delay the ferry ride (either to or from the statue) or your entrance into the statue. Expect to wait. If you don't have to, then your visit will be that much more pleasant.

6. See the museum! It's a must! It opened when the refurbished statue opened in July 1986. It's on two floors. The bottom level is devoted to the statue, its history, its construction, its image, and its symbolism. The upper level focuses on immigration. Allow a minimum of 90 minutes to see the museum. The best way to view the exhibits—depending on the time of year you visit—is to take a guided tour through either or both levels and then walk through the museum at your leisure later on.

By now, most everyone is familiar with the basic story of the statue.

Whether you have seen a film, such as Ken Burns's Academy Award-nominated *The Statue of Liberty*, or just got caught up in the net of hoopla during the centennial, you have heard that the statue was a gift from France and was largely the work of Frederic Auguste Bartholdi. It is made of copper and its torch symbolizes liberty lighting the world.

The statue museum, through photographs, videotapes, magazine covers, scale models, and what has got to be the world's biggest wrench, presents the statue's story in human terms.

Consider for example, that Bartholdi's model for the statue's face was his mother. Compare the full-scale reproduction of the famous face to that of Mrs. Bartholdi. Our guide, Jennifer Kavanaugh, said that visitors have claimed Mrs. Bartholdi resembles a host of celebrities from George Washington to Elvis Presley.

Bartholdi enlisted the assistance of another Frenchman, Gustave Eiffel, to create a support system for the statue, which he completed before creating his most famous work, the Eiffel Tower.

It wasn't pure altruism that caused France to give this gift to the United States; there were political motives. Bartholdi said that the original idea for the statue came from his friend and compatriot Edouard de Laboulaye, a French scholar and outspoken opponent of the ruling French Second Empire.

Laboulaye had cited the United States as a model of liberty and independence and anti-monarchical government. The gift of the statue to the United States accentuated these feelings. Bartholdi's name for the monument, "Liberty Enlightening the World," said Laboulaye follower Henri Martin, is "a sublime phrase which sums up the progress of modern times."

But we Americans also played a role in the lady's development, albeit an embarrassing one. It was up to the United States to supply the pedestal; this proved to be humiliating since several years went by before enough money was raised to build it. The museum exhibits a magazine cover depicting Miss Liberty as a decrepit old lady still waiting, a century later, for her pedestal. Enough money was finally raised in 1885 when publisher Joseph Pulitzer of the *New York World* said he would put names of all contributors in the newspaper. It proved to be a lot of names—the average contribution was less than $1.00.

The best-known symbol of the statue itself is the famous poem by Emma Lazarus that includes the lines, "Give me your tired, your poor, Your huddled masses yearning to breathe free." Most visitors are in for a couple of surprises when they encounter the poem.

The first is that these famous words do not start the poem. There are nine lines in the 14-line poem that precede them, and you can see for yourself when you read it on its original bronze plaque, displayed indoors as it has been since the beginning.

Yes, indoors. That is the second surprise. The poem was never displayed outdoors, and prior to its current spot in the museum, it was on an interior pedestal wall.

More words, these on the back of postcards, can be read in an ingenious display celebrating the statue's exploitation in pop culture. A mountainous display of postcards, looking like a crazy quilt, has been arranged so the yellow colors in the cards form the statue's image; walk behind it and you see a similar image of the statue made from postcards, this one in blue.

Look closer and you will see the many forms in which this allegorical figure of liberty has been portrayed on postcards. One has her waiting for a subway train; another shows Miss Liberty buried in sand up to her crown as in the final scene of *Planet of the Apes*. Others present her with famous faces such as those of Ronald Reagan and the Mona Lisa.

Notable examples of the statue as seen through the eyes of more pop culture creators are on videotape, including a Mad Magazine fold-out featuring Ms. Liberty as a bra-burning feminist, and the cover of Supertramp's 1979 best-selling "Breakfast in America" album, depicting her as a waitress in a coffee shop, raising high a tray of breakfast goodies.

Use of the statue's likeness to sell products didn't begin with the recent restoration. Bartholdi himself first licensed her image in 1875 before she had even been completed as a means of fund-raising, and her face has been used to sell Liberty Bonds and blue jeans ever since.

Her true meaning is explored, however, in the gallery devoted to the history of immigration in the United States. Between 1900 and 1914, a total of 2,000 immigrants a day arrived at Ellis Island, and just about all are praised somewhere in this extensive exhibit for both their contributions to their new country and the hardships they endured.

Immigrants who entered the United States from points other than New York City also are represented, as are those who came not by their own free will; witness the wrist irons used to shackle slaves imported in the 1700s.

A Jewish Kiddush cup from Czarist Russia is placed near a photograph of a sea of humanity packed into New York City's lower east side around the turn of the century. A model of a steamer similar to those that transported Irish immigrants sits not far from a warning from the anti-immigrant American Party (also called the Know-Nothing Party) of the 1850s advising others to watch out for "the Satanic Plot and Artful Crimes of Popery."

But the mood of the gallery overall is upbeat and praiseworthy, a paean to this melting pot, the likes of which are found nowhere else on the globe.

Location: The Statue of Liberty is on Liberty Island in New York Harbor. It is reached by ferries from Battery Park in Manhattan and from Liberty State Park in Jersey City, New Jersey. **Admission** is free for the statue and museum but charged for either ferry ride. **Hours:** Year round, daily. **Allow** three to six hours and expect to wait from a half hour to a few hours anytime except the dead of winter. (And even then!) **Information:** Statue of Liberty National Monument, Liberty Island, New York, NY 10004; (212) 363-3200. Contact Circle Line for information on either ferry, (212) 269-5755. For information on Liberty State Park in Jersey City, call (201) 435-8509.

Note: As of this writing, Ellis Island is closed to the public while refurbishing is taking place.

If you are staying overnight: Get information on conventional lodging and tour packages from the New York Convention and Visitors' Bureau, Inc., 2 Columbus Circle, New York, NY 10019, (212) 397-8222. For information on alternative lodging, contact City Lights Bed & Breakfast, Ltd., P.O. Box 20355, Cherokee Station, New York, NY 10028, (212) 737-7049. Another bed and breakfast service is Urban Ventures, P.O. Box 426, New York, NY 10024, (212) 594-5650.

FRANKLIN AND ELEANOR ROOSEVELT

Franklin and Eleanor, on the south lawn at Hyde Park in the summer of 1933.

FRANKLIN AND ELEANOR ROOSEVELT HAD COMMON GOALS BUT, FOR much of their married lives, separate houses. Franklin had the lavish and heavy Victorian big house, while Eleanor preferred the informal stucco home she named Val-Kill. Both are open to the public today in Hyde Park.

No member of the public would have been permitted to see the crude little wheelchair in FDR's dressing room at the Hyde Park big house. Not while he was alive. The president was concerned that should his handicap be seen by the public, his image as a strong and able leader would suffer.

Today, when visitors parade by the second floor dressing room and see the wheelchair, they don't recall FDR as a weakling or an incapacitated man. Most—whether or not they agreed with his political beliefs—still think of the only four-time presidential election winner as the leader who steered his country through a depression and a world war, who soothed us with words of comfort over the radio, and who embodied the spirit of a nation trying to land on its feet. All the wheelchair does is humanize the legendary statesman.

Amid the dark and heavy late-Victorian opulence are hints of the Roosevelt family's personality. Franklin's chair at the oak dining room table is turned back slightly in order that his wheelchair could be accommodated with little inconvenience.

Two high-backed leather chairs by the library fireplace are evidence of his two terms as governor of New York State; he was given one chair for each term and often sat in one while giving one of his famous fireside chats. The cozy room down the hall, known as the snuggery, was the domain of Franklin's mother, Sara, who was often found sitting at the desk, paying bills, or writing to friends.

It is said by those who knew the Roosevelt family that Sara Roosevelt's domination of the big house didn't stop at the snuggery. As a result, Eleanor spent much of her time in Hyde Park at Val-Kill. Even when she came home with her husband as president and first lady, she rarely stayed overnight here.

Her second floor bedroom is cold and empty. When you peer into the small, sparsely furnished room, you see a single bed, a wicker chair, a dresser, and a lonely writing table. It is not the room of a person who felt at home.

Not so for Franklin's room. He selected it because of its sweeping view of the Hudson River and of the distant Catskill Mountains. Pencil sketches of his mother and daughter are on the wall, and a picture of his well-known Scotty, Fala, hangs above his bedroom fireplace.

The president usually began his day holding court with his staff and advisers while still in bed. Within easy reach are two telephones, one on the nightstand and one on the wall. The wall phone was secretly coded with a direct line to the White House and was used many times during World War II.

Some of FDR's reading material from his brief fourth term still rests on a desk by a far window in his bedroom. The subjects reflect his concerns for the future. There is a biography of Italian dictator Benito Mussolini, a *Time* magazine dated March 5, 1945, a Bible, and a book titled, *Agenda for a Post-War World*.

Franklin D. Roosevelt never lived to see the post-war world. He died on April 12, 1945, at his Little White House in Warm Springs, Georgia, and is buried with Eleanor in the rose garden outside the Hyde Park home.

Like the big house, the museum of the Franklin D. Roosevelt Library next door helps visitors understand a complex man. Various items help tell his story.

The despised Scottish suit—kilts and all—that Sara made Franklin wear as a child, is displayed near a tongue-in-cheek election poster for the editorial staff of the Harvard University newspaper; both let observers know he had a privileged background.

The crutches and cane he used, emblems of his struggle against polio, are supplemented by his 1936 Ford Phaeton convertible, equipped with special manual controls.

The hard times of the 1930s are interpreted by bread line photos, National Recovery Administration posters with the famous blue eagle, and the first page of the 1933 inaugural speech containing the words, "The only thing we have to fear is fear itself," circled in bright red.

The rough draft of another famous speech also is displayed, the one given December 8, 1941. It was on this occasion that the president asked Congress for a declaration of war following the Japanese attack on Pearl Harbor. The first and most famous line which reads, "a date which will live in infamy," originally said, "a date which will live in world history." You can see where the bland "world history" is crossed out and replaced with the direct and hard-hitting "infamy."

What many find most memorable is the original desk and chair used by FDR in the White House. It is frozen in time, back to the date of his death. The desk is pleasantly cluttered with Democratic donkeys and Republican elephants, given by friends of both parties; miniature Scotties inspired by his own Fala; his renowned cigarette holder; and photos of his four sons in World War II service uniforms.

Two wings dedicated in honor of Eleanor Roosevelt were added to the museum in 1972, and here are several of her personal belongings, ranging from her christening outfit to her wedding veil to photographs of her as a delegate to the United Nations.

One would not expect to find a former first lady of the United States living in a converted factory off a dirt road in the woods. But of course, Eleanor Roosevelt was not a typical first lady.

To many, she was better known as a diplomat and a humanitarian than as the official White House hostess from 1933 to 1945. And it was her verve and energy that made her the most active, independent, and widely known first lady in the world.

It was that same independent spirit that drove her to her own Hyde Park home. But even after her private retreat was built, she had to share it with two friends and never truly had a place of her own until the death of her husband.

The idea for Val-Kill was born during the waning days of the summer

The Hyde Park big house, home of the man who led the country through its worst
depression and the second world war.

of 1924. Eleanor had invited two friends from the New York Democratic Committee, Nancy Cook and Marion Dickerman, to join the family for its last picnic outing of the season.

When Eleanor lamented that this would be the last such get-together before the big house was closed for the winter, Franklin suggested that his wife and her two friends build their own cottage nearby so they could enjoy the location all year.

By 1925, a little fieldstone house was built and named Val-Kill (valley stream), and accompanying it just a year later was a larger stucco building housing Val-Kill Industries, a furniture-making company started by the three friends plus another woman.

By 1936, when Val-Kill Industries closed, Eleanor had a falling out with Nan and Marion, so she let them have the little stone house and converted the factory building into two apartments—one for herself and one for her secretary. After Franklin's death, she lived there full time.

The building is a metaphor for Eleanor's self-image, plain as cardboard on the outside but warm and comfortable inside. Eleanor saw herself as awkward and homely, while the majority of Americans viewed her as a person of inner beauty and compassion that was truly uncommon.

The piano in the Val-Kill living room is emblematic of her care and concern for others. She couldn't play it but her children and grandchildren could, and she kept it there for their use. And like most grandmothers, she inconvenienced herself to accommodate them often, offering freshly baked cookies or reading aloud Rudyard Kipling tales as they relaxed on the flower-print chairs in the living room.

But her thoughtfulness extended far beyond close family members. Her home's five guest rooms were regularly occupied, and it wasn't unusual for her to put baked treats, flowers, or a book or magazine in a room for a special guest.

There were many: John F. Kennedy, Soviet Premier Nikita Krushchev, and Yugoslavia's Marshall Tito to name a few. But though she was an otherwise perfect hostess, she rarely cooked and freely admitted her weakness in that department. When the tour takes you into the dining room, you hear about the time she cooked for guests a dinner of macaroni, potatoes, and creamed chicken, topped off with pancakes and syrup.

The burled mahogany dining room table, as well as many of the chairs, tables, and other furnishings inside were made by Val-Kill Industries. The vintage Philco television set sits on a Val-Kill table and, for many visitors, brings back memories of their own living rooms in the early 1960s. It is one of many items that reflect both the period depicted here and her preference for the informal life.

That is especially apparent when you enter the screened-in porch upstairs. It was Eleanor's favorite place to sleep in summer—where she could enjoy the fresh night air, the sounds of the crickets, and the distant silhouetted views of the Catskill Mountains. It looks more like the bunk where your counselor at Camp Waxahachie slept, rather than a bedroom for the first lady of the United States.

That is appropriate though. This was a first lady who would rather pass up a formal party to sit on a wicker chair on her porch while family and friends cooked hot dogs in a fireplace or relaxed on the lawn enjoying nothing but the view and the sunshine. The atmosphere was such that Britain's Winston Churchill, for example, thought nothing of dropping formalities to take a soothing swim in the outdoor pool before grabbing a hot dog for lunch.

Location: FDR's big house, properly called Franklin D. Roosevelt National Historic Site, is on Route 9, about a mile south of the center of Hyde Park. The Roosevelt Library and Museum is on the home's grounds. **Admission** is charged for both attractions. **Hours:** Home: April through October, daily; November through March, Thursday through Monday. Museum: Year round, daily. **Allow** an hour to see the home and walk the grounds and another hour to tour the museum. **Information:** Roosevelt-Vanderbilt National Historic Sites, 249 Albany Post Road, Hyde Park, NY 12538, (914) 229-9115; Franklin D. Roosevelt Library and Museum, 259 Albany Post Road, Hyde Park, NY 12538, (914) 229-8114.

Events: January 30, Franklin Roosevelt's birthday, grave side ceremony, West Point color guard, Army firing team; early December through January 1, Christmas at Hyde Park, re-creation of family Christmas decorations based on historic accuracy, and tours relating to Roosevelt family Christmas celebrations.

Note: Your admission ticket is good for entrance into both sites.

Location: Val-Kill, properly called Eleanor Roosevelt National Historic Site, is two miles east of FDR's big house, accessible most of the season by shuttle bus only. **Admission** is free to the house but is charged for the shuttle bus ride. **Hours:** April through October, daily; March and November 1 through December, weekends. **Allow** an hour. **Information:** see above address for FDR site.

Events: October 11, Eleanor Roosevelt's birthday, grave side ceremony, special talks, exhibits; early December through January 1, Christmas at Val-Kill, re-creation of Eleanor Roosevelt's Christmas decorations based on photographs and written accounts, and tours relating to her Christmas traditions.

Note: Val-Kill is reached by shuttle bus only from April through October; the bus departs from the FDR home parking lot. In the off-season, the house can be reached only by car—signs direct you from Route 9— and since there is no shuttle bus, visitors pay no fee.

If you are staying overnight: Holiday Inn, Route 9 (two miles south of Poughkeepsie), (914) 473-1151; The Dutch Patroon Motel, Route 9 (a half mile north of the FDR site), Hyde Park, (914) 229-7141; The Roosevelt Inn, Route 9 (a mile north of the FDR site), Hyde Park, (914) 229-2443; Beekman Arms, Route 9 (at junction with County Route 308), Rhinebeck, (914) 876-7077; Fala: A Bed and Breakfast, 46 East Market Street, Hyde Park, (914) 229-5937.

THEODORE ROOSEVELT

"A bully tramp" led by Theodore Roosevelt.

IT WASN'T LIKE THEODORE ROOSEVELT TO GET HIS EXERCISE LIKE OTHER presidents—on a putting green or from the back of a horse. Roosevelt took friends and visiting dignitaries on point to point hikes on which they had to go over, above, or through, but never around, any obstacle in their way.

French ambassador Jean-Jules Jusserand was forced to swim naked across a stream too deep to ford, and British ambassador Sir Mortimer Durand once became stuck in a wooded mass of roots and hedges.

British diplomat and friend Cecil Spring Rice once responded to these treks by sighing, "You must always remember that the president is about six."

Roosevelt wouldn't have been hurt by that comment. He welcomed the chance to take his six children on point to point hikes near his home, Sagamore Hill, in Oyster Bay. In part, he enjoyed the hikes because he was finally getting a chance to be a child; his own youth was spent as a sickly asthmatic in a New York City brownstone.

In fact, he was on a hiking trip in the Adirondacks when he officially became president of the United States following the assassination of William McKinley. Roosevelt quickly journeyed to Buffalo for the swearing-in ceremony, and the house where it occurred is a national historic site open to the public.

Teddy Roosevelt was a dynamo, full of energy, unintimidated by blocks in his path. He grew from a weak child into a pillar of strength and determination, through years of tedious weight training and self-discipline.

As New York's governor he was a reformer, taking on the powerful machine of infamous boss William Marcy Tweed. As president, he was also a reformer, challenging and conquering J.P. Morgan and a slew of other robber barons.

Visitors to Sagamore Hill can see the acres of woodlands where TR led his guests and children on point to point hikes. Look past the trees that have grown since the turn of the century and the waters of Long Island Sound come into view, where the president would row his young ones down to a faraway stretch of beach for an overnight camping trip.

Sit on Sagamore Hill's peaceful piazza and you can view the outdoors as the Roosevelts did. It was on the piazza where Roosevelt received his nomination for governor of New York, for vice-president, and for president of the United States. It was here that he often spoke to groups like woman suffragists, servicemen, or Boy Scouts.

Politicking on a more personal note was reserved for the library, the first room seen inside Sagamore Hill. Ambassadors from two warring countries, Russia and Japan, met with TR in this room and came out agreeing on a treaty ending the war. The treaty was signed a month later in New Hampshire and earned the president the Nobel Peace Prize.

The silver candlestick on TR's library desk symbolizes the presidential peacemaker; it was used to seal the treaty. The animal trophies throughout the room—a bear skin rug and rhinoceros foot inkstand, for example—bear witness to the Roosevelt endorsement of the strenuous life.

It's hard to escape in Sagamore Hill his love of the wild and rugged. The hirsute head of an African cape buffalo stares blankly in the entrance hall, and in the North Room (a massive 30 by 40-foot reception area that looks more like a hunting lodge) are elephant tusks and antelope and buffalo heads; TR's Roughrider sword, hat, and revolver hang on an improvisatory pair of antlers turned hat rack.

Edith Roosevelt, the first lady, took it all in stride, once saying to her husband after he rushed indoors with a profusely bleeding scalp cut, "Theodore, I wish you would do your bleeding in the bathroom. You will ruin every rug in the house."

Edith's room was the downstairs drawing room, brighter and softer than the library and North Room. This is where she received her guests by the Beauvais tapestry screen and rosewood desk. But even her room has a polar bear rug given by Arctic explorer Admiral Robert Peary.

The six children also left their marks in Sagamore Hill, but their legacy is relegated to the second floor with its nursery, bedrooms, and red bathroom. A resident in the nursery is an original teddy bear, dreamed up by a shrewd toy maker after TR refused to shoot an old bear in Mississippi that was brought and placed before him for his hunting pleasure. Cartoonist Clifford Berryman immortalized the event in ink and before long, the teddy bear, an American institution, was born.

The president himself was born in a narrow Manhattan brownstone at 28 East 20th Street near Gramercy Park. The original house was razed in 1916, but three years later, a private group bought the property and reconstructed the birthplace. It is now a National Park Service site.

About 40% of the furnishings inside are original pieces; another 20% came from other Roosevelt family members. An adjoining building, on the lot where Teddy's Uncle Robert lived, is a museum that through personal belongings, photos, and political cartoons tells Theodore Roosevelt's story.

And what a story! Known as Teedie to his family, the sick and frail child was so weak he couldn't even attend school. Some of his earliest memories were of his father carrying him in his arms trying to help him breathe.

As a young boy, Teedie became an avid reader, craving books on nature and history and dreaming of the open outdoors. He chose a hobby, taxidermy, that a housebound boy could enjoy, and he called his collection of trophies the Roosevelt Museum of Natural History.

All along he had been gradually improving his physical condition inspired by the words of his father, "You have the mind but you haven't got the body. To do all you can with your mind, you must make your body match it." So Teedie began to work out regularly in a gymnasium his father had installed in the house's back piazza. When Roosevelt was born, his birthplace was on a quiet residential street, hard to believe when you pass in front of the house today. But upon entering, the noise of the city is locked outside and the world of Teedie Roosevelt, the child, surrounds you.

The black horsehair chairs that he recalled scratching his young legs sit around the dining room table. Young people touring the house can relate to such childhood annoyances, but adults are more interested in the furniture style, characterized by guide Kathryn Gross as "modified Gothic Revival." The china rose pattern prompted her to tell us the direct translation of the family name: "field of roses."

National Park Service photo by Richard Frear

It's hard to escape TR's love for the wild and rugged in Sagamore Hill's North Room.

Since the dining room runs the width of the house it affords visitors some perspective on its narrow frame. In 19th-century New York City, there were rows and rows of similar brownstones, and in most, as here, the parlor was the most elegant room.

This one is decorated in blue in the then-fashionable Rococo Revival style, and the ceiling sports a glass chandelier. Later in life, the president recalled that he once absconded with a glass prism that had fallen from the chandelier; perhaps, suggested Kathryn Gross, the nearsighted boy was mesmerized by the colors of the rainbow reflecting off it.

Theodore came into this world in the master bedroom one flight up. The rosewood and satinwood bedroom set is original and was purchased by the Roosevelt family in the 1850s for the exorbitant price of $3,000. Next to it is the nursery with its crib, sleigh bed, rockers, and a tiny chair used by Teedie to sit in front of the fireplace. Who would know that years later he would sit in a much bigger chair in the Oval Office?

Theodore Roosevelt actually became President of the United States at 2:15 A.M. on September 14, 1901, while he was on a train in the Adirondacks. President William McKinley died at that moment from wounds caused by an assassin's gun a week earlier in Buffalo.

Roosevelt took a train to Buffalo, and as soon as he arrived that afternoon, he was driven to the home of friend and philanthropist Ansley

Wilcox, where most of McKinley's cabinet waited. At the pie-crust table in the library of the Wilcox mansion, Theodore Roosevelt, dressed in borrowed clothing, was sworn in as President by Federal Judge John Hazel.

The library is preserved in the Wilcox home today, looking as it did on September 14, 1901. A transparent window wall permits a full view into the room. The filled bookcases, chandeliers, gas lamp, and Windsor rocker are all original, and the pie-crust table still stands in its loneliness.

To learn more about this day of destiny, step inside the parlor, now a small museum devoted to the assassination of McKinley and the inauguration of Roosevelt. The exhibits range from the grisly to the warm; there is the handkerchief McKinley assassin Leon Czolgosz used to cover up his handgun and samples of teddy bears sold by Sears & Roebuck during Roosevelt's administration.

Theodore Roosevelt is buried in Youngs Memorial Cemetery near his home and place of death, Sagamore Hill, in Oyster Bay.

Location: Sagamore Hill National Historic Site is on Cove Neck Road in Oyster Bay. From the Long Island Expressway (Interstate 495), take exit 41 to Route 106 north into Oyster Bay. Turn right at the third traffic light onto East Main Street, and about three miles east of town, turn left onto Cove Neck Road to the house. **Admission** is charged. **Hours:** Summer and early fall, daily; rest of year, Tuesday through Sunday. **Allow** an hour and a half to tour the home and walk the grounds. **Information:** Sagamore Hill National Historic Site, Cove Neck Road, Box 304, Oyster Bay, NY 11771; (516) 922-4447.

Note: An audio cassette guide to Sagamore Hill can be rented in the gift shop near the parking lot. We highly recommend it. The tape lasts about 40 minutes and consists of a room to room house tour by Theodore Roosevelt's daughter Ethel Roosevelt Derby. It provides fascinating insights and information you won't receive by just walking through the house on your own. There are no guided tours except for large organizations. If you have visited Sagamore Hill in the past, you will immediately notice that the home, once yellow and red, is now grey. According to former site Superintendent Loretta L. Schmidt, this accurately represents the house's color when Roosevelt was president.

If you are staying overnight: Howard Johnson's Motor Lodge, 270 West Jericho Turnpike (Route 25), Huntington Station, (516) 421-3900; Howard Johnson's Motor Lodge, 450 Moreland Avenue (Long Island Expressway, exit 54), Commack, (516) 864-8820; Holiday Inn, 215 Sunnyside Boulevard (Long Island Expressway, exit 46), Plainview, (516) 349-7400. Note that lodging is extremely expensive on Long Island. It is very difficult to find a double room priced less than $80 per night. If you are en route to another location, consider staying elsewhere.

Location: Theodore Roosevelt Birthplace National Historic Site is at 28 East 20th Street near Gramercy Park in Manhattan. The closest subway stop via the IRT and BMT is at 23rd and 14th Streets. **Admission** is charged. **Hours:** Year round, Wednesday through Sunday. **Allow** an hour to take the guided tour and see the museum. **Information:** Theodore Roosevelt Birthplace National Historic Site, 28 East 20th Street, New York, NY 10003; (212) 260-1616.

Events: Music concerts, Saturday afternoons throughout the year.

Note: A brochure, "Following Teddy's Footsteps," detailing a self-guided walking tour through the historic Gramercy Park area is available. The birthplace also maintains an excellent library of films and videotapes about Theodore Roosevelt and will show them on request.

If you are staying overnight: Get information on conventional lodging and tour packages from the New York Convention and Visitors' Bureau, Inc., 2 Columbus Circle, New York, NY 10019; (212) 397-8222. For information on alternative lodging, contact City Lights Bed & Breakfast, Ltd., P.O. Box 20355, Cherokee Station, New York, NY 10028; (212) 737-7049. Another bed and breakfast service is Urban Ventures, P.O. Box 426, New York, NY 10024; (212) 594-5650.

Location: Theodore Roosevelt Inaugural National Historic Site is at 641 Delaware Avenue in Buffalo. From Interstate 90 (New York State Thruway), take Route 33 (Kensington Expressway) to Route 198 (Scajaquada Expressway); take the Delaware Avenue exit and head south to the site, on the left. **Admission** is charged. **Hours:** April through December, Monday through Friday and Saturday and Sunday afternoons; January through March, closed Sunday. **Allow** 45 minutes to an hour. **Information:** Theodore Roosevelt Inaugural National Historic Site, 641 Delaware Avenue, Buffalo, NY 14202; (716) 884-0330 or (716) 884-0095.

Note: A parking lot for visitors is in the back of the site on Franklin Street, across from 547 Franklin.

If you are staying overnight: Best Western Inn–Downtown, 510 Delaware Avenue, (716) 886-8333; Holiday Inn–Downtown, 620 Delaware Avenue, (716) 886-2121; Buffalo Exit 53 Motor Lodge, 475 Dingens Street (Thruway exit 53 to South Ogden Street to Dingens), (716) 896-2800; Holiday Inn, Rossler and Dingens Streets (Thruway exit 53 to South Ogden Street to Dingens), Cheektowaga, (716) 896-2900.

MARTIN VAN BUREN

He was called the Red Fox—Martin Van Buren, eighth president of the United States.

T HE PACKAGING OF CANDIDATES AND SELLING OF THEIR IMAGES IS nothing new. It predates television, predates radio, predates the age of the professional politico, and predates the era of mass journalism.

In 1840, President Martin Van Buren, native of Kinderhook, New York, ran for a second term against the contrived but, for that age, very slick campaign of Whig challenger William Henry Harrison.

Harrison was portrayed by the Whigs as a man of the people, born in a log cabin and a drinker of hard cider. They cursed Van Buren as a high-living, champagne-drinking aristocrat. In 1840, the country was suffering through its first significant depression, and Van Buren was accused of living in the lap of luxury while the common man suffered.

In truth, Harrison was the scion of prosperous Virginia family; an ancestor signed the Declaration of Independence. Harrison was born at Berkeley, a grand Virginia plantation, and, at the time of the campaign, was living very much at ease on a comfortable Ohio farm.

It was true that Van Buren enjoyed a sip of champagne and had his share of the good life. But he came from a basic background, the son of a Kinderhook tavern keeper who supplemented his income as a farmer. And Van Buren was a true Jacksonian Democrat; he was, in fact, Andrew Jackson's hand-picked successor.

Van Buren lost the election overwhelmingly and went down in history as a one-term failure. After he died in 1862, he became an obscure figure. His home, Lindenwald, had no historic significance; it was just another home in the upper Hudson Valley.

The 20th century has been kinder to Martin Van Buren. The 1982 presidential rating survey of nearly 1,000 historians conducted by Pennsylvania State University Professor Robert Murray rated Van Buren 20th among 37 presidents, in the middle of the "average" category. Many historians agree that the depression was something he inherited rather than caused. He was an easy scapegoat.

Even so, it wasn't until 1987 that Lindenwald was open to the public on a full-time basis. A National Park System property, Martin Van Buren National Historic Site is the place to hear more about the 1840 campaign, learn what we know that 19th-century people didn't, and see one of the Hudson Valley's most eclectic, eye-pleasing early homes.

"Lindenwald," said Ranger Lee Ann Merrill, "was to be Martin Van Buren's retirement home. But retirement came earlier than expected."

In 1839, he picked out the neglected Georgian home built in 1797 on land that had belonged to a distant relative several generations back. To Van Buren, purchasing it symbolized a restoration of family holdings, and soon after the deal was closed, he began massive alterations to make it his retirement estate. It is thought he had hopes of turning Lindenwald into another Mount Vernon or Monticello.

One of the first actions was to demolish an entrance hall stairway and turn the hall into a large room for dining and entertaining. Van Buren wallpapered it with a French hunting scene, *Landscape of the Hunt;* the original paper still hangs on the room's long walls. On its short walls are accurate reproductions of the paper, which allow you to see what the colors looked like when Van Buren was master of the house.

Alterations took place over several years, but the most radical were orchestrated by the president's youngest son, Smith Thompson Van Buren, who moved to Lindenwald at his father's suggestion. Smith hired architect Richard Upjohn, designer of Manhattan's Trinity Church, to do the work.

While the former president had told his son he could change the home to accommodate his tastes, Van Buren was leery about the scope of them. Still, he kept a sense of humor about it and said, "The idea of seeing in life, the changes which my heir would be sure to make after I am gone, amuses me."

By the time all was complete, the house little resembled the simple Georgian home Van Buren had purchased and became the merry mix of Renaissance, Italianate, Romanesque, and Gothic Revival styles you see today. It also was one of the most modern houses in its time.

Van Buren's then brand new coal burning kitchen stove is still there. (Slaving **over** a hot stove was a literal thing; the stove is small.) So are the flush toilet, with its Wedgewood porcelain bowl, and Van Buren's most boastful modern touch, the zinc-lined bathtub.

Lindenwald was also one of the first homes to be equipped with running water. If you ever visit Calvin Coolidge's boyhood home in Vermont, you will see the crude two-hole wooden privy, used until the early 1930s. Keep in mind that Van Buren's plumbing was installed in the 1840s.

To maintain Van Buren's "simple, elegant lifestyle," extra help in the form of servants was needed. Van Buren had four—a cook, parlor maid, waitress, and laundress, all Irish women. Van Buren appreciated their work and treated them well—for the time.

They were given only a half day off a week, a work schedule more reflective of the period than Van Buren's attitudes. They lived in wall-papered rooms and ate meals off British Amoy china, similar to Dutch Delft, in their own sitting room, very plush for servants in the 1840s.

The additions to Lindenwald gave the servants a huge house to care for, 36 rooms in all. From the outside, the most noticeable feature is the four-and-a-half-story-high tower, purely ornamental. It's the magnet that initially draws visitors' eyes when they first set foot on the grounds.

The library was anything but ornamental. It was a room blessed with wonderful natural lighting and the view enabled the president to watch his children play on the estate lawn. Political cartoons deck the library walls as they did when Van Buren lived here. One depicts Van Buren as a red fox losing his tail as he is about to go down in political defeat; he was given the crafty nickname for his fluffy red sideburns. He was also called "The Little Magician," in honor of his ability to maneuver politically or, in the eyes of political enemies, be conveniently non-committal.

When not playing politics, Van Buren was commonly playing cards. A favorite game was whist, a forerunner of bridge, and the parlor card table is set up for it. Looking down on the table are photographic reproductions of Thomas Jefferson and Andrew Jackson, statesmen that Van Buren greatly admired.

Upstairs, several rooms are sparsely decorated for lack of authentic items. However, Van Buren's bedroom where he died at age 79 is filled with original possessions, including his sleigh bed, toilet set, and shaving bowl. His last few years were unhappy. The first president born under the American flag, he died in 1862, disheartened by the onset of the Civil War.

Martin Van Buren is buried in Kinderhook Cemetery on Albany Avenue (Route 21) in Kinderhook.

Location: Martin Van Buren National Historic Site is on Old Post Road, just off Route 9, southeast of the town of Kinderhook. **Admission** is charged. **Hours:** Mid-April through mid-October, daily; late March through mid-April and mid-October through early December, Wednesday through Sunday. **Allow** 45 minutes to an hour for the guided tour. Allow an extra half hour if you wish to walk the grounds. **Information:** Martin Van Buren National Historic Site, P.O. Box 545, Kinderhook, NY 12106; (518) 758-9689.

Events: June, Columbia County Coaching Society carriage show, 19th-century carriages and drivers in performances and on show; mid-summer, picnic, afternoon band concert in period clothing playing mid-19th century music; August, nature walk, naturalist leads walk on Lindenwald grounds.

Note: Parking is available on Old Post Road in front of the mansion. Each tour is limited to 15 people.

If you are staying overnight: Howard Johnson's Motor Lodge, Route 32 (off Thruway exit 20), Saugerties, (914) 246-9511; Carl's Rip Van Winkle Motor Lodge, Route 23B (off Thruway exit 21), Catskill, (914) 943-3303; Catskill Motor Lodge, Route 23B (off Thruway exit 21), Catskill, (914) 943-5800.

MILLARD FILLMORE

Millard Fillmore. Queen Victoria reportedly called him "the most handsome man in the world."

EVEN MILLARD FILLMORE SEEMED TO KNOW HIS NAME WAS DESTINED to be the target of mockery and ridicule.

When he visited England in 1855, Fillmore declined an offer of an honorary degree from Oxford University. Said he, "They would probably ask, 'Who's Fillmore? What's he done? Where did he come from?' And then my name would, I fear, give them an excellent opportunity to make jokes at my expense."

Among all of the 39 chief executives, none—not Franklin Pierce—not Benjamin Harrison—not Chester A. Arthur—has suffered the pointed barbs and cruel ribbing tossed at Millard Fillmore.

Fact: The Students Committee for the Glorification of Millard Fillmore was founded in 1965. Its actual intent, however, is to vilify, not glorify, Millard Fillmore. After the committee's convincing, former Maryland Governor Marvin Mandel issued a proclamation declaring Fillmore's birthday, January 7, Millard Fillmore Day in Maryland.

Fact: Another group, the Millard Fillmore Society, brought their campaign to bring "respectability" to the name of Millard Fillmore to the general public by appearing on "The Tonight Show" with Johnny Carson.

Fact: One newspaper columnist once said that Fillmore's most noteworthy accomplishment was being the only president ever to visit Elmira, New York. Others have stated that the high point in the Fillmore administration was the installation of the White House's first bathtub.

You can meet this much maligned man on a trip upstate and judge for yourself whether his impact on history deserves to be so derided.

Nobody who ever saw Millard Fillmore in his prime would have taken him for a loser. He was a tall and handsome man, with blue eyes and a light complexion, and it was reported that Queen Victoria called him "the most handsome man in the world." His character was mellow. He was rarely known to lose his temper and seemed to have the perfect temperament for a statesman.

But Fillmore, like John Tyler before him, was an accidental president. He was elected as vice president on the Whig ticket and ascended to the top office after the death of President Zachary Taylor in 1850. Fillmore was later denied his party's nomination for the 1852 presidential election and he stands as one of just five United States presidents never elected to the office.

Aside from a presidential visit to Elmira and the first White House bathtub, what is the Fillmore administration really known for?

Just months after taking office on July 10, 1850, Fillmore signed the Fugitive Slave Law as part of the Compromise of 1850. The law dictated that runaway slaves found in free states were still the property of their southern owners, and federal officials were responsible for recovering them. Though there were measures in the compromise that favored free states, the Fugitive Slave Law caused Northerners to dislike Fillmore almost from the start.

The Whig party weakened and crumbled during the mid-1850s, but instead of joining the ranks of the growing anti-slavery Republican party,

Fillmore ran for president in 1856 on the ticket of the American Party, also called the Know-Nothing Party, which developed as an anti-immigrant, anti-Catholic party.

Most historians say Fillmore didn't necessarily harbor nativist views but was more of an opportunist, using the third party as a vehicle for entering the 1856 campaign. But Fillmore finished a poor third in the general election, winning only one state, Maryland.

Fillmore lived 21 years after his term ended, speaking often on issues of the day, a favorite topic being the prevention of cruelty to animals; he even helped found a local chapter of the Society for Prevention of Cruelty to Animals. But according to several historians, his words were rarely noticed outside Buffalo. He died on March 8, 1874.

Sadly, none of Fillmore's Buffalo homes survive. But the first house he ever owned, a little Greek Revival cottage in suburban East Aurora still stands and has been restored to its 19th-century appearance. It is in this home that you hear another side to the story of Millard Fillmore.

The staff of the Millard Fillmore House will tell you that the Compromise of 1850 was a positive action. Muriel Case, our tour guide, pointed out that it delayed the start of the Civil War for ten years, allowing the North a decade of growth in which they became better prepared, militarily and economically.

Step inside the home and you enter the world of Fillmore as a newly married young lawyer. Millard built it for his bride, the former Abigail Powers, at age 26 in 1826, when his life was full of promise. The primitive desk and volumes of law books in the tiny cubbyhole he used as an office symbolize the struggling early days of his career.

The meager financial situation of one just starting out is brought to mind as you climb the steep and narrow staircase to the second floor bedroom. Some of the future president's white linen shirts are displayed on the bed, while adjacent to the bedroom in these tight quarters is a child's cozy playroom where it is thought Fillmore's son, Millard Powers Fillmore, was born.

You can judge for yourself if Queen Victoria was right when you enter the kitchen and see on the wall a sketch of dark and wavy-haired Millard, drawn when he was in his twenties. Next to his is a sketch of Abigail, with brown, curly ringlets dangling under a mop hat. The two young marrieds complement each other.

The wooden scrub-top table in the kitchen is one the Fillmores owned and Millard probably made. Should you be here at the right time you can sample goodies made in the Fillmore kitchen fireplace. Costumed guides are often baking delectables like cookies and bread, and a group of school children was once treated to a turkey feast, offered right from the authentically reproduced reflector oven.

The paintings on the wall give a clue to the identity of the master of this house.

You can examine the herb garden after leaving the house, but to study the roots of Millard Fillmore, you have to journey to the village of Moravia in the Finger Lakes region.

About five miles from the actual birth site of the 13th president—marked by a commemorative plaque—is Fillmore Glen State Park. Just past the entrance is a log cabin built in 1965 to represent the one in which Fillmore was born.

Fillmore was the son of a dirt-poor frontier farmer, and the cabin is emblematic of the luck and pluck that is the core of the American dream. Through determination and hard work, Fillmore rose from a log cabin to the White House. Step inside and you can shudder at the thought of raising a child is such sparse surroundings. The wooden box-like bed is reproduced, but other items like the crude chairs and tables are authentic to the period.

Fillmore is buried in Buffalo's Forest Lawn, a park-like cemetery that attracts its share of bird-watchers, joggers, and fall foliage seekers. A granite obelisk marks the site of the graves of Fillmore and his family, although his own grave is noted with nothing but a small stone bearing only his initials.

Location: To reach the Millard Fillmore House from Interstate 90, take Route 400 (Aurora Expressway) to the Maple Street exit; follow

Maple until the intersection with Main Street; turn right onto Main and take the next right onto Shearer Avenue. The Fillmore House is the second on the right at 24 Shearer. **Admission** is charged. **Hours:** June through mid-October, Wednesday, Saturday, and Sunday afternoons. **Allow** 45 minutes for the tour. **Information:** East Aurora Historical Society, 24 Shearer Avenue, East Aurora, NY 14052; (716) 652-0167 or (716) 652-4228.

If you are staying overnight: Open Gate Motel, 7270 Seneca Street (Route 16), Elma, (716) 652-9897; Transit Manor Motor Inn, 2831 Transit Road (north of Route 400 on Routes 20 and 78), Elma, (716) 674-7070; Roycroft Inn, 40 South Grove Street, East Aurora, (716) 652-9030.

Location: Millard Fillmore Birthplace is in Fillmore Glen State Park on Route 38, a mile south of the village of Moravia. **Admission** is charged to enter the state park but is free to the cabin. **Hours:** Warm weather months, daily. **Allow** 10 minutes. **Information:** Fillmore Glen State Park, RD3, Moravia, NY 13118; (315) 497-0130.

Note: Fillmore Glen State Park is beautiful and offers full park facilities such as camping, swimming, picnicking, hiking, and fishing, in addition to cross-country skiing in winter. Highlights are gorge walking trails that cross the stream on eight bridges.

If you are staying overnight: Camping in Fillmore Glen State Park is available mid-May to mid-October (see address and phone above); Econo-Lodge, Route 11 (off Interstate 81, exit 10), McGraw, (607) 753-7594; Lester's Motel, Route 11 (off Interstate 81, exit 10), Cortland, (607) 756-5476; Benn Conger Inn, 206 West Cortland Street (off Route 222), Groton, (607) 898-5817.

Location: Forest Lawn Cemetery is at the corner of Delaware and Delavan Avenues. Take Interstate 90 to Route 38 to Route 198. Take the Delaware Avenue exit off Route 198 and follow south. **Admission** is free. **Hours:** Year round, daily. **Information:** Forest Lawn Cemetery, 1411 Delaware Avenue, Buffalo, NY 14209; (716) 885-1600.

WASHINGTON IRVING

Courtesy: Historic Hudson Valley

Author, diplomat, and "the Bill Cosby of his day": Washington Irving.

"HE WAS THE BILL COSBY OF HIS DAY," SAID GERI HEISSER, SITE manager of Sunnyside, Washington Irving's gabled riverside home in Tarrytown.

"By the time he moved here, he was a well-known celebrity," continued Heisser. "He was 52, famous, and respected as much in Europe as here. The United States was not respected for literature until Washington Irving came along."

Irving first became known in 1809 when he published his satirical *History of New York*, for which he created his well-known character Diedrich Knickerbocker.

Short stories like the legendary "Rip Van Winkle" and "The Legend of Sleepy Hollow" followed. Then there were also sizable serious volumes like *The Life of Columbus;* there also had been years of public service as a diplomat at American posts in Madrid and London.

Although Irving's career was firmly established when he bought Sunnyside, his dream home was not; it was just a small stone cottage when he bought it in 1835. Irving added Dutch stepped gables, weather vanes, and various Gothic and Romanesque architectural features.

He later referred to his finished home in this manner: "a little old-fashioned stone mansion all made up of gable ends and as full of angles and corners as an old cocked hat."

There was one consideration Irving didn't take into account when he bought the house in 1835, the growing railroad industry. But how could he have ever known that track would be laid on the land between his home and the Hudson River?

Said Irving later in a Cosbyesque piece of cynicism, "If there was a Garden of Eden on the earth today, a train would run right through it."

The railroad is still there. Commuting suburbanites roll past Sunnyside daily on their way to and from fashionable Westchester County homes and midtown Manhattan offices.

If Irving were alive today, he would likely be taking the same train, since Sunnyside was as modern and innovative for his time as solar and modular homes are for late 20th-century residents. In the Sunnyside kitchen is a cast iron cooking stove, a brand new convenience in 1850's America, when the open hearth was still the rule for most homes.

Irving's pantry has a wooden drying rack, one of the first kitchen area space savers. Other modern marvels of Irving's day included a chest lined with zinc, sort of an ancestor of the icebox, and a bathtub—when even the White House couldn't claim one. But the most progressive of all Sunnyside's innovations was the hot water boiler and running water fed from the Sunnyside pond (which Irving called "The Little Mediterranean") through a gravity flow system.

After the kitchen and pantry, most visitors like Irving's study best. It's a snug little 19th-century work place loaded with books; ironically, it is in this room that you hear that Irving was not a good student. He hated school, but he liked the arts and loved having good times.

The study is the best-documented room in Sunnyside, since many artists who visited Irving here kept a visual record of it. His desk was a gift from his publisher, George P. Putnam, and a common first reaction from visitors is that the drawers are on the wrong side. Actually, the

Washington Irving's Sunnyside was one of the country's most modern homes for its time.

drawers that face you are fake; real drawers are on the side you can't see. In the rear of the study is the red divan where Irving often slept.

Irving never married, but he didn't live alone. Nieces Catherine and Sarah Irving resided with him, acting as hostesses, and were commonly found playing the mahogany piano in the parlor, the author accompanying them on flute. Much of Catherine and Sarah's original music can be found in the parlor, which abounds in Federal-style furniture.

One or the other niece often stayed in an upstairs bedroom with the work tables and serving equipment that signified a 19th-century ladies' room. The bed is adorned with frilly, feminine handmade bobbin lace hangings.

Irving opened his home to another family member, his brother Ebenezer, who stayed in the bedroom next to the nieces. It's a pallid, little room reflecting Ebenezer's conservative tastes.

On the other hand, the author's bedroom tells of a colorful extrovert. While Ebenezer was sleeping on a plain rope mattress, his more famous brother, when not asleep in his study, rested his weary bones on a lofty Sheraton tester bed with a bold and bright Jacquard double-leaf coverlet; the Jacquard loom had been developed in France and created patterns far more intricate than those previously crafted.

Irving's personal possessions or period pieces representing them are in this room: a walking stick, top hat, paisley shawl he used as a bathrobe, and bedside writing table supporting a pillbox.

On another table is an engraved likeness that haunted him until death. Though he never married, Irving had been engaged to Matilda Hoffman, daughter of onetime attorney general Josiah Hoffman, with whom Irving studied. Matilda died of tuberculosis before they could be married, and Irving kept her engraving next to his bed throughout his life; it was here when Irving died in 1859.

Outside is the fenced-in area called the kitchen yard where servants did laundry, chopped wood, and worked at other tedious jobs. Adjacent to it are the root cellar and wood shed, and nearby is the ice house, reconstruction based on a drawing done by a turn-of-the-century Tarrytown schoolgirl.

Walking paths crisscross the property—24 acres worth—and in nice weather an outdoor jaunt is a must. The River Path offers extraordinary views of the Hudson.

Location: Sunnyside is west of Route 9 of West Sunnyside Lane, one mile south of the Tappan Zee Bridge and one mile south of Interstate 87, exit 9. **Admission** is charged. **Hours:** April through November, daily; December through March, Wednesday through Monday. **Allow** 45 minutes for the tour; plan to spend a few hours if you wish to walk the grounds. **Information:** Historic Hudson Valley, 150 White Plains Road, Tarrytown, NY 10591; (914) 631-8200.

Events: Early February, Winter Weekend, early cooking, winter recreation; mid-October, Appletime at Sleepy Hollow, orchard visits, cooking authentic old apple recipes; late October, Legend of Sleepy Hollow Weekend, puppets, story tellers; Thanksgiving at Sunnyside; late December, candlelight tours.

Note: Buy admission tickets in the reception center before you reach the house. Discounted combination tickets for Sunnyside, Van Cortlandt Manor, and Philipsburg Manor, Upper Mills, are available. A picnic area is provided on the Sunnyside grounds.

If you are staying overnight: Westchester Marriott Hotel, 670 White Plains Road (Route 119, just west of Interstate 287, exit 1), Tarrytown, (914) 631-2200; Howard Johnson's Motor Lodge, 290 Tarrytown Road (Route 119, off Interstate 287, exit 4), Elmsford, (914) 592-8000; Holiday Inn, Tarrytown Road (Route 119, take Interstate 287, exit 1, or Interstate 87, exit 8), Elmsford, (914) 592-5680; County Center Motel, 20 County Center Road (Routes 100 and 119), White Plains, (914) 948-2400.

WILLIAM SEWARD

William Seward. The Republicans didn't nominate him for president in 1860, opting instead for Abraham Lincoln. They feared Seward would get the country into a civil war.

T HE BANKS AND SCHOOLS ARE CLOSED IN ALASKA EVERY YEAR ON THE last Monday in March in honor of William Seward, a New York native, who negotiated the purchase of Alaska from Russia in 1867.

Seward is as much of a hero to Alaska as George Washington is to the United States as a whole, and it is not unusual to find his home the target of many tourists from Alaska who travel 6,000 miles to see where the diminutive statesman slept, worked, and relaxed.

But Seward's accomplishments transcend the 49th state. In fact, he came very close to being nominated in 1860 for the Republican candidacy for president of the United States, only to lose the nomination to Abraham Lincoln.

"Seward thought he would win," offered our guide, curator Betty Lewis, "but the delegates at the Republican convention thought he was too radical and would get the Union into a war."

Prior to his bid for the presidency, Seward had won several elections, serving as state senator, governor, and United States senator from New York, while espousing rigid anti-slavery views. So it wasn't surprising that Lincoln selected him to be his secretary of state, a position he held through the term of Lincoln's successor, Andrew Johnson. It was during Johnson's presidency that Seward negotiated the purchase of Alaska.

The event occurred early on an Alaskan morning when, by gaslight, Seward and Russian minister Edward Stoeckl signed the treaty turning "Russian America" over to the United States. The event was immortalized in oil by Emanuel Leutze, the artist best known for *Washington Crossing the Delaware,* and today *The Signing of the Alaska Treaty* dominates the second floor stairwell of Seward's home, called the diplomatic gallery.

The gallery comprises Seward's collection of 132 prints and photographs of world leaders he met on diplomatic missions across the globe. As much as it is a who's who of mid-19th-century rulers, it is also a mosaic of humanity.

The colors and creeds of the world are showcased, each handsomely presented, orderly and unobtrusively. There is General Giuseppe Garibaldi of Italy, bearded and in native costume. Nearby is Benito Juarez, president of Mexico, looking forceful and determined. Side by side are the black leaders of Liberia, Stephen A. Benson and J.J. Roberts. Then there is the King of Siam, the same one immortalized in *The King and I,* appearing much unlike Yul Brynner.

Bearded Russian Edward Stoeckl, with whom Seward shook hands and traded Alaska for $7.2 million, is pictured, as is Seward's second boss, Andrew Johnson. Seward himself appears on this wall of fame, too, but likenesses of Seward also abound throughout the home. Most impressive might be the bust of Seward created by Daniel Chester French, best known for sculpting *Seated Lincoln* in Washington's Lincoln Memorial.

It is said that while leading one of his guests past the gallery, Seward once mentioned that many of the monarchs and elected officials pictured there had "passed from office or from earth in the brief period of eight years."

His guest answered, "It is a sermon on the instability of human greatness."

To which Seward replied, "Perhaps so. I can only hope that they all enjoyed the prospect of getting out of office as much as I do."

Seward's tenure as secretary of state was one of tragedy, caused indirectly by the war nobody wanted but which couldn't be avoided.

While John Wilkes Booth was shooting Abraham Lincoln in Ford's Theater, as revenge for the defeat of the South, a hulking half-wit of a man and compatriot of Booth's named Lewis Paine made an attempt on Seward's life. Seward was bedridden after suffering injuries in a carriage accident nine days earlier. Paine identified himself as a delivery boy bringing medicine to the secretary of state.

Seward's son Frederick answered the door and was promptly clubbed on the head by a gun Paine held in his hand. Paine then stabbed three people, including another son, Augustus, before reaching Seward and stabbing him repeatedly in the face and throat.

Paine was later captured and hanged along with three others found guilty in the conspiracy. Seward survived, thanks mainly to a steel and leather brace supporting his jaw from the earlier carriage accident. But the shock of this assassination attempt was too much for Seward's sickly wife, who died just two months later. One year later, his daughter died. Seward's spirit was broken, and he died in 1872.

Mementoes of his career stock the floors, halls, and walls of the handsome house. Since it was never sold out of the Seward family, most of the 15 rooms open to the public are filled with Seward's original possessions just as he had them.

There is a somewhat grisly display of the sheet on which Seward lay when he was attacked by Paine. There is also a military uniform he wore, looking as if it were custom-made for an adolescent but a perfect fit for the 5'4" slightly-built Seward. Also displayed are original letters written by Lincoln to his secretary of state.

The most eye-opening displays are the treasures Seward brought back from his diplomatic journeys to far-off places or collected from foreign guests visiting Washington. In a dining room cabinet is a cobalt-tinted 60-place set of china, a gift of Prince Napolean Joseph Charles Paul Bonaparte, the French emperor's nephew. On the buffet in the same room is a copper Russian samovar. Also ornamenting the room are an alabaster Buddah from Siam and a pair of porcelain garden seats from China.

Most of the room is decorated as was fashionable in early Victorian times when Seward was in his prime. The North Library is typically dark and heavy, but the drawing room, added in 1870, is lighter and airier; favorite pieces there include the Oriental carpet from Turkey and the family portraits. The basement kitchen, however, is a throwback to the house's initial construction date of 1816. It is colonial in appearance with a beehive oven, Sheraton bamboo chairs, and an oversized child's cradle that, when turned over, becomes a bench.

But no matter where you turn, you can't walk more than a few feet without encountering reminders of Alaska. You will see an Alaskan kayak not far from rare armor worn by Alaskan Indians. The biggest oddity is a product of more modern times: a 49-star flag, produced after Alaska was admitted into the union but before Hawaii achieved statehood. There were 49 states for such a short period of time (only eight months) that few 49-star flags were made. This one hangs upstairs and once flew over the United States Capitol.

Seward purchased Alaska with the country's national defense in mind, but immediate reaction to his deal was ridicule and mockery. Americans laughed at the place they called "Seward's Folly" and "Seward's Icebox." Yet although Seward knew he was onto something big, even he couldn't have foreseen the riches in gold, oil, furs, and fish we have reaped from the 49th state.

Location: The William Seward House is at 33 South Street in the center of Auburn, near City Hall. From the New York State Thruway (Interstate 90), take exit 40 onto Route 34, which becomes South Street in Auburn. **Admission** is charged. **Hours:** April through December, Tuesday through Saturday afternoon. **Allow** at least an hour for the tour. **Information:** William Seward House, 33 South Street, Auburn, NY 13021; (315) 252-1283.

If you are staying overnight: Holiday Inn, 75 North Street (Route 34), Auburn, (315) 253-4531; Sleepy Hollow Motel, Route 20 (east of town), Auburn, (315) 253-3281; Grant Motel, 255 Grant Street (Route 5, northeast of town), Auburn, (315) 253-8447.

ELIZABETH CADY STANTON AND SUSAN B. ANTHONY

Courtesy: Women's Rights National Historic Park

Elizabeth Cady Stanton (left) and Susan B. Anthony. Stanton forged thunder-bolts and Anthony fired them.

THEY CALLED IT "THE OTHER DECLARATION OF INDEPENDENCE."

But this one contained demands most Americans found ludicrous. The most laughable stated that women be allowed to vote. The Declaration of Sentiments, as it was officially titled, stated that "all men and women are created equal," and it was signed by 100 men and women in the Wesleyan Chapel in Seneca Falls on July 20, 1848; soon it was the cornerstone of the crusade for women's rights. Today, Seneca Falls is regarded as the birthplace of the women's rights movement.

The woman who started the chain reaction that resulted in the Declaration of Sentiments was Elizabeth Cady Stanton, a transplant from Boston who was bored with life in this out-of-the-way milling town.

Nearly a quarter century later, Susan B. Anthony put Henry David Thoreau's principle of civil disobedience and Elizabeth Cady Stanton's philosophy into action and voted for the Republican candidate for president, Ulysses S. Grant. She was promplty arrested.

The homes of both women are open to the public today, Stanton's in Seneca Falls and Anthony's in Rochester.

Stanton's home is part of one of the country's newest national parks, Women's Rights National Historic Park. Visitors, however, should not expect to see heirlooms, rare antiques, or even Stanton's household items; the main attraction is the story of the woman who lived here, the story of a radical whose then far-fetched ideas are part of today's routine life.

Stanton believed in equal education for both boys and girls, including physical education for girls and sewing and knitting for boys. She believed wages earned by a woman should be hers to keep; in 1848 all women's wages went to their husbands. And she believed women should be given the right to vote.

In most American communities, she would have been dismissed as a kook, an extremist. But Seneca Falls in the 1840s was different. There was a spirit of reform going on, due in part to an economy changing from agriculture to manufacturing and an influx of transient radicals and idealists sailing the Erie Canal on their ways west, making this mill town a perfect platform for Stanton's ideas.

She and other like-minded women decided to call a convention to discuss women's rights. Shortly afterwards, the Declaration of Sentiments was drawn up and signed by 68 women and 32 men; some convention attendees withheld their signatures rather than approve a document so extreme as to demand that women be allowed to vote. The approval of the declaration is considered the beginning of the women's rights movement.

At Stanton's house you see both the frustrated firebrand of 1848 and the family woman who gave crowd-pleasing parties and cared for seven children. One of her sons is on record as saying, "There was never an empty seat in the house."

As we stood in the formal parlor, guide Kim Raia described Henry and Elizabeth Stanton as community entertainers and listed a who's who of progressives, abolitionists, and feminists who gathered here: William Seward, William Lloyd Garrison, Lucretia Mott, and Wendell Phillips, for starters.

With seven children—who garnered the reputation as neighborhood hellions—the Stanton household was filled with mischief and misadventures that today's network sitcom writers in their most creative moods couldn't imagine.

It was in the nursery upstairs where Raia told us about the time when the three oldest Stanton boys decided to strap baby brother Theodore to the chimney. Watchful neighbors informed the Stanton parents that their youngest son was on the roof.

Then the boys, curious to see if baby Theodore could float, took him to the Seneca River and tied him with ropes and corks. Result: Theodore did float, and since he was used to baths in big tubs, he had a marvelous time splashing around until rescued by his mother, who described him as being "as blue as indigo and cold as a frog."

When you tour the six-room house—a wing has been removed—you will wonder how Stanton managed to find the time and space to write, speak, organize rallies, and raise seven children. It is said she had a flagpole in the front yard that her neighbors recognized as kind of a combination semaphore and birth announcement. She would raise a red flag after giving birth to a boy and a white flag for a girl.

Stanton did not meet Susan B. Anthony, the more famous of the two women's rights advocate, until 1851. At the time of the first women's rights convention, Anthony was still in Rochester, heavily involved in the abolitionist movement.

The two women became friends and worked well together, once giving an impromptu speech while stuck on a ferry caught in an ice jam on the Mississippi River.

Stanton excelled at writing and Anthony's skills were in organizing and speaking. Elizabeth Cady Stanton, it was said, forged thunderbolts. And Susan B. Anthony fired them.

It's only natural that the most popular room in Anthony's home among today's visitors is the Victorian parlor, the room in which she was arrested after voting for president. Anthony's defense was that her right to vote was guaranteed by the new 14th and 15th Amendments.

The 14th Amendment, passed in 1868, read that "all persons born or naturalized in the United States . . . are citizens" and "no State shall make or enforce any law which shall abridge the privileges of immunities of citizens."

The 15th Amendment, added two years later, barred any state from withholding the right to vote from any citizen "on account of race, color, or previous condition of servitude."

You hear the story of Susan B. Anthony, her suffragist ideals and her fight for them, when you tour her brick Madison Street home. She had friends and enemies of both sexes, said guide Katherine Thompson, and it wasn't unusual for women to bemoan "the foolish notions of this old spinster" or men to befriend her; one was Henry Selden, a former New York judge, who defended her in court.

Anthony's first cause was not woman suffrage but temperance, and she championed it for 15 years. She was often at a disadvantage, though, because fellow supporters wouldn't allow women to speak. Once, Thompson told us, Anthony spoke for a half hour while a debate ensued whether or not she be allowed to speak. These experiences and her friendship with Stanton led to her involvement in the women's rights movement.

Stanton and Anthony's friendship is emblematized in the Anthony parlor by a duplicate of the table on which the Declaration of Sentiments was written, given by Elizabeth to Susan as an 80th-birthday present. She had gifts from other famous people, too, not the least of which was the lace collar given by Queen Victoria; a portrait of Anthony wearing it hangs in the parlor.

Anthony lived here 40 years, most of that time with her sister, Mary, and her mother. Unlike Elizabeth Cady Stanton, Susan Anthony never married; she had offers, Thompson said, but none appealed to her, and she didn't want the life of a housewife.

Thanks to grandnieces and other non-direct descendants, personal possessions of the Anthony sisters stock the home. Mary's bedroom still claims her bed, dresser, and washstand. Their mother's room, on the other hand, has been turned into a museum room with portraits of people involved in the women's rights movement; included are Elizabeth Cady Stanton, Lucretia Mott, Abigail Adams, Harriet Beecher Stowe, and the family of Mrs. Thomas N. Hepburn of Connecticut; young Katherine, who grew up to become a world famous actress, is there, too.

The aftermath of the trial? Susan B. Anthony was found guilty and fined $100 plus costs. Henry Selden appealed to both houses of Congress for remission of her fine but it was rejected. The three male inspectors who allowed her to vote were also found guilty and fined lesser amounts.

Anthony died in 1906, fourteen years before the 19th Amendment giving women the right to vote was ratified.

Location: The visitor center of Women's Rights National Historic Park is at 116 Fall Street in the center of Seneca Falls. From the New York State Thruway, take exit 41 onto Route 414 south to Routes 5 and 20 (Fall Street) in Seneca Falls. To reach the Stanton home from the visitor center, head south on Fall Street, then take a right onto Ovid Street and cross the bridge over the Seneca River; take an immediate left onto Bayard Street, then the second left onto Washington Street; the Stanton house is at 32 Washington Street. **Admission** is free. **Hours:** Stanton house: June through September, daily; rest of year, by appointment. Visitor Center: April through November, daily; rest of year, Monday through Friday. **Allow** an hour to 90 minutes to explore the visitor center and tour the Stanton home. **Information:** Women's Rights National Historic Park, P.O. Box 70, Seneca Falls, NY 13148; (315) 568-2991.

Events: Mid-July, Convention Days, boat tours of canals, bicycle tours, evening walking tours, speakers, reenactment of first women's rights convention; August 26, Women's Equality Day, speakers; November 12, Elizabeth Cady Stanton's birthday, tea with speaker, birthday cake.

Note: Although it is not necessary to visit the visitor center before touring the Stanton house, we strongly recommend you do so to familiarize yourself with the background of this underpublicized part of American history. In summer, free walking tours of the Seneca Falls historic district are offered. Keep in mind though that the park is relatively new and still developing; future plans are to open more important buildings to the public. In case you are curious, Superintendent Judy Hart says that in its first few years, the park drew mostly women but now draws as many male as female visitors. A related site is the National Women's Hall of Fame, 76 Fall Street, Seneca Falls, 13148, (315) 568-2936.

If you are staying overnight: Holiday Inn, Mound Road (Route 414, east of town), Waterloo, (315) 539-5011; Starlite Motel, 101 Auburn Road (Routes 5 and 20), Seneca Falls, (315) 568-6149; Locustwood Inn, 3563 Route 89, Seneca Falls, (315) 549-7132.

Location: To reach the Susan B. Anthony House from the west take Interstate 490 east to the Brown Street exit, follow Brown Street and after the overpass make a sharp left onto Silver; go one block, turn right into Madison Street and follow three blocks to the house. From the east take Interstate 490 west to the Broad Street exit, follow Broad, then turn left onto West Main and follow a half block; turn right onto Madison Street and follow for a half block. The house is at 17 Madison Street. **Admission** is charged. **Hours:** February through December, Wednesday through Saturday afternoons. **Allow** an hour to an hour and 15 minutes. **Information:** Susan B. Anthony House, 17 Madison Street, Rochester, NY 14608; (716) 235-6124.

Note: Parking is available along Madison Street.

If you are staying overnight: East Avenue Inn, 384 East Avenue, Rochester, (716) 325-5010; Red Roof Inn, Route 15 (at junction with Thruway exit 46), W. Henrietta, (716) 359-1100; Genesee Country Inn, 948 George Street, (716) 538-2500. For bed & breakfast accommodations contact Bed & Breakfast Rochester, P.O. Box 444, Fairport, NY 14450; (716) 223-8510.

GEORGE EASTMAN

Courtesy: International Museum of Photography at George Eastman House

George Eastman made taking pictures a household pastime.

IF YOU RECALL THE ADVERTISING SLOGAN, "YOU PRESS THE BUTTON, we do the rest," you are likely older than you care to admit. You're also familiar with "The Father of Amateur Photography," the man who made it possible for any person, no matter how clumsy with machinery, no matter how unskilled as an artist, to take family and vacation pictures with the ease of well . . . pushing a button.

Rochester's George Eastman did not invent the camera. Professionals had been using cameras years before Eastman first saw the light of day in 1858. But the key word is "professionals." The process of taking photographs was lengthy and awkward and involved massive equipment, fragile and cumbersome glass plates, and serious know-how. The average man in the street did not take photographs until Eastman developed his first Kodak camera in 1888.

Eastman's Rochester home, which contains the International Museum of Photography, is open to the public as a memorial, a showcase for the world's best photography and a tribute to his invention that made taking pictures a household pastime. Formal tours are limited to one or two a day, but docents are stationed in most rooms to tell you about Eastman and his 1905 Greek Revival house.

The photo galleries are primarily on the second floor but the main floor is the concern for most casual visitors. It's here that you learn of Eastman's lifestyle and life's work.

It was in the conservatory where we heard the story behind the naming of his company. "Kodak" is basically, a nonsense word. Eastman wanted a word for his company that could not be translated into any other language. He liked the letter K and arrived at the magic word as casually as brushing his teeth.

"In France, it's Kodak, in Russia, it's Kodak, in any language, it's Kodak," said the docent, acknowledging that Eastman got his wish.

Another docent volunteered that Eastman's fondness for the letter K stemmed from his closest female relatives, sister Kate and his mother, Marie Kilbourn Eastman. So he took the Ks from his sister's first and mother's maiden names and threw in the middle letters.

Eastman never had any closer female family members; he never married. His home companion was to be his mother. He had the house designed with her in mind, giving her the east side with its airy and feminine feel. But she only lived here two years before dying at age 82. From then on, Eastman lived alone.

He did, however, have many friends, four of whom were women he called the lobster quartette, after a favorite meal they often enjoyed together. He often went shopping with them, buying them clothes they liked, and, as a skilled horticulturist (the west garden has been restored in the manner in which Eastman kept it), he would give each an orchid corsage upon their visits. They discussed a wide variety of subjects, we were told, ranging from birth control to suicide.

It wasn't idle talk. Eastman committed suicide in his bedroom at age

Courtesy: International Museum of Photography at George Eastman House

Eastman was a skilled horticulturist. The west garden has been restored to its appearance in his day.

78, shooting himself with an automatic Lugar. He was in poor health and had left a note that read, "My work is done—why wait?"

In life he was a generous man, a loved and respected philanthropist who gave large sums of money to colleges, such as the Rochester Institute of Technology and the Massachusetts Institute of Technology, and to area charities. He opened five dental dispensaries where any person could have a tooth pulled for a nickel. All totalled, it is said he gave away $100 million.

The one room that most reflects his character is the library, left just as it was during his lifetime. There is his collection of Japanese ornamental fasteners called netsukes, and each of his books has his own bookplate, an image of Eastman sitting in front of a warm fireplace with book in hand. Titles include Thoreau's *The Maine Woods* and *Theodore Roosevelt's Letters to his Children*, underlining Eastman's diverse interests.

But the subject with which we associate him most is photography, and you will find cameras upon cameras in two downstairs galleries. It's a trip down memory lane as you remember your first Brownie (which Eastman named after a fictional character in a children's story) or, for post-baby boomers, your first Instamatic. These fascinating exhibits are not limited to Kodak products; you will probably recognize the first model Polaroid Swinger, dated 1964, a modern convenience in its day.

In 1839, the state of the art was the invention of Louis Jacques Daguerre, the world's first commercial camera; there is one on view. Contrast it with the dime-a-dozen children's and novelty cameras in the shapes of Mickey Mouse, Snoopy, and a can of Budweiser beer.

Leaving behind the can of beer, head to a glass case where Kodak's 25 millionth disc camera lies completely dismantled and exposed—all 14 solid parts of it. Contrast it with Eastman's bulky first camera from 1888. America's first amateur photographers paid $25 for a fresh-from-the-factory Kodak camera, complete with a role of film with 100 exposures. When it came time to develop the film, the camera owner did not remove it; instead, he sent the entire camera to Kodak, who returned it with developed photographs and a fresh role of 100 exposures.

There are gadgets on display you can handle, including a zoetrope and a mutoscope, which the curious looked inside to see the steady flow of drawings, simulating continuous action; these were the great-grandparents of the cartoon.

The best in still photography are hung throughout the second floor, in bedrooms and other rooms. The collection spans the years from the advent of photography to modern times. Included are early Daguerreotypes, which are pictures on silver coated copper plates dating from 1839, to the works of 20th-century photographers like Lewis Hine, Alfred Steiglitz, Margaret Bourke-White, Edward Steichen, Lee Friedlander, and Richard Avedon.

Location: The George Eastman House and The International Museum of Photography is at 900 East Avenue. Westbound from the New York State Thruway (Interstate 90), take exit 45 to Interstate 490 west. Eastbound from the New York State Thruway (Interstate 90), take exit 47 to Interstate 490 east. From Interstate 490, take the Culver Road exit; take a right onto Culver Road, then a left onto East Avenue and follow for three blocks to the mansion, which is on the right. **Admission** is charged. **Hours:** Year round, Tuesday through Saturday and Sunday afternoons. **Allow** an hour and a half to two and a half hours. **Information:** International Museum of Photography at the George Eastman House, 900 East Avenue, Rochester, NY 14607; (716) 271-3361.

Note: Films from the museum's collection are shown often at the adjacent Dryden Theater. A new building to house much of the collection is currently being constructed next to the Eastman house.

If you are staying overnight: East Avenue Inn, 384 East Avenue, Rochester, (716) 325-5010; Red Roof Inn, Route 15 (at junction with Thruway exit 46), W. Henrietta, (716) 359-1100; Genesee Country Inn, 948 George Street, (716) 538-2500. For bed & breakfast accommodations contact Bed & Breakfast Rochester, P.O. Box 444, Fairport, NY 14450; (716) 223-8510.

NEW YORK'S
FINEST
MANSIONS

OLANA

Courtesy: Olana State Historic Site

High in the Hudson Valley stands the Persian palace called Olana, an astounding sight to eyes used to Victorian homes and Greek Revival mansions.

WE STOOD IN THE GALLERY IN OLANA, A MASTERPIECE OF A MANSION built by artist Frederic Church, a master in his own right from the Hudson River School of Art.

To the right and left of a door leading from the gallery to the studio are portraits of Church and his father.

"You can see who was the artist and who was the businessman," said guide Jack Thorne.

Church's father, a Hartford insurance executive, is depicted as clean shaven, stern, and gray. The artist is bushy haired but balding and with a walrus mustache; his eyes are tender and his expression is questioning.

We left the gallery and entered a long hallway, catching a glimpse of the Charter Oak chair, which will strike a chord in anybody who grew up in Connecticut. The Charter Oak was a tree that served as the hiding place for Connecticut's royal charter in colonial Hartford and is to this day Connecticut's most famous symbol. The tree was destroyed in a storm in the mid-1800s and chairs made from its roots and branches were given to members of the seven families that originally settled Hartford.

Appropriately, the chair represents the severing of the artist's roots to Hartford. He shunned insurance and answered another calling, which made the world of art the beneficiary of his talents.

The tour of Olana (derived from an Arabic word meaning "our place on high") begins with a 10-minute introduction of the man and his house. Frederic Church is regarded as the first American artist to receive international recognition. A worldwide traveler, Church intended to model his home after a French chateau, until a trip to the Middle East in the late 1860s inspired him otherwise. Impressed by the region's architecture, with its massive bearings, sense of eternal presence, and relationship of muted stone shades with highly decorated patterns, Church's dream house plans took on a distinctly Middle Eastern air.

The Persian carpets, the Arabic script on the walls and over the main portal, and the Syrian tiles make this a mansion unlike all others in the Hudson Valley. In fact, the first sight of Olana from the crest of the access road that climbs 460 feet above the river is a reckless Persian palace of Islamic arches and exotic stenciling set amongst a valley of mansard roofs and belvederes.

Once inside, you can study the spellbinding style in detail. Examine the Persian tile around the fireplace in Church's studio; did you ever think there could be so many shades of blue?

Yet this architectural style, while an oddity in Columbia County, was not totally unheard of in Victorian times. There is an Ottoman smoking room in Victoria Mansion in Portland, Maine. Longwood, the unfinished home of cotton magnate Haller Nutt, brings a bit of Middle Eastern flavor to the magnolias and cotton boll of Natchez, Mississippi. Amid the palm trees and Spanish colonial homes of St. Augustine, Florida, is Villa Zurada with its Persian-style floor plan.

As a dutiful citizen of Victorian America, Church collected wherever he went. So it's not surprising to see South American and Mexican baskets and pottery in Church's studio and tables from Egypt and Morocco in the east parlor, which served as the formal guest reception room.

Church painted the doors in the east parlor silver and gold and their busy rectangular decorations of intricate designs simulate the markings he saw among the Middle Eastern upper middle class.

He also admired Persian homes for their central courtyards. The Court Hall, seen early on the tour, was his attempt at duplicating this feature. But New York is not the hot, dry Persian Gulf region, and Church ultimately abandoned the courtyard idea.

At one time he also considered skylights but again the area climate dissuaded him. So he decided to add an effect that couldn't be upset by the elements—Church painted the ceiling a light blue and varnished it to create the effect of a clear, open sky.

A bona fide nature scene is yours by looking through the ombra, a massive window with a shape falling somewhere between a Hershey's kiss and a Turkish turban, towards a vista unparalleled by any oil on canvas. The ombra frames the woods, the rolling river, and the blue mountains beyond.

Church was as proud of the natural setting around his home as he was of any man-made feature inside it, and he considered the combination of the window and the vast open outdoors a three-dimensional painting. Come here in the fall and you willl find the old adage true—you won't believe your eyes.

This, however, is not meant to detract from Church's best works, many of which hang proudly on the walls of Olana.

Solitary Lake in New Hampshire is typical of the Hudson River School's subdued style; it was painted by Church's mentor, Thomas Cole. Church's *Autumn in North America*, on the other hand, is unusually vibrant. In the sitting room is the sketch for *The Great Fall, Niagara*, which was the painting that signalled the beginning of Church's career.

Church was intrigued with all types of art and it is not surprising to hear that he saw Olana itself as a distinguished work of art. He believed that art was never finished—that any effort could be altered and improved, and, as such, Olana was in a state of eternal improvement.

"As long as I live, this house will never be finished," Church is reported to have exclaimed. Guide Jack Thorne said, "Church had a very tolerant wife."

The biggest change Church made was the addition of the studio wing between 1888 and 1891. By that time, he was suffering agonizing pain from arthritis and, as a result, taught himself to paint with his left hand. His easel, palettes, brushes, and other tools of his trade are set up for a left-handed artist in this studio.

The deteriorating conditions of both Church and his wife curtailed any future expansion plans he might have had for Olana. They spent the winter months where temperatures were warmer, and not long after he had built his studio, Church hired his son to manage the estate. Church gradually devoted less and less time to Olana; his wife died in 1899 and he died one year later.

Location: From the Taconic Parkway, take the Hudson-Ancram exit to Route 23 west to Route 9G south. The entrance to Olana is on Route 9G, five miles south of Hudson. From the New York State Thruway (Interstate 87), exit 21, cross the Rip Van Winkle Bridge to Route 9G south to the entrance to Olana. **Admission** is charged. **Hours:** Mansion open Wednesday through Sunday, Memorial Day weekend to Labor Day;

Courtesy: Olana State Historic Site

Church's studio in Olana, set up for a left-handed artist.

variable hours in September and October; grounds open year round. **Allow:** 45 minutes for the guided tour, up to two hours if you also explore the grounds. **Information:** Olana State Historic Site, RD 2, Hudson, NY 12534; (518) 828-0135.

Events: August, Victorian Picnic, brass band, period food.

Note: Because guided tours are limited to 12 persons, tickets can sell out early. According to James Ryan, site manager, the busiest months are July, August, and October. On weekends in those months, tickets for the last scheduled tour at 4 P.M. can sell out as early as 2:30 or 3 P.M. Wednesday is usually the busiest weekday. Tours on a summer weekday usually sell out by 3:30 or 3:45 P.M. Some reservations are taken, but most tours are first come first serve. A few picnic tables are on the grounds, but visitors are also welcome to bring a blanket to spread on the lawn or bring their own lawn chairs.

If you are staying overnight: Howard Johnson's Motor Lodge, Route 32 (off Thruway exit 20), Saugerties, (914) 246-9511; Carl's Rip Van Winkle Motor Lodge, Route 23B (off Thruway exit 21), Catskill, (914) 943-3303; Catskill Motor Lodge, Route 23B (off Thruway exit 21), Catskill, (914) 943-5800.

LYNDHURST

Photo by Louis H. Frohman

American "royalty" ate meals fit for a king in the Lyndhurst dining room.

GEORGE WASHINGTON REJECTED THE NOTION THAT HE BECOME THE first king of America, and so our country is without official royalty. That is why we create unofficial royalty—commercial and political royalty— people with money and power, whether they earned it the hard way or the old-fashioned way . . . through an inheritance.

Like British royalty, American royalty resides in palaces and castles. Of all those built alongside the Hudson River, Lyndhurst in Tarrytown is credited as the earliest and regarded as the first of many mansions classified as Hudson River Gothic.

As the architectural label hints, Lyndhurst, with its Gothic trademarks of arched doors and windows, finials, bosses, and ribbed and vaulted ceilings, looks the part of a royal family's castle. As icing on the structural cake, it sports turrets, lushly landscaped grounds, and a tower.

What American "royalty" lived here? First there was a politician, former New York City Mayor William Paulding, who commissioned Andrew Jackson Davis in 1838 to design the mansion. The grounds were designed based on the progressive ideas of Andrew Jackson Downing, recognized as America's first professional landscape architect.

Paulding called the home Knoll and it was a humble one, small but perfect as a retirement home for the ex-mayor who lived here until 1864.

But when the next owner, wealthy New York City merchant George Merritt, moved in with his wife and six children, it was obvious the place had to be enlarged. So Merritt called back Davis, who raised the roof line and added a wing, a porte cochere, and the striking tower, giving the place its distinct castle-like feel.

It was the final owner, the famous (and in some minds, infamous) Jay Gould, railroad magnate and Wall Street speculator, who best fit the role as American commercial royalty, though his improvements on the mansion, by then called Lyndhurst, were minor.

A painting of Jay Gould hanging in the vestibule is a metaphor for his perceived stature. He stood only 5' 2" but his posture and the positioning of his chair in the painting makes him look taller. Surely this man who, in 1884, controlled Western Union Telegraph, the New York El, and the Erie Railroad could hardly be perceived as small; he was worth nearly $72 million when he died in 1892.

Until 1961, when the home was willed to the National Trust for Historic Preservation, Lyndhurst never left the Gould family's possession. Daughter Helen took charge of Lyndhurst after her father's death, and after Helen died in 1938, her sister Anna, Duchess of Talleyrand-Perigord (at last, some genuine royalty!) returned from France to live her last years here.

In the late 19th century, long before swimming pools and Porsches, wealthy people had other ways to broadcast their status that you will encounter throughout Lyndhurst, from the cork floor in the kitchen to the disguised pine wood in the dining room.

The lowly pine has been dressed up to fool your eyes and to the eyes of most visitors, it succeeds. The marble columns in the dining room really are pine; the rosewood and oak ceilings there are also pine.

You will find this pattern throughout Lyndhurst. Our guide, Juliette, pointed out wooden doors in the porte cochere painted to appear bronze. In the vestibule, plaster walls have been painted to resemble yellow marble, and plaster ceilings to resemble white marble.

The purpose of disguising common wood to make it look valuable, was not, as we first thought, for Lyndhurst owners to fake out guests. On the contrary, said Juliette, status-conscious people went through this trouble to show they could afford to hire artists who could make the ordinary appear expensive.

Courtesy: Lyndhurst

Regal Lyndhurst sits snug among the lush greenery of the lower Hudson Valley.

An abundance of stained glass—some Tiffany, some Bohemian—is an additional hallmark of the time. But the stained-glass dining room alcove windows are energy efficient as well. The window on the right is red, in order to help heat the room in the morning; on the left, it's blue to cool down the room in late afternoon.

Upstairs bedrooms sport a Tiffany look with a desk set and a number of lamps, and the music room, with Tiffany glass and an Aeolian organ—pipes poking out of the floor—holds the favorite piece of many visitors and the ultimate in prestige: a Steinway piano. Actually, the Steinway was a gift from Helen Gould to the Brooklyn Naval Yard and was returned to Lyndhurst when that facility closed; it's not original to the house.

Other highlights of Lyndhurst? There's the library that has tiered bookshelves, a clever method of displaying as many books as possible. It also has two doors, one that opens into the music room and another that opens into a blank wall, all done for the sake of symmetry.

The art room, which was a library before the Merritts enlarged the house, is the only room with a true Gothic ceiling. Here is the Goulds' art collection, some 40 paintings lining the walls; the most famous is *First Caress* by William Adolphe Bouguereau, created in 1866. Look above the framed art to see the faces of classical writers and philosophers like Voltaire, Shakespeare, Dante, and Rousseau carved into the walls.

You end the tour where there is no art nor stained glass or other trademarks of the 19th-century rich and famous. Step into the butler's pantry and you have a servant's eye view of the dining room. But there is a touch of the high class here, too. The floor is made of cork, making it less likely to be damaged, and cushioning the tired feet of the butler and head footman. Downstairs was a scullery, workplace for the lowly scullery maid, often a girl from the slums who with a little old-fashioned luck and pluck, could work her way up to the respectable position of head housekeeper. You exit through the kitchen, set for an early 1900s dinner, a royal one, no doubt.

Location: Lyndhurst is on Route 9, about a half mile south of the New York State Thruway (Interstate 87) at the Tappan Zee Bridge. **Admission** is charged. **Hours:** April through October, Tuesday through Sunday; March, November, and December, weekends. **Allow** 45 minutes for the tour and up to two hours if you also plan to walk the expansive grounds. **Information:** Lyndhurst, 635 South Broadway, Tarrytown, NY 10591; (914) 631-0046.

Events: There are several including these: spring, antique show; June, Children's day, 19th-century entertainment such as puppet shows, stilt walking, hoop rolling, refreshments; weekly in Summer, classical and semi-classical concerts; fall, craft show; October 31, Halloween For Children, costumed guides, hay rides, ghost stories; weekly in December, Christmas at Lyndhurst, Victorian holiday music, refreshments, and decorations.

Note: There are picnic tables on the grounds. The Lyndhurst gift shop has a fine selection of Victorian-style gifts. People with an interest in horticulture should plan some time to walk the grounds.

If you are staying overnight: Westchester Marriott Hotel, 670 White Plains Road (Route 119, just west of Interstate 287, exit 1), Tarrytown, (914) 631-2200; Howard Johnson's Motor Lodge, 290 Tarrytown Road (Route 119, off Interstate 287, exit 4), Elmsford, (914) 592-8000; Holiday Inn, Tarrytown Road (Route 119, take Interstate 287, exit 1, or Interstate 87, exit 8), Elmsford, (914) 592-5680; County Center Motel, 20 County Center Road (Routes 100 and 119), White Plains, (914) 948-2400.

VANDERBILT MANSIONS

Courtesy: Roosevelt-Vanderbilt National Historic Sites

This was the mansion of Frederick Vanderbilt, whose introversion was surpassed only by his altruism.

THE VIEW FROM THE NORTHPORT PORCH IN CENTERPORT AT LONG Island's Vanderbilt Museum mansion is to many worth the price of admission alone. In the foreground is the patio. Look past the patio and you see the calm waters of Northport Harbor. Beyond is the expansive Long Island Sound and when it is extraordinarily clear, Norwalk, Connecticut, 10 miles away, is visible.

The Vanderbilts always had a way of incorporating aquatic views into their property. Up in the Hudson Valley there is Vanderbilt Mansion National Historic Site in Hyde Park, which offers from the backyard a picture book vista of the rolling Hudson River.

These are the two mansions once owned by the Vanderbilt family that are open to the public in the Empire State. But there is more to the admission price at Centerport's Vanderbilt Museum than a look at a mansion.

Here, visitors explore what could stand on its own as a formidable natural history museum. William Kissam Vanderbilt II, adventurer, conservationist, and builder of this 24-room residence he called "Eagle's Nest," started a collection of animal and marine specimens that he willed to the public with his home. Also on the property is the Vanderbilt Museum Planetarium, constructed in 1971 on the site of the family tennis courts.

It's the mansion that initially draws the curious, and as far as houses of the rich and famous go, this one won't disappoint the average visitor. But don't expect the palatial splendor and architectural braggadocio of the estates in Newport or the one at Hyde Park. This home is showy but livable. It will impress but won't overwhelm.

The owner, William Kissam Vanderbilt II, was the great-grandson of Commodore Cornelius Vanderbilt, the railroad and shipping magnate who founded the family fortune. The lush Vanderbilt mansions open to the public elsewhere were the homes of various members of the third generation; that includes Marble House in Newport, built in 1892 at the cost of $11,000,000 which was the summer "cottage" of William's father. (Perhaps by the fourth generation, wealth was no longer as new and it was no longer necessary to lavishly impress.)

But don't worry, there are still plenty of treasures from throughout the world to admire within the white stucco walls and under the red tile roof of this three-story Spanish Revival building.

The list of the lush and luxurious includes the limestone and marble 15th-century sitting room fireplace that came from Portugal and depicts knights of the crusades. Also from Portugal are the brown and turquoise floor tiles in the dining room. Sitting upon those tiles are 17th-century Flemish carved walnut chairs, a sacristy cabinet, and a 16th-century wooden monastery sidetable. The ceiling of hand-carved, painted Florida cypress adds to the medieval feel.

Mr. Vanderbilt's master bedroom is dominated by French Empire-style pieces with a bust of Napoleon on the desk and the seal of Napoleon embossed on the front of the bed. It is a touch of the far East though—a 19th-century Chinese screen—that aesthetically blocks the bathroom from the casual visitor's view at the entrance to the room.

This lengthy list of lavishness is not to imply that all you see is centuries-old. The organ room is appropriately named for the 2,000-pipe Aeolian Duo-Art organ that Vanderbilt installed in the 1920s. You will notice other evidence of the 20th century as your guide conducts you through the home: a wicker toilet seat cover and hamper in a bathroom and art deco closets in a dressing room.

While on the tour, keep your eyes out for the maritime decorations signalling William Vanderbilt's great love for things nautical. Try to spot the scallop shell replicas on the front door, the shell moldings around the master bedroom ceiling and the wood carvings of sea horses, snails, and scallops on the stairway columns of the courtyard's bell tower.

Following the mansion tour, you will be left on your own to take your time and inspect the museum exhibits. Plan to come face to face with brightly plumed birds, seemingly representing every color of the spectrum, and grotesque marine life, which could only have been hauled up from the depths of the ocean.

There is a red macaw from Brazil, a green festive parrot from the upper Amazon River, and a sharp, light blue-capped fly catcher from the Fiji Islands. The plumage of Count Rossi's Bird of Paradise looks amazingly similar to a spiked orange punk haircut, while the long, flowing white feathers of the Greater Bird of Paradise, from Papua New Guinea, resemble the powdered wig of a colonial merchant.

Shells and sea creatures take up eight rows on each wall in the next gallery. Clams, sponges, sea urchins, crayfish, and starfish in innumerable varieties are displayed, all specimens collected while William was on three voyages from 1926 to 1932 in which he visited all of the world's seas and oceans.

In order to make the most out of his opportunities at sea, he took with him an artist and curator, a taxidermist, a photographer, and a doctor. His yacht, *Alva*, named for his mother and built in Germany in 1930, was designed solely for his hobby of collecting marine life.

On the opposite side of the estate is the Vanderbilt Museum Planetarium. One of the largest planetariums in the United States, it can show the appearance of the sky with the sun, moon, planets, and stars in their proper places from any location on earth, during any time of year, and from the beginnings of time onward into the future. Its "skyshows," open to the public, are changed three or four times a year with talks planned periodically.

Step back a generation and make a jaunt north to Vanderbilt Mansion National Historic Site in Hyde Park. The owner of this Gilded Age mansion, the only one operated by the National Park Service, was Uncle Frederick to the owner of the Centerport estate.

His name was Frederick W. Vanderbilt and, there's a ten-minute-long slide show and a series of exhibits where you learn that Frederick was a painfully shy man but that his introversion was surpassed only by his altruism.

For example, after noticing laborers on a job with no protective hand covering, he ordered and paid for gloves for all; in another instance, he and his wife, Louise, threw a special dinner for the hard working but poorly paid paperboys in Newport.

Vanderbilt, however, like the rest of his family, spared no expense in building his own summer palace. Whereas his brother William in Newport went in for marble, Frederick had a passion for tapestries, and you will see them throughout the three-story mansion.

Guests were greeted in the main hall and this is where you will see your first tapestry. It hangs above the fireplace and depicts the coat of arms of the Medici family of Florence, Italy. Another in the south foyer on the first floor brings the Trojan War to life and was crafted in 16th-century Brussels. Still more are opposite it in the north foyer and upstairs, blanketing Frederick's bedroom walls.

Like most wealthy Americans of the time, Frederick and Louise emphasized French with a shade of Italian styles in furnishing their house's interior; and like other Vanderbilts, Frederick built a home that members of European royalty would find as comfortable as the throne rooms in their own palaces.

The lush rococo style of the reception room, also known as the gold room, bathes it with an elegance that's the hallmark of continental luxury. Gold leaf decorates the wood-paneled walls, and the Louis XV furniture fits in perfectly. This room was meant to convey the feeling of a mid-18th-century French salon. It succeeds.

Upstairs, Louise had a white and gold railing built around the bed in her second floor room. After all, that is the way things were done at Versailles.

We learned as we peered into this room that it was modeled after a French queen's bedroom of the Louis XV period. The queen, too, would have had a railing encasing her bed since it was a custom for ladies of nobility to hold receptions in the morning while still in bed. Eager tradesmen, standing outside the railing, would present flowers, ribbons, gloves, or other goods to her while her majesty's friends would sit inside the rail on folding stools or cushions.

Genuine royalty made their presence felt here. The Duke of Marlborough was entertained in the living room, also called the drawing room, which was the scene of innumerable elaborate fetes and formal dances. The expansive living room had enough space for a small orchestra to provide live entertainment.

How did the other half live? You are given a peek as you finish your tour.

"We came in like the upper crust and we leave like the servants," our guide smiled as he led us down a spiral staircase into the basement.

Actually, servants lived well in the Vanderbilt mansion. Their dining room table is set with Royal Copenhagen china with place settings for eight, and, although the kitchen appears small for such a huge house, we were told that a visitor from the nearby Culinary Institute of America said he could fix a meal for 100 people in it with little problem.

We were led outdoors by way of the hired hands' quarters but were

Courtesy: The Vanderbilt Museum

Not all Vanderbilts lived at Hyde Park or Newport. This lush home is on Long Island.

invited to walk the mansion grounds on a high bank above the river, savoring a view that a millionaire could appreciate.

Location: To reach the Vanderbilt Museum in Centerport, Long Island, take the Long Island Expressway (Interstate 495) to exit 51N (Deer Park Avenue), and follow Deer Park Avenue (Route 231) north for six miles; turn right onto Broadway and continue past Route 25A where Broadway becomes Little Neck Road. The museum is at 180 Little Neck Road. **Admission** is charged. **Hours:** Year round, Tuesday through Sunday. Call for planetarium schedule. **Allow** an hour to 90 minutes to take the guided tour of the mansion and see the museums. **Information:** Vanderbilt Museum, 180 Little Neck Road, Centerport, NY 11721; (516) 261-5656. For planetarium information only, call (516) 757-7500 during the school year and (516) 757-7501 in summer.

Events: Numerous special activities take place annually. A partial list includes: spring concerts in the library (a room not seen on the regular tour); courtyard concerts in summer; yacht race in fall; lectures throughout the year; carol sing in December.

Note: Buy tickets in the reception center, to the left as you walk from the parking lot to the mansion. There is a limit of 20 persons per tour. Picnic tables are by the main gate in front of the parking lot.

If you are staying overnight: Howard Johnson's Motor Lodge, 270 West Jericho Turnpike (Route 25), Huntington Station, (516) 421-3900; Howard Johnson's Motor Lodge, 450 Moreland Road (Long Island Expressway, exit 54), Commack, (516) 864-8820; Sheraton, 110 Vanderbilt Motor Parkway (Long Island Expressway, exit 54), Smithtown, (516) 231-1100. Note that lodging is extremely expensive on Long Island. It is very difficult to find a double room priced under $80 per night. If you are en route to another location, consider staying elsewhere.

Location: Vanderbilt Mansion National Historic Site in Hyde Park is on Route 9, two miles north of the entrance to the Franklin D. Roosevelt National Historic Site. **Admission** is charged. **Hours:** April through October, daily; November through March, Thursday through Monday. **Allow** an hour to tour the visitor center and the mansion. You may also want to allow an extra half hour to an hour to explore the grounds. **Information:** Roosevelt-Vanderbilt Mansion National Historic Sites, 249 Albany Post Road, Hyde Park, NY 12538; (914) 229-9115.

Events: Mid-June, antique auto show; lawn concerts in summer; mid-December through early January, Christmas at the Vanderbilts, gilded age decorations.

Note: Up to 75 people can be accommodated on one tour, which means that at busy times you may have to sacrifice personal attention. On summer weekends, tours are offered every 20 minutes; at other times, they are every half hour. Picnics are permitted on the grounds.

If you are staying overnight: Holiday Inn, Route 9 (two miles south of Poughkeepsie), (914) 473-1151; The Dutch Patroon Motel, Route 9 (a half mile north of the FDR site), Hyde Park, (914) 229-7141; The Roosevelt Inn, Route 9 (a mile north of the FDR site), Hyde Park, (914) 229-2443; Beekman Arms, Route 9 (at junction with County Route 308), Rhinebeck, (914) 876-7077; Fala: A Bed and Breakfast, 46 East Market Street, Hyde Park, (914) 229-5937.

BOLDT CASTLE

Photo by Michael Schuman

This was to be George Boldt's castle on his own fantasy island. But tragedy cut short Boldt's dream.

Bᴏʟᴅᴛ ᴄᴀꜱᴛʟᴇ'ꜱ ꜱᴛᴏʀʏ ɪꜱ ᴀ ᴘᴀʀᴀʙʟᴇ ᴏꜰ ʟɪꜰᴇ ᴀᴛ ɪᴛꜱ ᴍᴏꜱᴛ ᴋɪɴᴅ ᴀɴᴅ most cruel, a towering testament to the ancient adage that money can't buy happiness.

The turreted, stone, Rhenish-style castle and its surrounding outbuildings, which are as magnificent as the castle itself, occupy all of Heart Island in the St. Lawrence River in New York State's Thousand Islands region.

The castle was built around the turn of the century during the peak of America's Gilded Age. It was to be part of a millionaire's gift to his wife; she was also to be presented with the entire island, which her husband arranged to have reshaped to resemble a heart.

The millionaire was George C. Boldt, a name long lost in oblivion, but in his day, the best-known and most successful hotelier in the country. Boldt was a Prussian immigrant, arriving in America at age 13 and gradually rising from a menial laborer in a New York City hotel kitchen to the proprietor of the city's world-renowned Waldorf-Astoria Hotel and Philadelphia's landmark Bellevue-Stratford Hotel.

Boldt and his wife, the former Louise Kehrer of Philadelphia, began vacationing in the Thousand Islands in 1894 and, after several years, decided to buy property.

As a child in Germany, George Boldt admired the medieval castles along his country's Rhine River and dreamed of someday acquiring enough wealth to build his own. While his castle in America was to be a present for Louise, it was also confirmation of his life-long dream, a Horatio Alger story come true.

He went back to Europe on buying trips, searching out the continent's best treasures in the form of chandeliers, sculptures, marble mantelpieces, and tapestries. He scoured Italy, France, and Germany for paintings to bring the most impressive masterpieces back with him. He hired skilled artisans, masons, electricians and landscape architects from around the world to lend their professional touches to the castle and the ten buildings surrounding it.

In 1900, work on Boldt's fantasy island began. The crew first built the Alster Tower, resembling an old defense tower on Germany's Alster River. Boldt lived in the tower while the castle was being constructed.

The powerhouse, which held the generating plant that provided power for the rest of the buildings, was built next, and, keeping it in fashion with the rest of the estate, Boldt built it in a medieval style with a 90-foot-high carillon clock tower. He purchased 15 silver bells formerly used by Wanamaker's Department Store in Philadelphia to announce the hours to the same tones as London's Westminster chimes, so no one near the island could miss it.

An arch of triumph planned to be the formal entryway for launches was then raised. All the while the main castle, six stories of granite walls, steel and concrete roofs and floors, and cast terra cotta decorations, was taking shape. The bottom two floors included a ballroom, dining room, library, billiard room, and reception rooms. Bedrooms—each with private bath and fireplace—were to occupy the upper floors. In total, the Boldts' dream home would contain 120 rooms.

By the end of 1903, the castle structure was complete, and the interior was filling up with luxurious furnishings. All was proceeding normally with more than $2.5 million of George Boldt's money invested in it.

Then, just after ringing in what promised to be another happy and prosperous new year, 1904, George Boldt rushed a telegram to the superintendent of construction. Louise Boldt was dead. A grieving and disheartened George ordered the crew to stop construction immediately. They did. The castle was about 18 months from completion.

And not so much as a single nail was hammered in the castle for the next 70 years.

Boldt lived until 1916 and while he visited the Thousand Islands after his wife's death, the story says that he never again set foot in the castle.

Today the castle sits on Heart Island (originally spelled "Hart," the new spelling is accepted since Boldt changed the island's shape) and 160,000 tourists a year explore its interior. There are no lavish furnishings, no rich tapestries from the looms of Flanders, no smooth marble mantelpieces from Italy, no sculptures from the artisans of France. There is hardly any furniture; what is there, period pieces like 17th-century carved wooden Tudor-style chairs, were donated by local organizations.

But there are photographs of and commentaries on the castle's decorative idiosyncrasies, like carved hearts (for Heart Island), clovers (for Philadelphia's Clover Club where Boldt once worked—he named his daughter Clover), and shells (for the Shell Room at the Waldorf). There is also a quality craft shop and a well-produced slide show, telling in first person the story of Boldt and his castle and the mood of the Gilded Age.

There are broken dreams here, too. It nearly hurts to follow markers labeled "Miss Clover's Room" and "Mr. and Mrs. Boldt's Suite" only to find rooms as bare as the winter woods and walls scribbled with graffiti, remnants of 70 years of neglect when the elements and vandals had their way with Mr. Boldt's dream.

One's imagination, however, has a way of filling in the gaps. Enter what would have been the library and imagine it furnished in Flemish Oak, or visit the ballroom, which would have contained its own pipe organ and keyboard controlling the chimes in the powerhouse. Look up towards the domed ceiling that was to be enclosed with colored glass, lit by the bright sky in the day and by the new wonder of electricity at night.

Then walk the island's grounds, past the arch and the Alster Tower, and examine the castle's many angles; there is no better pastime on a sunny day than to sit on any of the many benches and watch the multitude of boats sail by.

You can approach the powerhouse, too, but to see the 90-foot carillon clock tower, you must once again use your imagination. The entire tower and a portion of the house were destroyed by a skyrocket in 1938 during the celebration marking the opening of the Thousand Islands International Bridge.

As if Boldt's Castle was crying, "Enough is enough," the Thousand Islands Bridge Authority took control of the castle in 1977 and has been operating it ever since. A restoration project is expected to take several years to complete; in the meantime you can wander through the magnificent and silent castle, examining one man's glorious Gilded Age dream stopped cold by a happenstance that even his millions of dollars couldn't alter.

Location: Boldt Castle is on Heart Island and is accessible by shuttle or tour boat operated from Alexandria Bay by Empire and Uncle Sam Boat Lines and out of Clayton by Thousand Islands Seaway Cruises. (See pages 61 to 64). **Admission** is charged. **Hours:** Mid-May through early October, daily. **Allow** an hour to 90 minutes. **Information:** Thousand Islands International Council, P.O. Box 400, Alexandria Bay, NY 13607; (315) 482-2520 or (315) 482-9724.

Note: Picnic tables are on the grounds; you can buy food at the castle or bring your own picnic.

If you are staying overnight: Thousand Islands Club Resort, Wellesley Island (follow signs from Interstate 81, exit 51), (315) 482-2551; Pine Tree Point Resort, Anthony Street, Alexandria Bay (a mile northeast of town), (800) 253-9229 (in New York state), (315) 482-9911; Captain Thomson's Motor Lodge, James Street, Alexandria Bay, (315) 482-9961; Bach's Alexandria Bay Inn (bed and breakfast), 2 Church Street, Alexandria Bay, (315) 482-9697.

MILLS MANSION

Courtesy: Mills Mansion State Historic Site

It took 24 servants to keep this palatial 65-room home in full operation when owners Ogden and Ruth Mills were in residence.

IF YOU LIVE IN A TYPICAL SUBURBAN AMERICAN RAISED RANCH OR split-level house, it is safe to say that your house could comfortably fit inside the dining room of the Mills Mansion in Staatsburg.

You will likely hear that as you proceed on the guided tour through this emblem of Gilded Age wealth and style just north of Hyde Park. It is a comparison declared in order to let visitors know the sheer size of the place where Ogden and Ruth Mills had their evening meals, since the numbers 50 by 30 feet may not by themselves get the point across.

The dining room rug is 35 feet long, and when 18 leaves are added the table extends as long as the rug. When you tour you will probably see the table with seven leaves, a perfect size for the occasions when the house wasn't quite half-filled with guests. You also will observe four rich Flemish tapestries ornamenting the walls of Italian marble; it is said that the room was decorated around the tapestries.

In a similar manner, this Gilded Age mansion was built around an 1832 Greek Revival home located on the same spot. The Greek Revival home was built by Morgan Lewis, a Revolutionary war colonel and the state's third governor, and his wife, Gertrude, sister of Chancellor Robert R. Livingston, to replace another house that was destroyed by fire in 1832.

The home passed through generations of the family, and in 1888 it was inherited by Lewis's great-granddaughter, Ruth Livingston Mills, wife of financier and philanthropist Ogden Mills. They felt the property needed to be enlarged and remodeled, so they chose the New York architectural firm, McKim, Mead and White, who designed many millionaires' mansions during the Gilded Age, to do the work.

They added two large wings on opposite ends of the house and embellished a new exterior with floral swags, pilasters, and balustrades. Inside, they brought in the styles of Louis XV and Louis XVI with gilded ceilings, ancient objets d'art, the tapestries, and marble fireplaces. The finished product was a 65-room mansion Ogden Mills was proud to call his country retreat.

The Millses also kept a seaside retreat in Newport, Rhode Island, a California retreat in San Mateo, a European retreat in Paris, as well as an apartment in Manhattan. This Hudson River mansion was their home when a chill invaded the air and the leaves began to lose their green coating; they would come here in September after closing their Newport home for the season and leave about four months later.

When the urge to go skating or ice boating struck them in the dead of January, they would use this place as a mid-winter getaway, and on rare occasions they would come here for a spring fling. Most of the time, however, this was their autumn home.

Considering aesthetics alone, the Millses were luckier than most of their neighbors. The railroad that crawls up the Hudson River Valley passes by the front of this house, close to Route 9, rather than through its backyard on the fringes of the river, making it one of the few estates in this vicinity in which the river view is not obstructed by the railroad.

The best river scene may be from the round room, part of the original 1832 house. This vantage point boasts a stunning view of the late afternoon sun setting over the glistening Hudson with the faint outline of the Catskill Mountains in the distance.

Companion to the round room is the drawing room, also part of the original Greek Revival mansion. A Ming Dynasty teak and jade incense burner joins five Greek drinking vessels dating from 500 to 400 B.C. as a few of the plentiful fine furnishings in the drawing room. Women would withdraw to this room after dinner—the name drawing room was a shortened version of withdrawing room.

The drawing room was used by most American commercial royalty as a showcase for their most valuable ornaments and objets d'art. Modern home owners apparently take a dim view of such ostentation; Site Manager Melodye Moore reports that the most often heard comment from visitors on tours is that the drawing room is "too busy."

As women were leaving the dining room table for the drawing room, men were likely heading downstairs to the billiards room, which unfortunately is not open to the public. But in a house boasting 65 rooms and 14 bathrooms, no tour could exhibit all.

The library, architectural companion to the dining room, is on the tour and its collection of 1,800 volumes will impress even seasoned veterans of mansion-hopping. The collection represents five generations of the Lewis-Livingston-Mills families, and many volumes are personalized. If the books don't make an impression upon you, perhaps the 19th-century Steinway piano and the silk damask draperies will.

Even when the Mills family wasn't entertaining, they had a full house on their hands. They travelled with 19 servants from home to home; five additional servants lived at this mansion year round, so when in residence there were 24 servants keeping the owners company.

But that two dozen pales in comparison to the ten dozen people employed to care for the grounds. There were greenhouses, outbuildings, and a full compliment of livestock, including cattle and horses, to care for.

The mansion and grounds have become Mills-Norrie State Park, actually two connecting state parks comprised of land donated by the daughter of Ruth and Ogden Mills and the sister of Margaret Lewis Norrie. The park has 18 holes of golf, a campground, cabins, the Norrie Marina, the Dutchess Community College Environmental Site, a fitness trail, clubhouse restaurant, hiking trails overlooking the Hudson River, and picnic areas, all operational in warm months. In winter the park is open for cross-country skiing on groomed trails and sledding on the mansion's lawns.

Location: Staatsburg is three miles north of Hyde Park. Take Route 9 to Old Post Road (a side street to the left as you head north) to the mansion. Mills-Norrie State Park can be reached from either Route 9 or the mansion. **Admission** is free for the mansion, the park, the environmental site, and for cross-country skiing. Admission is charged for golf and camping. **Hours:** From late May to Labor Day, the mansion is open all day Wednesday through Saturday and on Sunday afternoons; Labor Day through late October, afternoons only, Wednesday through Sunday. The park is open daily, year round. Call to check on specific activities. Camping season is mid-May through late October. **Allow** 50 minutes for the tour, considerably longer to walk the grounds or use any park facilities. **Information:** Mills Mansion State Historic Site, Staatsburg, NY 12580; (914) 889-4100. To contact Mills-Norrie State Park call (914) 889-4646.

Events: Summer in Mills-Norrie State Park, musical concerts and family films; October, Scottish Tattoo and Highland Fling; October, antique auto show.

Note: Restoration on the mansion began in 1986 and is planned to be ongoing for several years. However, public access is not blocked and the mansion is open for tours as usual. Tours, even in the heart of vacation season, are given every half hour. The good news for golfers is that according to the park staff, there is usually no lengthy wait on the courses even on the busiest days.

If you are staying overnight: Holiday Inn, Route 9, Poughkeepsie, (914) 473-1151; The Dutch Patroon Motel, Route 9 (a half mile north of the FDR site), Hyde Park, (914) 229-7141; The Roosevelt Inn, Route 9 (a mile north of the FDR site), Hyde Park, (914) 229-2443; Beekman Arms, Route 9 (at the junction with County Route 308), Rhinebeck, (914) 876-7077; Fala: A Bed and Breakfast, East Market Street, Hyde Park, (914) 229-5937. Camping and cabins at Mills-Norrie State Park: in peak season, fourth Saturday in June to Labor Day, minimum reservation for one week, maximum reservation for two weeks; in off-season, opening day to fourth Saturday in June and Labor Day to closing day, minimum reservation for two nights (three nights when holiday falls on Friday or Monday), maximum reservations for two weeks.

SCHUYLER MANSION

Dining rooms were rare in 18th-century Albany but that didn't stop William Schuyler from having one.

WHEN PHILIP SCHUYLER RETURNED HOME FOLLOWING A HARD DAY at work in the mid-18th century, he went to an isolated part of Albany high on a bluff overlooking vast acreage of pastureland that included property of the nearby Dutch church.

The church, boxy and with an angled roof, was far more typical of Schuyler's surroundings than was his Georgian-style mansion. As late as 1789, Albany still resembled a cozy medieval Dutch town; a sketch of it is reproduced in the Schuyler Mansion visitor center.

Plan to spend some time in the visitor center where a small exhibit area and brief video presentation serve as the introduction to Philip Schuyler, his house and time.

The reason why Schuyler chose to build his home in the Georgian style is unclear, but it's thought he may have been inspired by other similar buildings already existing in the colonies; Philipse Manor Hall State Historic Site in Yonkers is a prime example. Whatever the reason, Schuyler Mansion was an anomaly in Albany in its day.

On the other hand, the chief occupant of the house fit perfectly in this elegant version of home sweet home. Philip Schuyler was an aristocrat, a member of a family that had been in the colonies for a century, and a patriot who had entertained the likes of George Washington, Benjamin Franklin, Benedict Arnold, and Alexander Hamilton during the American Revolution.

But Schuyler's ardor towards the colonists' cause was never as fervent as that of his more famous guests. In the tense years prior to the firing of the shots at Concord and Lexington, Schuyler was a moderate, opposed to the radicals who fiercely defied England. When fighting broke out, Major General Schuyler was put in command of the Northern Department of the Continental Army, but his partiotism was questioned when he was accused of abandoning Fort Ticonderoga.

He was later cleared of charges of neglect of duty and once more took an active role in the war. Following the signing of the Treaty of Paris, he became a well-known statesman, serving in the New York State and United States senates as well as holding other noteworthy positions.

It was in Schuyler's mansion that General John Burgoyne and his staff were simultaneously guests and prisoners; following Burgoyne's defeat at the Battle of Saratoga in October 1777, he and his aides-de-camp were sequestered here for some time.

Two famous weddings also were held here. Family friend Alexander Hamilton married Schuyler's daughter, Elizabeth, in December 1780. Then in 1858, Caroline McIntosh, widow of a later owner of the mansion, married former President Millard Fillmore.

Keep these stories of the mansion in mind when you go through it and what could be just another old mansion tour will come to life with the ghosts of the Schuylers, Hamiltons, Burgoynes, and Fillmores.

The elaborate formal parlor where Elizabeth Schuyler and Alexander Hamilton married is typically Georgian. Much of the furniture is Hepplewhite style and chairs are pushed against the walls as was the custom at the time; they were only brought out to the center of the floor when needed. There's a portrait of the groom, Hamilton, and a piano, circa 1810, complete with 68 keys, far short of today's standard 88. Letting in light are massive windows, each with 24 panes, unusually big considering that glass was taxed during Schuyler's day.

The room believed to be the one where Burgoyne was sequestered is the southeast bed chamber upstairs. The bed is covered by a vivid and colorful bed curtain in the chinoiserie style of Chinese intricacy; it reflects Schuyler's social standing as one of Albany's upper crust, since less fortunate 18th-century residents would never have been able to afford such lively decor.

It is known through his letters that Schuyler had gout as well as other ailments. So along with the bed in which he slept in the northwest bedchamber is a day bed, used mainly for lying down when suffering from an attack. On the fireplace mantle is a spring-loading lancet, commonly used to bleed sick patients like Schuyler, since bad blood was believed to be at the root of many maladies.

More than likely, there was a dining room in the Schuyler Mansion, rare though they were when Schuyler was alive. The ball-and-claw-foot table there is set formally and symmetrically, with oyster shells on the plates. Receipts, said Falk, show that oysters were one of Schuyler's favorite foods; he bought them by the barrel.

The mansion is also unusual in that it is believed to have had a detached kitchen, common in the South but rare in the Northeast where uncomfortable intense summer heat was less of a problem. In addition, evidence indicates there was a detached smokehouse, used to flavor and preserve meat, and a separate ice house to refrigerate foods; the nearby Hudson River produced much in the form of fresh bass, sturgeon, and other fish, making for sumptuous suppers that needed to be kept cool for mealtime.

Location: Schuyler Mansion State Historic Site is at 32 Catherine Street, two blocks west of South Pearl Street. From Interstate 787 north, take the Port of Albany exit and follow signs for Route 32N; turn left onto Rensselaer Street (which becomes Morton Avenue), then left onto Clinton Street and right onto Catherine Street; mansion parking lot is on the left. From Interstate 787 south, take the Madison Avenue/Port of Albany exit, turn left onto Green Street, right onto Rensselaer Street (which becomes Morton Avenue), left onto Clinton Street, and then right onto Catherine Street; mansion parking lot is on the left. **Admission** is free. **Hours:** April through December, Wednesday through Saturday and Sunday afternoons. **Allow** 20 to 30 minutes to see the visitor center and one hour for the house tour. **Information:** Schuyler Mansion State Historic Site, 32 Catherine Street, Albany, NY 12202.

Events: May, Springfest, decorative arts, farm animals, and demonstrations such as sheep shearing and cow milking; December, Christmas Open House, candlelight tours, colonial crafts, music, and holiday greens (no Christmas tree, however, since there was none in Schuyler's day).

Note: Parking is available in a lot at the rear of the mansion.

If you are staying overnight: Albany Hilton, Ten Eyck Plaza, State and Lodge Streets, (518) 462-6611; Albany Marriott, 189 Wolf Road (off Interstate 87, exit 4), (518) 458-8444; Jeremy's Inn, 500 Northern Boulevard (off Interstate 90, exit 6), (518) 462-5562; La Siesta, 1579 Central Avenue (off Interstate 90, exit 24, and Interstate 87, exit 2W), (518) 869-8471.

SONNENBERG GARDENS

Photo by Michael Schuman

The gardens are the main draw here, but Mary Clark Thompson's turreted mansion will grow on you, too.

"WITH MY GARDEN FAIR AND SWEET,
My thoughts full often stray,
To greet again the lovely flowers
Along the accustomed way."

Mary Clark Thompson

We walked along, ten of us and tour leader Florence Richardson, from a greenhouse by the parking lot up the sloping walkway to benefactress Mary Clark Thompson's formal gardens, better known as Sonnenberg Gardens, in Canandaigua.

As we walked uphill, we could see fragments of the estate's Richardsonian-style mansion. Turrets, chimneys, windows, and bits and pieces of geometric patterns came into view. But like the famous plantation gardens of Charleston or other parts of the South, the gardens are the primary attraction here, the mansion secondary. And so Richardson identified all the trees on the grounds as we strolled past them.

"There's a weeping beech, similar to a banyan, but it doesn't take root like one."

"Here's a Kentucky coffee tree. It grows a pod with big brown beans that were brewed for a beverage. And over there is a purple beech. In wet weather, the leaves take on a dark reddish tint."

As we reached the mansion, Florence asked us to turn around and look into the distance. Here we discovered the inspiration for the name of the grand estate. Sonnenberg means "sunny hill" in German. In between the trees on this bright, blue western New York day were the waters of Canandaigua Lake and blue-grey domed hills in the distance.

It was then that we embarked on the formal garden tour, made up of jaunts to several small gardens on the grounds: the Italian garden, the sub-rosa garden, the pansy garden, the Japanese garden, the rose garden, the moonlight garden, the colonial garden, and the rock garden.

Ironically, casual neglect was responsible for saving much of the floral kaleidoscope at Sonnenberg today. The story begins shortly after the turn of the century when Mary Clark Thompson started the gardens as a memorial to her husband, banker and philanthropist Frederick Ferris Thompson, who died in 1899.

Mary continued to practice his charitable ways, donating large sums of money to colleges, museums, and other worthy causes, and regularly opened the floral wonders of Sonnenberg to the general public; she often saw up to 7,000 visitors a day ambling along the footpaths, admiring the fragrant roses, studying classic Greek statuary, and gazing at the placid, clear waters of the reflecting pool.

When she died in 1923, Sonnenberg was inherited by a nephew who later sold the estate to the United States government. A veterans' administration hospital was constructed on the grounds with the mansion serving as a nurses' dormitory.

The gardens and grounds were neglected and fell into disuse but were never destroyed. So when restorers came here in the early 1970s, following the closing of the hospital a few years earlier, they already had a living skeleton sketch of the estate. In addition, old photographs from the early 1900s and a 1916 description of the grounds from the director of the New York Zoological Gardens further enhanced the restoration project, letting planners and workers know exactly what went where.

The restored Sonnenberg Gardens opened to the public in 1973 and have gradually been brought back to full bloom since then. Although there is still work to be done—a Roman bath along with its marble pillars and flooring sits as a silent victim of upstate New York winters—the gardens are 95% completed; in fact, the Smithsonian Institution has recognized them as "one of the most magnificent late Victorian gardens ever created in America."

Each of the individual gardens was designed so it could be viewed apart from the rest. We took notice of that during our tour, when the blue sky darkened and a drizzle began to fall. Richardson led us to the belvedere separating the Italian garden from the rose garden.

In one direction, we looked upon a classic European garden, which reminded us of those we had seen at Old World palaces like Versailles and Nymphenberg, with its four sunken parterre forming a modified fleur-de-lis design; despite its name, the Italian garden borrows greatly from French influence.

In the other direction, we saw rows of roses: pink, red, and white. The rose garden was the first of those restored when more than 4,000 rose-bushes were planted by volunteers, reestablishing the original beds.

We turned a corner and there was the sub-rosa garden, the term meaning "under the roses," referring to its hidden chapel-like location. The hedges bordering this garden, Richardson reported, were supposedly so thick that the family cat couldn't even sneak through them.

The tour continued, the rain let up, and we reached *Diana Robing*, a 19th-century sculpture modeled after a 4th-century Greco-Roman statue now in the Louvre in Paris.

That's not all the statuary here. The Italian garden is garnished with *Hercules Slaying The Hydra* while the Japanese garden is dominated by the soft visage of a bronze, meditating Buddha.

The Japanese garden, complete with a tea house based on one in Kyoto, Japan, was designed and built by a man named K. Wadamori with seven workers whom Mary Thompson brought over from Japan; the remainder of the landscaping was the work of Ernest W. Bowditch, a well-respected Boston landscape architect.

Bowditch was a firm believer in variety, as evidenced by Sonnenberg Gardens' multiformity, which doesn't let up even as you approach the tour's end. That's when you come across the colonial garden, the rock garden, and the moonlight garden.

The colonial garden is similar to those you likely have visited at places like Colonial Williamsburg and Mount Vernon, Virginia; its design, however, has been traced as far back as Pompeii. The moonlight garden, predominantly white, is arranged so its blossoms are illuminated by the moon; of course you can't see this on the guided tour in full daylight, but it's not difficult to imagine.

Circular in shape, the rock garden is composed of pudding stone and Onondaga limestone, two conglomerate rocks selected for their natural indentations and pockets, which make perfect homes for rock plants. Geysers and simulated springs shoot up, and a climbing hydrangea wraps around the walkway up to the Lookout Tower, a favorite spot for children. A statue of the mythological creature Pan, with his human body and goat's legs, horns, and ears, can't help but fascinate kids.

As Richardson left us and the garden tour came to an end, we were invited to enter the mansion. Staffpersons are on duty inside, but there is no guided tour. You move at your own pace and read about the house on posted descriptions.

An elk head, a bear skin, and a minstrel gallery all draw your attention in the medieval Great Hall. Next to the hall is the Tudor-style front room with its arch and half-timbers, while down the hall is the drawing room used to entertain guests on formal occasions.

Like many of the wealthy in her time, Mary Clark Thompson collected treasures from the Orient, and you can see the melange of jades, porcelains, and ivories in the tiny trophy room. But her favorite room was the library since the axis of the Italian garden lined up directly with its French doors, and the view of the garden from inside was commanding.

Location: From the New York State Thruway (Interstate 90) heading west, take exit 43 onto Route 21 into Canandaigua where it becomes Gibson Street, then follow the signs. From the Thruway heading east, take exit 44 onto Route 332 into Canandaigua where it becomes Main Street; take a left onto Gibson Street (Route 21) and follow the signs. From the south, take Interstate 390 to exit 2 at Cohocton onto Route 21; follow Route 21 north 37 miles into Canandaigua and follow the signs. **Admission** is charged. **Hours:** Mid-May through mid-October, daily. **Allow** two to three hours to take the guided garden tour, walk the grounds, and explore the mansion. **Information:** Sonnenberg Gardens, 151 Charlotte Street, Canandaigua, NY 14424; (716) 394-4922.

Events: Late June, Rose Sundays; July 4 weekend, Americana Weekend; Labor Day weekend, Old-Fashioned Weekend.

Note: Admission fee admits you inside the property. You can either take the 90-minute-long guided garden tour or walk around on your own. There is no extra charge for the tour, but tours are offered only three times daily. The tour may be lengthy for children or adults with little interest in gardens but you are permitted to leave the tour at any time. Buy admission tickets in the greenhouse closest to the parking lot. Picnic tables are available for your use by the duck pond next to the greenhouse.

If you are staying overnight: Sheraton Inn, 770 South Main Street, Canandaigua, (716) 394-7800; Econo Lodge, 170 Eastern Blvd., Canandaigua, (716) 394-9000; Wilder Tavern (bed and breakfast), 5648 North Bloomfield Road (two miles west of intersection of Route 332 and North Road), Canandaigua, (716) 394-8132; Finger Lakes Bed & Breakfast Association, P.O. Box 862, Canandaigua, NY 14424.

Other Books About New York State

Written for people of all ages and experience, these popular and carefully prepared books feature detailed trail and tour directions, notes on points of interest and natural phenomena, maps and photographs.

Long Island to the Hudson Valley

*20 Bicycle Tours in and Around
New York City* $6.95

*Walks and Rambles in Westchester and
Fairfield Counties* $7.95

Fifty Hikes in the Hudson Valley $9.95

Upstate New York (including the Adirondacks)

*State Parks and Campgrounds in Northern
New York* $9.95

Fifty Hikes in the Adirondacks $9.95

"Discover" guides are four-season, multi-use guides featuring fishing and picnic spots, walks, hikes, bushwhacks, x-c ski & snow shoe routes, and canoeing.

Discover the South Central Adirondacks $8.95
Discover the West Central Adirondacks $13.95
Discover the Central Adirondacks $8.95
Discover the Eastern Adirondacks $9.95
Discover the Southeastern Adirondacks $8.95
Discover the Southern Adirondacks $10.95
Discover the Southwestern Adirondacks $9.95
Discover the Northeastern Adirondacks $9.95

Central New York State

20 Bicycle Tours in the Finger Lakes $7.95
Fifty Hikes in Central New York $8.95
Canoeing Central New York $9.95
25 Ski Tours in Central New York $7.95

Recreational Guides to Other Regions

New England

New England's Special Places $10.95

Vermont on $500-A-Day (more or less) $10.00

Explorer's Guides are an alternative to mass market guides. They feature inns, B & Bs, restaurants, things to do, shopping, entertainment -from budget to top drawer.

Vermont: An Explorers Guide $14.95

Maine: An Explorer's Guide $13.95

*The Other Massachusetts, Beyond Boston
& Cape Cod: An Explorer's Guide* $12.95

Walks and Rambles in Rhode Island $8.95

50 Hikes in Connecticut $8.95

50 Hikes in Massachusetts $9.95

50 Hikes in Maine $8.95

25 Bicycle Tours in Maine $8.95

50 Hikes in the White Mountains $9.95

50 More Hikes in New Hampshire $9.95

25 Bicycle Tours in New Hampshire $6.95

50 Hikes in Vermont $9.95

25 Bicycle Tours in Vermont $7.95

Mid-Atlantic Region

50 Hikes in New Jersey $10.95

25 Bicycle Tours in New Jersey $8.95

25 Bicycle Tours in Eastern Pennsylvania $7.95

50 Hikes in Eastern Pennsylvania $9.95

50 Hikes in Central Pennsylvania $9.95

50 Hikes in Western Pennsylvania $9.95

*Walks and Rambles on the
Delmarva Penninsula* $8.95

25 Bicycle Tours on Delmarva $8.95

50 Hikes in West Virginia $9.95

Also available are ski-touring, canoeing, canoe camping and other books about these regions.

The above titles are available at bookstores, certain sporting goods stores, or they may be ordered directly from the publisher with $2.00 added for postage. For complete descriptions of our books, write to THE COUNTRYMAN PRESS, PO Box 175, Woodstock, Vermont 05091